WITHDRAWN

LOSING GROUND

Agricultural Policy and the Decline of the American Farm

Hugh Ulrich

Chicago Review Press

Library of Congress Cataloging-in-Publication Data

Ulrich, Hugh.
   Losing ground : agricultural policy and the decline of the
American farm / Hugh Ulrich. —1st ed.
            p.   cm.
   Includes index.
   ISBN 1-55652-059-X : $18.95
   1. Agriculture and state—United States. 2. Agriculture—
Economic aspects—United States. 3. Farms—United States.
I. Title.
HD1761.U38 1989
338.1'873—dc19   89-783
                                                       CIP

Copyright ©1989 by Hugh Ulrich
All rights reserved
Printed in the United States of America by BookCrafters
First Edition

1 2 3 4 5 6 7 8 9 10

Published by Chicago Review Press, Incorporated
   814 North Franklin Street, Chicago, Illinois 60610

ISBN 1-55652-059-X

Contents

U.S. Farm Population 1910-1987

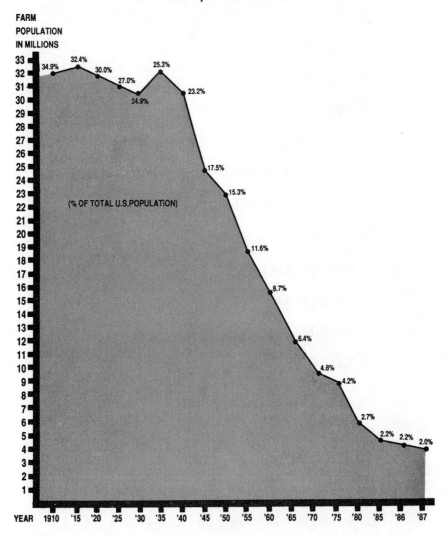

FARM
POPULATION
IN MILLIONS

(% OF TOTAL U.S.POPULATION)

34.9% 32.4% 30.0% 27.0% 24.9% 25.3% 23.2% 17.5% 15.3% 11.6% 8.7% 6.4% 4.8% 4.2% 2.7% 2.2% 2.2% 2.0%

YEAR 1910 '15 '20 '25 '30 '35 '40 '45 '50 '55 '60 '65 '70 '75 '80 '85 '86 '87

INTRODUCTION

Over the past five years, the United States has experienced two major farm crises on a scale that used to
occur only once or twice in a lifetime.

In three short years we went from a full-scale farm
depression with unsold grain piled in fields and park-
ing lots, to a drought which has left us with tight
supplies of wheat and soybeans, and dwindling stocks
of corn that may well be loaded with cancer-causing
aflatoxins.

Corn, soybeans, and wheat are renewable resources,
but look a little deeper and you'll see they weren't the
only things in short supply after the drought of 1988.
A 72-year downtrend in the farm population has left it
at barely 2 percent of the U.S. total, and still falling
fast.

Even that number is overstated. Knock out the large
number of part-time farmers who need jobs off the

farm to stay afloat, as well as those thousands getting the latest round of pink slips from farm creditors, and you'll find the number of full-time farmers has already dropped below 2 percent well in advance of the Census Bureau statistics. Is it wise to concentrate food production in the hands of 1–2 percent of the population?

The losses don't stop there. For decades, the United States has been losing its topsoil to water and wind erosion at a rate that in sheer volume rivals drought-stricken areas of the Sahel in sub-Saharan Africa. In its 1988 review of soil and water conservation the USDA said that topsoil on 173 million acres of cropland (out of a total of 420 million) is eroding faster than nature can replace it.

The USDA follows this statistic with one of the great understatements of all time. The loss of topsoil, "reduces the ability of the soil to support future plant growth." And how! It is this topsoil that allows basic crop production to occur. Its loss eliminates the production of wheat, corn, and soybeans—crops on which much of the human food chain depends.

Topsoil is not all that deep to begin with. Much is measured in inches, not feet, and the only reason the United States is still in the game after decades of rapid erosion, is that we started out with so much more than the people of places like Chad and the Sudan. In no sense can our vaunted modern agricultural system claim to be any less destructive than the methods of those primitive Africans.

American agriculture is also depleting groundwater and the water in aquifers across several hundred thousand square miles in the center of the North American continent. It has tainted much of what remains, the drinking water on which more than half the U.S. population depends, with cancer-causing residues from pesticides, fertilizers, and herbicides.

As the chemical residues of the 1950s, 1960s, and 1970s percolate downward into deeper and deeper groundwater, a new chemical bath is sent down behind them each spring and summer. This adds to the chemical levels of the water near the surface and gives the people with deeper wells a little something extra to drink in ten to twenty years. Agriculture is responsible for more of the pollution of the nation's supply of fresh water than any other industry by far.

Let's see, we're losing replaceable crops and irreplaceable farmers, as well as soil and clean drinking water. Is that it?

No. The United States has also lost farm export market share to tougher and more sensible competitors. It has lost scores of billions of tax dollars that were spent on farm subsidies to no avail; in fact they were spent to our harm. We are losing the small towns, cheap housing, and good schools that can no longer be properly supported in many rural areas because of the declining farm population. Things are not going well down on the farm.

How did this happen? How *could* it happen? When did it start? Who is responsible? Has the worst passed? Is this precious part of our national birthright beyond recovery?

Well, therein lies the story. The decline of the American farm, that most basic building block of both our economy and our culture, did not happen by accident, and it didn't happen overnight. It was neither inevitable nor the result of a colossal run of bad luck. No, this disaster, like so many others, is a human product. It has come to us through sins of commission and omission. Most of all, it's the result of federal farm policies that were designed for a world that never existed.

Our flawed policy foundation was first laid down in 1933. We've spent the more than half century since preserving all of its original flaws, adding an occasional new one, and passing the mess on. With time, that flawed foundation achieved sacred-cow status.

Everything constructed on top had to be twisted, turned, and jammed into place to fit the original flaws.

Of course the great droughts that punctuated the troubled 1980s weren't a human product, but droughts of one sort or another have been part of every farm cycle since farming began. Why was it that the policies of the United States were always doing precisely the wrong things when each major drought occurred?

Why do we always seem to be busily slashing acreage, or in the process of selling off the last of a major surplus on the very eve of a drought year? Why did we just finish stripping the landscape of tree rows and wetlands in time for the decade of droughts? At times our knack for bad timing seems almost eerie, but in fact it's the legacy of that flawed foundation.

We can't even take cold comfort from the fact that everyone shares our dismal trends. No industrialized food exporter has suffered waves of farm foreclosures like those in the United States. None have lost up to a third of their export market share in a basic commodity like wheat since 1981. No major exporter except perhaps Brazil has done anywhere near as much damage to its environment in such a short period of time. Worst of all, these destructive trends show no sign of reversing. All are still merrily underway.

As if to add insult to injury, American taxpayers have paid top dollar for all of this. The United States has had the world's most costly system of agricultural subsidies during the decline, with the possible exception of the wretched farm economy on which the people of the USSR depend.

The blame lies everywhere. Much of it lies with the farmers themselves, who have had a measure of political control over their destiny enjoyed by few others. Plenty of blame lies with a weak and reactive federal establishment. Mostly, though, the blame lies with us, the American people, and our embarrassing level of disinterest and ignorance.

As with so many of the other basics of education—history, geography, grammar, mathematics—the average American citizen is so poorly educated in the area of the food system, that he barely belongs in the same category with the rest of the industrialized world. Add to this ignorance our endless fascination with the short term, and you get American farm policy. Under the circumstances, how could things have turned out any differently?

But we don't have to keep this up. We don't have to let topsoil erode to zero on 40 percent of the nation's cropland over the next generation. We don't have to continue the contamination of our water supply with farm chemicals, until every last bit has been tainted. We don't have to continue subsidizing what amounts to a new landed aristocracy in the United States by paying farm subsidies to wealthy nonresidents while an increasingly poor and landless population is left behind to perform the labor. We can recognize the fact that basic agricultural policies have the power to set in motion powerful forces for either good or ill.

The effect of our farm policy decisions is often epic; they are played out on hundreds of millions of acres across a million square mile chunk of the North American continent. No other single area of the national policy can have such a broad and immediate impact on local economies, the national environment, and the price each of us pays for food. No other federal agency has the power to turn the lights on or off in the 1,000 formerly prosperous small towns stretching across a 1,000-mile arc from Ohio to the Dakotas, where fewer and older people now live.

In an era when it takes two incomes to maintain a household in cities where the decent jobs exist, a cheap and magnificent housing stock is being abandoned because we can't match it with the jobs. Agriculture can make this connection.

Non-farm taxpayers, along with their elected representatives, have a social and financial contract with the farm population and agribusiness. This isn't any old contract. It involves our food and water. We tax-payers are the paying customer, and we have not gotten the return we have a right to expect.

At one time America could afford a farm policy that was deeply flawed because we were so rich and our resources seemed limitless. After a decades-long battering, however, we have become weak, off balance, and poor. The farm economy, and the rest of us, can no longer afford our ignorance and arrogance. We need instead to see ourselves as we truly are, and learn to be wise.

Wisdom can only come from a clear understanding of the past, some brutal honesty, and a solid plan. That is the purpose of this book.

1

BALANCE

The story of how we got into the current farm mess is a sort of "How the West Was Won" in reverse, and it weaves itself very neatly through the changing fabric of the American culture and world events in the twentieth century.

The question is, when did the story begin? Agriculture, even American agriculture, has obviously been around for a long time. We could legitimately start as early as 1800, with the dawn of the Industrial Revolution and the genesis of the modern grain export markets. The rapidly growing industrial centers of Britain and northwestern Europe, no longer able to feed themselves domestically, needed to import grain, and larger and larger quantities began to travel greater and greater distances to reach their final markets.

Or we could start in America itself, with the inven-

tion of the steel plow by John Deere of Illinois in
1837—the invention that allowed the American grain
farmer to quickly "bust" the very tough prairie sod on
a large scale, enabling him to tap the hundreds of
millions of acres of rich black topsoil that were locked
away beneath it.

Or we could begin right after the American Civil War
with the dramatic entry of those prairie sodbusters
from the United States and Canada, (who had multiplied greatly in number), into world grain export
markets that were then just beginning to explode in
size.

But this is not a history of European markets or
modern technology so much as a critical look at the
events, perceptions, and decisions that have struc-
tured American agricultural policy. Thus we should
begin the story by examining the circumstances that
first inspired the durable but flawed thinking currently endangering the American farm.

I think that the best place to start is at the big pivot
point in the history of the American farm at the beginning of the twentieth century, the five years just prior
to the First World War. Those years, 1910–14, formed
an historic pause of sorts, as most of the social and
economic farm trends of the nineteenth century played
themselves out, and the seeds were quietly sown for
the major new trends that would make their own great
runs through the twentieth century. It is these trends
in turn that seem to be maturing today.

Calling the great agricultural forces of the
nineteenth century "trends" almost trivializes them.
They were actually events of epic, even romantic
proportions that were unprecedented in world history.
In the span of one lifetime, millions of American
citizens and immigrants, steel plows in hand, had
poured into the American Midwest and ventured out
onto the trackless Great Plains. They had cultivated
hundreds of millions of virgin acres; raised millions of

cattle, hogs, and chickens; built the hundreds of farm towns that were needed to trade with the big new farm population; revolutionized farm technology for all time; and established a rural standard of living that far surpassed anything found in the rest of the world, including other parts of the United States.

The farm economy of the Grain Belt—stretching from eastern Ohio to the Great Plains—had just finished this historic job in 1910–14, and it was settling in to enjoy the first fruits. These years turned out to be a period of prosperity and balance, calm and relative ease that was idyllic compared to what had come before and to what existed elsewhere.

During this little golden age, the supply of grain seemed to consistently match up with the demand, a bit of a miracle in farming history, and most farmers who produced a good crop of wheat, corn, hay, and oats made a nice profit when they sold it. The average price that the farmer received for wheat (the major U.S. cash crop) held in a very steady range of 80–90 cents a bushel, with the exception of 1914, when it shot up to an even more profitable 97 cents.

With these prices, that average farmer managed to run what for him was a substantial positive cash flow. He put that cash flow plus his growing borrowing power within the growing American capital markets to good use. It went toward the improvement of his business; he purchased more land and livestock that he could breed and fatten in order to take his crop to market in a value- added form. The cash flow also went into the latest generation of labor-saving farm equipment which was being invented and manufactured right then and there in the industrial centers of the American Midwest by industrial concerns like John Deere. This farm equipment had long since begun the process of eliminating the most backbreaking farm labor, and while the farmer still put in an exceedingly tough day by our standards, it was no longer the killing work that it had been in the nineteenth century.

This remarkable national achievement was very fresh in 1910–14. In fact, it was still underway. For instance, tractors didn't become common until after 1900, but by 1914 only a fraction of land in the Grain Belt was still being planted or harvested with a team of horses. People living on farms and riding on those tractors could therefore vividly remember farming behind a team of horses. They could see a few others still doing so. Nothing of the kind was happening to the vast majority of the world's other farmers and farm workers. Most of the farmers in the Grain Belt knew this very well since there was a generation still alive who had emigrated from those other countries. They knew the contrasts from personal experience.

Best of all, the ownership of the most basic asset of the farm economy, the land, was spread with remarkable evenness among the men and women who actually worked it, at least in the Grain Belt of the Midwest. This too stood in sharp contrast to the rest of the world where land had long since concentrated itself into estates of large landowners, and where the vast majority needed to labor on someone else's land to get by.

National policy had been specifically designed to accomplish this even distribution of land with the Homestead Act and other federal land policies. The government had given land or sold it very cheaply to individual families in parcels that were about all that one family could handle, so the center of the continent would be populated and each of those families could be self-reliant. The plan had worked.

In those years before the First World War, there was plenty of reason to think that things might just keep getting better and better. While the best of the land was already under cultivation, it was still relatively cheap. A hardworking non-farmer could still save money, find a good farm for sale, and get into the game on a fairly solid footing with a couple of good crops. (The idea of an average citizen having access to the multimillion-dollar business of farming these days is almost inconceivable.)

That abundant and still fairly cheap land was, by the grace of God, more fertile than most of the lands of western and central Europe. The American Grain Belt was also blessed with a growing season that was longer than that of America's biggest competitor, Russia, and rainfall that was more ample and consistent than that of Russia, Canada, and Australia. Of all the major grain exporters, only Argentina was equally blessed with soil and climate, but there the land was owned by a tiny minority.

The American farmer/exporter was closer to the major importing centers of western Europe than were his competitors in either South America or Australia. And unlike his counterparts in Canada, he enjoyed the use of an inland water system of navigable rivers on which his grain could be easily and cheaply shipped. To fill in the blank spaces between navigable waterways, he had the best network of railroads outside of Germany and Great Britain.

Above and beyond all of these natural advantages, he could deliver his grain to a domestic milling and processing industry that was the world's largest and most modern, which could in turn add considerable value to his raw commodities. Those aggressive and modern processing plants then could find additional domestic and foreign markets for the finished food products they cranked out, spreading everybody's marketing net that much wider.

The American farmer was the world's healthiest farmer. He lived longer and reproduced more rapidly than any of his counterparts. Birth and survival rates on the farms of the Midwest and Great Plains from the end of the Civil War until World War I were among the highest ever recorded—in large part because the population was well fed, better educated, and isolated from many of the diseases that regularly tore across Europe and Asia.

Add all of these advantages together, and our average American farmer in 1910 could produce more bushels of grain than any of the world's other farmers. In most cases, he produced more bushels than his parents had on the same farmland and very often, more bushels than he himself had produced just a few years before.

Of course, as marvelous as all of this was, those five years wouldn't have been golden, and everyone wouldn't have been so busy producing all those bushels of grain, if there had not been markets big enough to absorb the growing supply. In 1910–14, the American farmer had such markets as well.

The cities of America were among the largest in the world, growing rapidly and rich enough to afford one of the best average diets in the world. The huge, growing farm population itself helped to absorb a big chunk of the food surplus.

The industrial population centers and middle classes of Europe were also growing in size and prosperity, and they absorbed the bulk of the surplus. The American farm economy exploited all of its competitive advantages to gain a greater disproportionate share of the growing western European business and to gradually start nudging aside the less fit among the competition—countries like Russia, Romania, and Poland that soon would be nudged out of the ranks of major food exporters for good.

By the immediate prewar years, these successes and advantages had begun to snowball in a classic example of how the rich get richer. The profits that these markets generated for the well-positioned American farmer were plowed by that farmer right back into the business. The more he could improve his productivity, the more grain he had to sell, and the more cash he earned. The more cash he earned, the more he had left after basic expenses to buy more land and to invest in improving equipment. Since the system was broken down into small and fairly uniform units, these small businessmen were able to apply their profits with a speed and efficiency that only small businessmen with a consistent cash flow can hope to match.

The more money the farmer had to apply to the purchase of modern farm equipment, the more it stimulated the inventors and manufacturers of the Midwest to develop the next generation of even better and more productive machinery for an affordable price. The more productive they both became, the more grain one farmer could produce. The more grain one farmer could produce, the more cheaply he could sell it and still earn a profit. The more cheaply he could sell his grain at a profit, the better his competitive advantage in the growing export markets.

During that five-year span, things just clicked. The grain surplus did not turn into a glut; it was an asset.

In 1910–14, the American farm was even perfecting its "look." Most of the ten million people living on Grain Belt farms had personally made the transition from sod houses and cabins to the comfortable Victorian farmhouses that dot the landscape to this very day.

The white farmhouses with red barns and outbuildings built by this generation still form the stage setting of the American farm mythology for many of us. The props that filled the stage were all there in force as well: the big extended families, the farmyard filled with chickens and pigs, the business of getting up before dawn every day to milk the cows, shoveling out the barn and spreading it on the fields. All of this comprised an integral part of the scene, and I suspect that a lot of non-farmers still have this agreeable image fixed in their minds. But the fact is that this lovely version of farm life has steadily eroded over the past seventy years. Little of it remains.

Although it is not too surprising that many of these romantic details have been burned into the American conscious, it is remarkable that they have also been burned into the conscious of the federal bureaucracy. In the 1930s, Congress decided to try to freeze the return that a farmer got for his work back in 1910–14. They instructed the Department of Agriculture (USDA) to compile an official index that quantified those years as a standard against which the USDA could compare the state of the U.S. farm economy each year. The name of the index and the concept is parity.

To the economists and bureaucrats that designed basic policy in the 1930s, the parity years stood out from the forty or so years of mostly low prices that came before and the turbulence that followed. They became mesmerized by the idea of recapturing them.

The gist of the parity index was that it estimated how high the prices of various farm commodities should be in order to give the farmer a return for them that is equivalent to, or at *parity* with the price farmers got in those five balanced years. It also attempted to recapture the economic relationship between rural and urban workers. (Technically the calculation was modified in 1948. It's now a compilation of a current index, multiplied by a ten-year moving average of the farm price in question, multiplied by the 1910–14 index. The result, however, is almost exactly the same.)

Although the concept of parity has been modified and moved a bit to the sidelines through the years, the index itself and the rather spooky thinking behind it lives on. It is updated and published for a broad range of commodities each month. As recently as the 1970s basic support prices for the grains were still pegged to it. Even today, full parity prices are guaranteed to farmers in case of a political embargo. In the case of wheat and corn, those prices are above the highest levels at which those crops have ever traded. It's a dangerous little index to have rattling around.

We can look at the whole parity concept as a red flag, an early sign that there was some seriously flawed thinking going on among those who were constructing the farm policy of the United States. Farm policy took years to build. There were many such built-in flaws to come, and parity itself didn't get locked in until the 1930s, but I think that we should bestow on parity the title of Flawed Building Block Number One.

Nothing lasts forever, and the years of balance could not have lasted either. As attractive and promising as farming and the future of farming appeared to be getting across the American grain belt in 1910–14, many of the seeds of change were already planted and starting to sprout.

The variables that had created the years of balance to begin with were revolutionary in nature: dynamic changes in technology, population, and world events that had placed American farmers in the first rank.

Unfortunately, dynamic variables often have too long a life. They don't just go away or stop dead in their tracks the moment they've created the sort of world we want. They stay on to play themselves out in the time allotted to them. In the end they may not be nearly as comfortable to have around as they were in the beginning.

The seemingly comfortable old nineteenth century variables are a case in point. Things like improving technology seemed to be all to the good of the farmer as it first came onstream, but it was bound to become a mixed blessing at some point because eventually greater productivity always makes somebody obsolete.

Things that have always gone up, like land prices and population, can instead start heading down. Your

best customers who have done nothing but grow and
prosper for decades might suddenly fall on hard times.
Things change.

By 1914, there were already such changes aplenty
cooking away, unseen below the surface of the farm
equation, and with a little more time, they surely
would have bubbled to the surface and manifested
themselves in a different and less balanced set of
circumstances for the American farmer.

Sometimes, however, the passing of time is not what
changes the equation around. Sometimes, the process
is greatly accelerated by an unexpected catalyst from
outside of the basic equation, and all of those unseen
variables come to the surface much more quickly.

In 1914, a catalyst to end all catalysts was right
around the bend.

2

BOOM

Most of the customers were about to go to war—a world war.

When it began in August of 1914, that First World War was greeted with wild enthusiasm by most of the combatants in Europe, but with a profound sense of detachment in the United States. America was determined to stay out, no matter who started winning. This was the result of a mixture of self-interest, wisdom, and the time-honored American habit of ignoring European affairs as a matter of course. The United States, and most sectors of the U.S. economy, pretty much liked the way things were going. They considered the American economic and political systems superior to those of Europe. They believed that Europe was fighting about issues that simply didn't exist for the American people, and that the United States was on an altogether separate path. President Wilson agreed, and he urged his fellow citizens to remain "strictly neutral in thought and deed."

This was excellent advice, but it probably flew in the face of reality, because the Great War instantly became the central event on the world stage.

Both sides immediately fielded the largest armies that had ever faced off. The French alone sent more than three million troops to the front in the course of a two-week mobilization effort in late July and early August (a number that would reach a grand total of 8.4 million by the war's end). July and August are right in the middle of the summer growing season, and while most European crops of 1914 were easily brought in with the help of women and the men who were left behind, the war did end up disrupting the planting of winter crops that first year, along with the myriad activities that need to occur in a labor-intensive farm economy before the next spring planting.

Agriculture was affected in other ways that were even more profound than that early loss of manpower. The war also used up a lot of good agricultural land. By 1915 the armies of Britain, France, and Germany were dug in several million strong along a western front that zigzagged for some 600 miles through the farm land and forests of France and Belgium. You can't grow grain on a battlefield.

The front lines, plus a broad no man's land, plus the area behind both lines that was constantly threatened by artillery barrages and used for staging areas added up to many hundreds of thousands of acres that were to be taken completely out of farm production for the next four years. The heavily populated and industrialized areas of northwestern Europe had been running a chronic food deficit for a long time, and this deficit immediately began to widen.

On the eastern front, the battle lines weren't so stationary, but even more farmland was probably disrupted since battles raged back and forth over a broader swath of territory, uprooting far larger populations, mainly in Poland and Russia. Since these territories traditionally produced a grain and meat surplus upon which northwestern and central Europe depended, the effects of the lost production in the east were serious for the populations on both fronts.

At first this created what seemed like a bonanza for the American farmers. Here they were, fresh from the single most consistent stretch of farm prosperity in the country's history, and prices shot even higher as soon as war broke out in August 1914.

Wheat and wheat flour were the focus of the food problem because they formed a much larger percentage of European and American diets during World War I than they do today. Cash wheat in Chicago had traded at just over 90 cents a bushel in the months before the war, and it reacted to the start of the war by nearly doubling in price to about $1.70 a bushel by mid-to-late winter.

Winter wheat gets planted in the fall and since the rally got started before planting began, the American wheat farmer responded as you might guess—with expanded acreage. Harvested wheat acreage rose from a record 55.6 million acres in June–July of 1914 (the last wheat crop harvested before the war), to another new record of 60.3 million acres harvested in 1915. However, as the market began to recognize that it had both record acreage and excellent growing conditions, it realized too that it had overreacted. It commenced a slide that took wheat prices all the way back to $1 a bushel as the record crop started coming in from the fields during June and July of 1915.

The balance of the parity years had not been disrupted so badly at this point. Cash wheat traded for the rest of the year in a range of about $1.00 to $1.30 at Chicago—a very good price, but certainly not of the windfall variety. Many farmers seemed to think that even this would not last. Most had not received the big

Chicago price of the previous winter at their local
grain elevator in any case. As the big 1915 crop rolled
in that summer, some local markets had plunged even
more steeply in the country than in Chicago, and many
a farmer had ended up selling his portion of the big
crop for what he considered a disappointing price.

This plus some weather problems discouraged plantings of winter wheat in the fall of 1915. In fact, planted
acreage for wheat dropped all the way back below the
1914 totals. As the growing season wore on, the crop
deteriorated. Taken together, this eventually resulted
in a drop in production of over 35 percent from the
record 1915 crop.

The summer crops in Europe were down again in
1916 for all of the same reasons they were down in
1914 and 1915, so there was no way for the continent
to even begin to overcome the unexpectedly large U.S.
shortfall. Prices at Chicago reacted after the 1916
summer wheat harvest by racing up through the initial wartime high of $1.70, and they spent the
remainder of 1916 trading in a range from $1.50 to
$2.00 per bushel—the highest U.S. wheat prices since
the post–Civil War Reconstruction. *This* was a boom.

Clearly these prices had to bring a big acreage expansion in winter wheat plantings in the fall of 1916.
Prices appeared high enough to generate record
acreage and more, but for a variety of reasons U.S.
wheat acreage actually dropped again—this time to
only 46.8 million (harvested), the lowest level since
1910.

The market was probably not entirely aware of this
at first, not until after the cold winter weather started
setting in. Winter wheat is planted in the fall, comes
up by late fall, and then becomes dormant through the
winter. In the spring, it greens up, ripens, and is
harvested in June–July. Given the low plantings of the
fall of 1916, that sequence meant that the next chance
the United States had to plant major crops would be

the spring (1917) when crops like corn, oats, and
spring wheat go in the ground. Those crops in turn
can't be harvested until late summer/early fall, so the
Western world was suddenly looking at serious
shortages of grain stretching out till the end of 1917,
with no way to catch up.

There was certainly no way to catch up in Europe,
where the downtrend in farm production had started
to gain momentum. By 1916, spot food shortages were
becoming common on the western front, and they were
already the rule all over eastern Europe. Even the seed
needed to plant future European crops was being con-
fiscated and eaten by hungry soldiers and refugees in
some areas, as is often the case when food shortages
deepen. Once this process starts, shortages tend to
feed on themselves, and they literally cannot be fixed
internally. Even if the war had ended with the great
stalemate of 1916, the variables that had already been
injected into the food equation were going to produce a
staggering European deficit in 1917.

The markets reacted to this no-win series of events
with a "price shock." The scale of the shortfall was so
great that the market reacted by bursting out of its
historic price parameters. Wheat vaulted up to $2.00
in late 1916, then past the Civil War highs to $2.50,
and then finally to a new all-time high of just under
$3.50 in March as it waited for the wheat crop to
mature.

This reaction of the central U.S. market in Chicago
was not just an abstract one in the futures. It represented a very real scramble among buyers—in this
case by the belligerents on both sides—to secure
desperately needed supplies of wheat in North
America. The market price is a simple reflection of the
average state of the supply and demand. When that
"reflection"—the price—is registering shock and
panic, it's safe to assume that all of the other elements
that go into that equation are suffering varying

degrees of shock as well. Harmony and balance were out the window.

"He Kept Us Out Of War"

As the war dragged into 1917, the United States still maintained its remarkable resolve to stay out, despite mounting pressure to enter on the side of Great Britain and the Allies. The sinking of the passenger ship *Lusitania* by a German U-boat in 1915 was the most serious early test of that resolve. That incident killed 114 Americans and generated a great deal of anti-German sentiment, but it never came close to generating an actual declaration of war.

The United States was also subjected to an intense pro-British propaganda blitz that commenced right at the start of the war, and basically never stopped. This was greatly abetted by incredibly bad public relations efforts on the part of the German government and the consistently unappealing persona of Kaiser Wilhelm II himself.

Still, the United States held out. President Wilson put the country's antiwar resolve to the test by making his 1916 campaign slogan, "He kept us out of war," and got reelected. Even as late as January 22, 1917, he formally proposed to both sides that they declare a "peace without victory," but there were no takers.

So the United States, with its short wheat crop, soaring food prices, and booming wartime manufacturing economy, sat and watched that winter from across the Atlantic Ocean. There was a growing awareness among the Americans that they would eventually be in the war if it didn't end very soon, but the aversion to actually taking the plunge kept winning out.

It was the Germans who essentially made the choice for the United States. They decided that it was still possible to break the stalemate and win with one last desperate gamble; so they announced on January 31, 1917 that their U-boats would henceforth sink all shipping in a war zone around Great Britain, regardless of nationality or cargo.

They reasoned, with some justification, that this would starve Great Britain into surrender by the fall of that year. They reasoned as well that this might finally push the United States into the war against them, but they felt this was a risk worth taking on the theory that the United States would not be able to field a large enough army in France to make a difference, until it was too late.

The United States simply protested at first by severing diplomatic relations with Germany (on February 3). The Germans were hardly interested in diplomacy at this juncture of course, and they flung themselves into the U-boat campaign, which was an enormous early success in terms of the gross tonnage sunk.

By late March the German plan seemed to be working like clockwork, and it was estimated that British food stocks were down to a six-week supply. The price of wheat reached its $3.45 a bushel high in Chicago which was about three and a half times the prewar level. The British owned a significant amount of wheat in North America, but there was serious doubt over whether it could be brought across the Atlantic in sufficient quantity and in time.

As the numbers of ships being sunk increased during February and March, so did the loss of civilian and American lives. This coincided with the release of an alleged letter from the Kaiser's government to the government of Mexico, offering Mexico a chunk of U.S. territory in the southwest if it declared war on the United States. This combination finally swung public sentiment in America decidedly and permanently against Germany, and on April 6, 1917, the United States finally declared war.

Wheat prices plunged over $1 in the next two months, in part because Britain wasn't the only foreign government that owned some wheat in North

America; Germany did too. All of their contracts were voided by the government, and this grain was thrown back onto the market. Combined with the market's annual skittishness about the approach of harvest and the fact that U-boats were making it difficult to deliver wheat to the customer, it was enough to make the market wonder what on earth it was doing at over $3 a bushel.

At one point during the harvest, prices appeared headed back to $2 or lower in Chicago. While this was an excellent price historically, the government feared that a further drop would once again curtail farmers' planting plans that fall. Wheat acreage was no longer a matter that could be left to chance with an American army to feed and millions of civilians on the brink of starvation in Europe, so the federal government instituted controlled or guaranteed prices in August. They were very high guarantees that fell about midway between the prewar levels, and the price-shock high.

The government prices were plenty high enough to encourage a big expansion since that farmer now could rest assured that he faced little or no financial risk, no matter how heavy local supplies happened to be when he brought his grain to market. Wheat plantings rose to a big new record that fall that would result in 61.1 million harvested acres the next spring and summer.

Meanwhile, the Allies were eliminating the roadblock to efficiently moving the grain that was presented by the U-boats. In February to April the Germans were sinking ships faster than the Allies could build them, but by summer the U.S. Navy had developed a system of grouping merchant ships into convoys that were escorted by ships of the British and U.S. navies equipped with recently developed submarine detection devices. Convoys became a very dangerous thing for the U-boats to attack, and by November the ratio had been dramatically reversed in the Allies' favor—only one ship was being lost out of every two hundred that sailed.

Not only did the Americans enter the war against the Germans, but they mobilized far more quickly than the Germans or anybody else thought possible. This was done with a national draft that was widely supported and backed up with a heavy rate of volunteerism. About two-thirds of the Americans who entered the war came from urban areas and towns and one-third from the farm. By the time the war was over just eighteen months later, their numbers would swell to nearly 4.4 million.

In one fell swoop, this mobilization ended one of the greatest of all nineteenth century American farm trends and jump started another in the opposite direction. For the first time since the Civil War, the U.S. farm population declined in 1917. It had declined in the Civil War too, but that had proved temporary. The downtrend in farm population that began in 1917 would last for seventy-two years and still counting as of this writing. In fact, if we carry this to its logical extreme and ignore all of the temporary fluctuations of the past, this wartime drop ended a demographic trend that went all the way back to 1621 when the Pilgrims made it through that first New England winter.

The title of one of the most popular songs of the war acknowledged the great sea change that was occurring in the countryside. "How you gonna keep 'em down on the farm, after they've seen Paree?" it asked. How indeed? The obvious answer after 1917 was that you no longer could.

The combination of reduced manpower and increased acreage produced a modest manpower shortage on the farm after 1917, in relation to the increased demand for food and the production targets being set by the government. While this was a minor farm influence compared to all the rest, it was nevertheless a stimulus toward even more mechanization. Naturally, most farmers couldn't and didn't upgrade all of their farm equipment during the eighteen months that the United States was in the war, but this added incentive became a sort of lagging economic effect, and it gave another boost to farm productivity for the long haul—an acceleration that the grain market only needed while the emergency lasted. Needed or not, however, this lagging effect spilled on over into the postwar period when the boys were on their way home and the manpower shortage was over.

(Of course, some boys never came home. Most who died carried a government insurance policy which paid lump sums to widows and other beneficiaries. In the case of farm families, this was usually applied to the farm mortgage, and in many cases it enabled that mortgage to be paid in full. That's why people came to say when someone died in the war that he had "bought the farm.")

All the pieces were now in place for the biggest farm "boom" of all time. It had all the price stimulation needed for expansion. This was solidly backed by virtually unlimited (albeit temporary) demand, and with the success of the convoy system there was also an almost unlimited ability to load up that grain and deliver it.

Any chance that the boom and its disruption of the "balance" would come and go quickly was lost in 1917, as one event after another guaranteed its longevity— the refusal of the Europeans to do the obvious thing and declare a truce, the German decision to escalate the war with unrestricted U-boat attacks, the potential starvation of the British people, the resulting American declaration of war, and the institutionalization of the boom with the high guaranteed prices that began in August 1917.

Since there seems to be some sort of economic law of farming which states that boom is always followed by bust, I suppose it was now inevitable that the biggest of all booms would be followed by the biggest of all busts.

3

BUST

Garrison Keillor of Lake Wobegon fame tells a funny story about the first settlers of that mythical little town in Minnesota. The first it seems were Unitarian missionaries from Boston who came to teach the natives interpretive dance. They were followed in turn by Norwegians on their way *back* from North Dakota and then by a bunch of Germans who refused to admit they were lost.

The Germans of World War I were also nothing if not stubborn. Like their American cousins in Lake Wobegon, they (and the other Europeans for that matter) refused to admit that the war was hopelessly stalemated by 1916. Then they took the last desperate gamble, initiating unrestricted U-boat warfare in 1917. When that failed and the United States entered the war against them, their position deteriorated from one of mere stalemate, to certain defeat. Still, they came up with yet another last desperate gamble, and in April and May of 1918, they unleashed three more major offensives on the western front.

This was made possible by an armistice they signed with the new revolutionary (Bolshevik) government of Russia in December 1917, followed in March by a formal treaty to end all hostilities between the two. This allowed Germany to transfer nearly all of its troops from the defunct eastern front to the western, and on paper this gave them the hope of overwhelming exhausted British and French armies before the newly arriving Americans could take the field.

The first two major German assaults were eventually stalled by the British and the French alone despite promising early gains. The third, however, broke through Allied positions shielding Paris, and the Allied retreat that followed was quickly in danger of becoming a rout. It was here that the fresh American troops were first pitted in large numbers against the onrushing Germans. The Americans held, and by the end of May, even the Germans knew that the war was lost.

They still refused to surrender though, and this last sad sequence of events resulted in the disruption of a fourth straight planting and growing season in western Europe. The same vast farm areas were still blanketed by the western front all through the summer of 1918. There were even fewer men and farm animals left at this point to do the field work on the still functioning farms that were not physically disrupted by the front. There was less seed to plant and less functional equipment; there would be less of everything to harvest come fall.

The enormous pressure put on the Allies during the German assaults of 1918 once again commanded all of the resources that the western Europeans could muster, which in turn kept the British and French from even starting to think about diverting their thin industrial and financial resources to the revival of their farm economies. Even in the east, the cessation of hostilities between Russia and Germany did not mean a return to normalcy in 1918. There, world war was replaced by revolution and civil war.

In June and July, the United States harvested the first big wheat crop under price control. It was big, but weather had been less than ideal and despite the record acreage, total production fell about 10 percent short of the record crop of 1915. The food problems in western Europe could therefore be alleviated, but just barely, and since the crop was being shipped across the Atlantic at a record pace there was suddenly a danger of shortages in the United States as well.

The federal government stepped in to manage the food supplies by directly negotiating export contracts with the Allied governments and being both buyer and seller within the domestic cash markets. As buyers, their role was to pull grain off the market, especially in remote areas where a flood of newly harvested grain threatened to overwhelm buyers and depress prices. This propped up prices, and they could easily sell it into areas that were being drained too quickly by export demand, or they could ship it directly to Europe.

Price controls were raised again in 1918 in time to stimulate yet another acreage increase in wheat since the European food deficit was expected to widen even further after the war ended. Acreage expanded to 73.7 million (harvested) acres, a jump of about 20 percent above the record set the previous year, which enabled the American farmer to catch up with the world deficit in wheat.

These weren't the only reasons that grain supplies were brought back into sync with demand after the United States entered the war. Private grain companies were no longer able to sell American grain to the increasingly hungry tens of millions in Germany, as they had done on a spotty basis before 1917. Out-

standing sales to the German government were canceled. A lot of German grain was sent to Britain.

After the U-boat blockade of Great Britain was
broken that summer and fall, the British (and
Americans) were finally able to tighten their own surface blockade of Germany until it was almost total. It
must have been ironic to the Germans as they waited
for the war to end, that their attempt to starve Britain
had brought the United States into the war, saved the
British from defeat, and in the end enabled the Allies
to turn around and starve the Germans into surrender
instead.

There was another large and hungry market that
was more or less crossed off the demand side of the
world grain equation after 1917. The Allies entered
into a virtual state of war with Russia after the Bolshevik Revolution of November, in the hopes that the
Communists could be ousted and Russia brought back
into the war against Germany. Therefore, despite the
fact that there were millions more hungry and starving potential customers for American grain in the east,
the politics (and the vast geography and distribution
problems) of Russia kept this very needy market off-
limits and out of the price equation.

These dark variables combined with the expanded
acreage to rebalance the grain supply/demand equation, albeit in a very perverse sense, and at a much
higher price than where it had been balanced in the
parity years before the war. Having these markets
off-limits was probably the factor that kept the price of
wheat from going on up to a second, even higher price
shock after the United States entered the war.

The U.S. food policies of World War I fell under the
auspices of the newly created Food Administration
Grain Corporation which was under the direction of a
Mr. Herbert Hoover (who had also directed the food
relief drive for Belgium in the first year of the war).
They were the first full-scale price supports that had

been implemented by the federal government, and
they were widely credited at the time with saving lives
in (western) Europe, protecting U.S. farm income, and
preventing hyperinflation for the American consumer
at home. That assessment seems deserved in
retrospect as well.

When the war finally dragged to a close on November
11, 1918, it was with the complete defeat of Germany
and the Austro-Hungarian Empire and the near ex-
haustion of all of the energies and finances of all of the
peoples of Europe. (This in itself presented a potential
long-term problem for the United States since Europe
had been its largest grain customer by far for some
fifty years at that point.)

There were other more pressing problems in the
short run, however. For one, the people of Germany
came back into the world supply and demand equation, and this added demand was clearly going to
tighten supplies in the United States at least until the
1919 summer crops could be planted in Europe, which
in turn brought up another problem. The farm and
non-farm economies of Europe had sunk to such a low
point that it became clear soon after the war that there
was little hope of getting normal crops into the ground
in 1919 either.

As a result, prices started edging higher from their
officially set levels during the last half of 1918, and
they spent all of 1919 in a highly volatile state, flinging
back and forth between the support offered by the
official government price and the price shock high of
April 1917. By the end of 1919, cash wheat prices in
Chicago had pushed just past that two-year-old high,
to touch $3.50 per bushel. Shortage, disruption, and
boom would not go away. Like a fox in the chicken
coop, once these variables were let inside, they ran
amok.

With their high price levels of 1918–20, the markets
reflected the difficulty that Europe was having in

starting its recovery. With their extreme volatility, they reflected their difficulty in gauging its progress. Each of the belligerents seemed to be on such a different path.

Take France. Despite the fact that the western front had been focused in France, it was this country that fared best, first. It had one of the largest farm populations in Europe, and the ownership of French farmland was spread fairly evenly among that farm population—a factor made possible by the French Revolution. This wasn't true of other major countries in Europe, and it gave them the strongest base for recovery.

After the French army demobilized, a large percentage of its men could immediately return to specific places and start making themselves productive without waiting for any sort of government planning or for the gearing up of a large estate. This is the beauty of a small business. Since they had the most efficient system, the French were able to start feeding the majority of their population first.

Britain of course had been the world's greatest wheat importer for more than a century before the war, and the events of it had only served to widen the food deficit. The British were hampered in their farm recovery (especially in comparison to France) in large part because Britain was locked into a social and agricultural system that concentrated farmland heavily in the great estates of its upper classes. By the time World War I rolled around, those estates, and the upper classes, were becoming an anachronism. This was not a farming system and these were not people likely to gear up and suddenly turn productive in a crisis.

In addition, the war had reduced the financial means of the old social order in Britain, which for good or ill had sheltered and supported large numbers of its citizens in and around the great estates. The returning soldiers found that many of the estates from which they had come were no longer able to support the same large staffs after the war, and likewise could not support the villages that serviced the great estates. The British therefore were less able than the French to efficiently disburse their manpower. The men could not simply go home and become productive under their own steam. Large numbers of Britons migrated to the cities where unemployment was already high, so food imports remained heavy.

Germany and the rest of central Europe had it far worse. They continued to face both political upheaval and famine in the early postwar years. The average German soldier was far more likely to have come from a factory floor, the middle class, or the estate of one of the landowning Junkers of Prussia, than was his French counterpart, so he too had less of an opportunity to just go home and start producing food.

Adding to the woes of the German farm economy was the fact that a large chunk of the former Empire's better farmland was lopped off and given to the newly created state of Poland to the east, disrupting both the production of food and its distribution to Germans. Over it all loomed the French insistence on huge war reparations that the Germans strained to pay. The need to import food was great in the first years after the war, but the means to pay for them were inadequate. Hunger persisted until 1920.

It was Russia, however, that had it worst of all. That country had suffered most during the course of the war, and they continued to suffer the most after it had ended. The Russian Revolution of early 1917 overthrew the Tsar, and that quickly gave way to the Bolshevik Revolution of November. When the smoke cleared from the revolutions, there ensued a bloody civil war between Communists and conservative White Russians which lasted until 1920.

Russia had been the world's biggest exporter of wheat before the war, but fierce famines stalked the country from 1916, right on into the 1920s. As if the disruptions of warfare were not enough, after the Bolsheviks defeated the Whites they proceeded with their goal of completely reordering the new "Soviet" farm economy. The Bolsheviks viewed the conservative peasantry as a natural enemy of the revolution, and so Lenin was eager to diminish their economic power. He moved quickly to concentrate all ownership of land in the hands of the state.

Under the new system the peasants were expected to work the land to the full extent of their ability, keep and eat only what they needed, and turn over their surplus grain to the state after each harvest—a real life translation of Karl Marx's famous credo, "from each according to his ability, to each according to his need." This made the food problem even worse than it needed to be in the aftermath of war, and many of the peasants thwarted the Bolshevik policies by producing only what they needed.

In addition to suddenly being saddled with a brand new and much less efficient farming system, the USSR was struck by twin disasters: a massive crop failure in 1919, and an invasion by Poland during the planting and growing season of 1920. The Soviets lost the brief war with Poland and with it, by the fall of that year, some four million Russian ethnics, thousands of square miles of crop and pasture lands, and the crops and animals that were on them.

The net result was a famine that probably threatened the lives of some twenty million Soviet people at one point or another. America had become the world's granary of last resort, so an American relief effort was undertaken at the unofficial urging of the Soviets themselves. This drive delivered nearly one million tons of foodstuffs under the direction of the very able and very busy Mr. Herbert Hoover, and it has been estimated that it helped save as many as ten million lives.

These were the events that took the wheat market
up to the $3.50 a bushel at Chicago at the end of 1919
and the beginning of 1920. In the end, however, the
Russian famine turned out to be the last great
European food crisis of the war years, and as such it
was a somewhat misleading event for the American
farm markets as they traded near those all-time highs.

They had become accustomed first to consistent farm
profits, then to windfall profits, then the very lucrative
government price guarantees, followed in the end by
the highest prices of all. The Russian famine just
seemed like another event in a well- established trend.

Instead, by 1920 the world food equation was in the
process of reversing itself. With the exception of the
Soviet Union, the world was by then producing as
much grain as it needed to survive. Since the recovery
had barely started in 1920, it clearly had the ability to
start producing even more than needed, given continued stability and a little more time.

Just as the wheat market was figuring this out, the
U.S. government dropped its price controls (supports)
in 1920. Cash prices in Chicago fell from the all-time
highs at $3.50 in January, to less than $2.30 in about
two months, a drop of about one-third. From there the
market made one more run at the highs, but failed. It
started to collapse as the winter wheat crop matured.

The plunge was abetted by "bad" news from Europe.
The crops of 1920 progressed much better than expected, and as the year wore on, the European buyers
realized that they had already purchased more
American wheat in advance than they needed. They
abruptly withdrew from the U.S. and Canadian
markets just when these markets most needed buying
support to stem the decline. Prices fell through the end
of the year, and they kept falling right on through the
end of 1921, when they stopped just short of $1 per
bushel.

This in no uncertain terms signaled the end of the

long and prosperous run by the American farmer, a run that could be traced back to at least 1910. It was over so quickly that by 1921, farmers in the western U.S. Corn Belt burned corn for fuel, partly in protest, but also because for some the price it fetched on the open market was less than their cost of production. Things were much the same for many wheat producers.

How could $1 a bushel for wheat be less than the cost of production in 1921, when it was above the prices that had been so profitable for so many before the war started? The answer was that farming had gotten progressively more expensive during the boom, and it now cost more to produce a bushel of wheat. The added expense came on all fronts: higher land prices, the debt incurred to buy that land, and the more sophisticated equipment required to play the game.

Expenses were highest for the new and expanded farms because they tended to contain poorer land. With poorer land came lower yields. Since it cost about the same amount to plant and harvest on both good land and poor, the profit gets decided in a low priced year by how many bushels one can squeeze out of each acre. On the more recently planted lands with their poorer soils, there was no way to get a top yield.

Some farmers with poor land, a lot of recently acquired debt, or a long way to haul their grain to market found it difficult or even impossible to meet basic operating expenses after the plunge. Some who could meet their operating expenses couldn't pay their interest or else couldn't support their families with what was left.

The vast majority who still remained profitable in spite of the plunge tried to compensate by maintaining their own high acreage numbers of 1918–20, but this just brought more grain on the market to depress prices even further.

On top of that, it soon became apparent that U.S.

farmland prices were going into a protracted downtrend. They first fell for two years after the first mad scramble to expand sent land prices to their all-time peak in 1916. That first drop didn't cause too much concern at first. Most farmers and lenders were confident that they would resume the historic uptrend, and land prices did in fact flatten out in 1919 and 1920. However, they then moved slightly lower in 1921, and slightly lower again in 1922, before commencing a relentless downtrend that lasted until 1933, when the average price of farmland finally stopped falling and bottomed out at only about 50 percent of its value in the peak year of 1916! The new and expanded farms of the war years had "bought the highs."

When revenues won't cover costs, and the value of the basic assets of your business no longer covers existing debts, that pretty much leaves just one option. Foreclosure. Farmers were forced off their land in relatively small, but highly publicized numbers. This was all the more poignant when it was land that the family had homesteaded and "busted" out of virgin prairie sod.

The supply news from overseas was no better. Once the corner had been turned on crop production in western and central Europe with that first good crop of 1920, the push for greater food production was on with a vengeance everywhere. For starters, the Europeans could no longer afford the level of imports they had been forced to accept during the war. They were on the other side of that price shock.

After the war, they were all nearly broke, and the U.S. dollar was very strong as a result of the new postwar status of the United States as the world's biggest creditor. For economies that needed to rebuild and upgrade so much of their economies, there were precious few of these expensive American dollars left over to buy food, unless it was absolutely necessary.

As if that weren't enough, the big new creditor wasn't

cutting anybody any slack. The United States expected the war debts of the European Allies to be paid in full, and on a fairly tight schedule. (There was much grousing, but the schedule was largely maintained by the Allies.)

When you're in the business of selling things, you can only do well when the customer is able to buy. Combine oversupply with broke customers, and you get the general American farm picture of the 1920s.

Gradually, some healthier spots emerged in the economies of Europe, but this too worked to the disadvantage of the American farmer. More capital soon became available to European farmers along with more modern farming methods; the study of which became very popular. There was also a limited introduction of commercial fertilizers and better seed to replace seed stocks that had been wiped out in the last years of the war.

The fact that major (and minor) European debtor currencies were much lower versus the dollar than they had been before the war, also worked to the advantage of the Europeans. They could produce and sell food at a profit in Europe for less than the Americans. European farmers also hadn't had the luxury of expanding and improving their operations with heavy borrowing during the war years as had some of their American counterparts, so they weren't as burdened with expensive debt in the 1920s.

Another "advantage" was that as a result of near economic collapse and the postwar scarcity of capital, land prices in Europe were very low after the war in comparison to land prices in the United States. The cost of start-up and expansion was therefore lower than in the United States. Mechanization made itself felt in Europe, too. It didn't quite burst onto the scene, but the healthier and more advanced farm economies concentrated on beating their swords into plowshares by investing more of their industrial capacity in better farm equipment, and this brought some enormous localized gains in productivity per farmer.

Just as the American gains in farm output and farm income had come from one strength piled on another before 1920, so it was now in a weird backward sense with the Europeans. Weaknesses became strengths.

Governments sensibly chose to accelerate this process by promoting increased food production with all their might. Italy proved to be one of the more startling examples as the decade wore on. Mussolini's Fascist government came to power in 1923, and it did a lot more than make the trains run on time. The Fascists made self-sufficiency in basic food commodities one of their primary national goals. Acreage was expanded by draining ancient swamps and wetlands just as Americans were to do fifty years later. These acres were planted in particular to wheat. In fact it was called "the battle of the wheat," and as a result of it, Italian wheat production leaped by an astonishing 70 percent.

(The Fascist state in Italy was not, however, motivated entirely by humanitarian concerns. It believed in the glorification of the state and war. It considered food production one of the pieces that had to be put in place before a state could hope to successfully wage a war of expansion.)

Even the desperate food shortages in the USSR evaporated. Lenin realized after the famine of 1920 that he was moving too far and too fast with Marxism; his government and its experiment was in danger of collapse in any case if the country could not feed itself. He therefore did a complete about-face and introduced a broad economic liberalization called the New Economic Policy (NEP). This eliminated the confiscation of grain surpluses and allowed the peasants to raise and sell whatever they wanted after paying a fixed tax.

NEP was a smashing success. A food surplus

returned, starvation was basically eliminated, grain was once again exported from the fertile Ukraine, and the class of prosperous peasants called kulaks became an important economic force.

The powerful forces that were at work expanding food output in Europe were more than just economic and political, of course. Otherwise they could never have been applied with such urgency, and the tables could not have been turned so quickly. Ten million people had died of starvation and disease during the war, and the numbers were even higher if you counted the troubles of 1919 and 1920.

The reaction of the peoples of Europe to their food deficit therefore came not only from financial circumstances, logic, and dogma, it came from the gut. Both government and people shared this as a top priority, whether it was to glorify the state or save lives. People shared the goal of making sure that their countries would never be so vulnerable again, and the domestic production of food was the obvious first step. A stimulus like that puts down deep roots, and that results in a long life.

Farming is such an ironic business. On the one hand, it's about as fine an occupation as one can imagine, yet it does best in the countries like the United States that produce an exportable surplus only when large numbers of people elsewhere don't have enough to eat, and when they are willing and able to pay up for the finite world surplus.

Even when you get past that one very unpleasant irony and simply look at the booms as rare and wonderful opportunities for the farmers' financial position to be enhanced, there is still another layer of irony. Booms inject great volatility into an otherwise stable environment. They set capital to flowing into the farm economy all right, but it tends to naturally flow to those who are on the soundest financial footing in the first place (and who wisely choose to ignore the urge to expand with borrowing). To the weaker players, flows debt.

Booms have this amazing knack of simply churning up the industries that they hit. When the boom goes bust, the debts endure. It's as true of farming as it is of oil drilling.

4

WHAT TO DO?

The advent of the farm crisis in 1921 quickly brought
a spate of political proposals to turn it around. The one
that first gained a national base of support was being
promoted already in late 1921 by Messrs. George N.
Peek and Hugh S. Johnson, both late of the Moline
Plow Company. I say "late" because the Moline Plow
Company had already failed by 1921, a testimony to
the swiftness of the decline. As Mr. Peek put it, "You
can't sell a plow to a busted customer."

Their plan centered around paying the farmer something called a "fair exchange value" for eight major
farm products ranging from wheat to sheep. They were
actually to be paid this value only for those goods that
were marketed within the United States. The rest, the
surplus, was then to be "segregated" by a government
corporation, exported, and sold at the prevailing
(lower) world price. Expenses were to be paid by the

growers themselves, with the cost to be split among them via an "equalization fee."

This was, I think, very much a legacy of the four-year period of price controls during and after World War I when the government made the export sales. (Both men had worked for the government during the war, and in starting a plow company immediately afterward, they too had "bought the top." It was probably natural that they would retreat to the comfort of a system of government marketing.) Their plan was first proposed to the Congress in 1924 as the McNary-Haugen Bill. With modifications it remained in circulation until May 1928, when President Coolidge vetoed it for the second and final time.

The plan had structural problems aplenty, starting with the fact that official high domestic prices would clearly stimulate even more U.S. production, just as they had after they were instituted in August 1917. On top of that, as the ever larger surpluses got "segregated" and then marketed (dumped) abroad by the government corporation, the world price was likely to sag even further. As it did, the spread between the high domestic "fair exchange value," and the low world price would almost certainly widen. The dollar totals needed by the government corporation to bridge that gap would grow and grow.

Since the cost for all of this, plus the bureaucracy to administer it was to be paid by the farmer himself, it seemed clear that there were other financial problems or twists to the functioning of this plan. One was that the plan depended on the availability of large sums of money. If this money was truly to come from farmers, it meant that the government would have to take money from wealthier farmers and pay it back to poorer ones. One didn't have to mull this over too long to realize that there was bound to be some resistance from the payee.

Even if the bill was passed, it could only continue to

function over the long haul if there continued to be large numbers of farmers who could operate at a profit and who were willing to keep working hard to do so indefinitely, in order to generate the money needed to keep the less profitable farmer in business. The experience of the Ukraine in 1918–20 offered a real life example of what was likely to occur. Prosperous farmers would refuse to produce under such a system. It was an unintentional form of "from each according to his ability, to each according to his need." By 1921, even Lenin had temporarily abandoned this sort of economic planning.

The second major plan to make it to Congress called for creation of a Federal Marketing Board which would purchase 90 percent of estimated domestic needs of wheat, corn, and cotton each year, and sell them for farmer's cost of production, plus a fair profit. Again the proponents wanted the federal government to resume a role as marketer of the farmer's crops.

It sounds like a very fine thing: give the farmer what it cost him to produce a bushel, plus a "fair" mark-up. The big flaw, however, was that there were nearly 6.5 million separate small businesses that made up the farm economy. They had paid different amounts for their land. Some rented land; some owned. They had different sized debt loads with different rates of interest. They received varying amounts of rainfall during the course of the growing season, and they would invariably end up with different yields per acre come harvest. Some had better soil, and that simply yielded a bigger crop each year, regardless of rainfall.

As a result, each would have his own individual cost structure, and that could even vary on a given farm from one year to the next. There was no way for the federal government to sort it all out.

If the government just went ahead (as the bill intended) with a high subsidy rate that would guarantee a profit to the highest cost farmers, and then spread

that subsidy around to one and all, it would make very
wealthy men out of those farmers with the best land,
no debt, and the lowest cost of production per bushel.
This was introduced in 1925 by Senator Lynn Frazier
of North Dakota, and it died in senate committee.

The third major plan that made it to Congress called
for a system based on the payment of "export-deben-
tures." Proposed by an economist, of course, this plan
proposed that a "bounty" be paid for the export of farm
products in the form of a negotiable debenture, or
certificate. This debenture could then be sold to an
importer who could in turn use it to pay U.S. custom
duties on other, unrelated imports.

This one certainly seemed to have a chance to function since it involved a fairly straightforward and
simple-to-operate transaction. It could also have had a
very desirable impact on the farm economy in terms of
an expanded export market for grain. The problem in
the eyes of the more militant farmers was that this
sort of plan would only work over the long haul, and it
would spread its benefits over the general farm
economy. It was not going to get the higher prices into
the hands of farmers who needed (or wanted) them
today to help cover operating expenses.

The export debenture plan might still have been
passed by the Congress as a partial solution, if it
weren't for the other snags. For one, it was likely to
strike other countries as being aggressively interventionist in the world grain trade, as it was intended to
directly subsidize the export of cheap American grain.
They were likely to react with protectionist or interventionist measures of their own, or they might have
simply decided to stimulate their own grain production even more. That particular pot didn't need any
more stirring in the mid-1920s.

Furthermore, as far as the Congress was concerned
the plan tended to rob Peter to pay Paul. The debenture could be paid in lieu of U.S. import duties, so the

federal government would lose the tax revenues brought by those duties in the first place. The export-debenture plan was proposed in 1926, and it too failed to even pass the Congress.

Even without all of the obvious (and subtle) structural flaws of these proposals, none of them had much chance of flying given the political mind-set of the country in the postwar period. Warren G. Harding was elected president in 1920 with the slogan, "a return to normalcy," and this seemed to pretty well sum up the basic desires of the people of United States all through the decade.

Normalcy meant an unfettered economic system. It meant progress toward a better life. It meant allowing the American economic system to follow its natural course and pull everybody into a better future.

Most Americans had started getting their first taste of serious material progress before and during the war. Now they wanted more. People wanted an icebox and a radio. They wanted store-bought clothes and a car. Plenty of people on the American farm wanted to get off and go to the city, where these things seemed easier to acquire.

America had not sought its involvement in the European war. After the war ended, the country wanted to close the books on it as soon and as completely as possible. People consciously desired to return to the less complicated days that existed before the war, and that dream included uncomplicated free markets. In general, people saw the big farm proposals as the sorts of convoluted experiments that the Europeans were prone to conduct, and as such to be viewed with great suspicion.

Most important perhaps, the farm crisis of the 1920s lacked a true sense of urgency. It may sound harsh, but the problem didn't seem that big to the American public, at least in comparison to the gigantic and destructive events of 1914–20. Nobody was out there

dying of the farm crisis, as so many people had so
recently died in the midst of troubles elsewhere.

There were other explanations for the lack of urgency. Prosperity was breaking out all over the non-farm
sector. This was, after all, the Roaring Twenties. The
more than two-thirds of the country's economy that
was non-farm had barely even paused after the wartime manufacturing boom, before it roared on into the
new decade.

The flow of capital that came from America's new
status as a major creditor gave the country a steady
cash flow that it could spend, save, and invest. Housing, commercial construction, steel, autos, com-
munications, entertainment, and banking all boomed
even more than they had during the war. This greatly
expanded the middle class, and the goods that were
then demanded by all of the new people in that new
middle class caused the prosperity to start to feed on
itself. The prosperity provided round after round of
new jobs as the decade wore on.

The booming non-farm economy was therefore well
able to absorb the steady stream of people moving from
the farm to the city. Since the number of foreclosures
were few in a given year, it was believed by many
non-farmers (with justification) that the farmers who
got forced off their land could pick up stakes and get a
decent job elsewhere, maybe even a better life. Under
the circumstances, the country was awfully hard to
convince that it needed to chuck its desire for "normalcy" in favor of complicated and interventionist
economic farm schemes. Then, when the schemes
revealed themselves to be so flawed, the proponents
lost what little momentum they had.

Also, food was very cheap, and the American diet was
changing and improving rapidly in the 1920s.
Americans liked that for some very obvious reasons.
Calvin Coolidge hit the nail on the head when he ran
for president in 1924 promising, among other things,

"a chicken in every pot." When you got right down to it, most of the farm schemes were specifically designed to raise the food bill of the average citizen at a time when a middle class lifestyle and a middle class diet were within their reach for the first time. The farm programs were not going to find their momentum out among the upwardly mobile. It all added up to a political knot that the farmer just couldn't untie until the end of the decade.

Actually, those dietary improvements were still another important new economic variable that had to be digested by the farmer along with all of the other profound changes in the 1920s. The improvements consisted of more per capita consumption of dairy, eggs, and poultry. For the most part the growth in those higher- ticket categories came at the expense of wheat (bread).

These changes started ending the age of wheat. The modern world grain markets had been overwhelmingly dominated by the wheat trade since they started to evolve in the late 1700s with Russia exporting the stuff to England. The crop that was produced and exported by the prairie sodbusters after the Civil War was wheat, and it was wheat and wheat flour that had dominated exports all through the war and postwar years.

The changing American eating habits of the 1920s, however, allowed corn to gradually shoulder its way into a more central position in the markets, at least in the United States. Poultry, dairy, and meat are animal products, and animals tend to thrive on corn. Cattle can be fattened up to slaughter weight much faster by eating corn in a commercial feedlot, than they can by staying out to pasture to graze on grass. Commercial poultry production is even more dependent on corn and other commercial feeds. Chickens needed to spend their entire lives on some sort of formal feeding plan, and confined in a coup in order to be a viable product

in the competitive food market of the 1920s. Corn fit
the bill for the new diet, and it was abundant and
cheap.

This new demand for meat and dairy was unfortunately not enough to overcome the world's oversupply of all the basic ingredients that went into them, and
corn prices, just like wheat, remained somewhat
depressed. What the new diet did, however, was give
the corn farmer more options than the wheat farmer.
He could bring corn to market in two different forms:
as grain or as an animal product. This had always been
the case, but now the market for the second option was
widening rapidly and providing many farmers with
their best shot at turning a profit.

Wheat got left out of this shift. Oh, it could be used
for animal feed too, but the feeding of wheat to livestock and poultry wasn't as cost-effective as feeding
them corn. For one thing, wheat tends to cost about
twice as much per bushel. In the 1920s that was
mainly because corn yielded about twice as much per
acre, as it had since the nineteenth century. That
priced the wheat farmer out of the new consumer
demand for meat and dairy products. His major option
was to keep selling the raw product into the same old
shrinking markets. The calories now being consumed
by Americans in the form of meat and dairy, were for
the most part calories that had formerly been consumed in the form of wheat (bread).

All of which is to say that in the 1920s, it was the
wheat farmer who was more vulnerable to bust. Since
wheat had been the crop most in demand during the
boom, and since most of the acreage expansion that
resulted from the boom was planted to wheat, and
since a lot of this wartime expansion had occurred out
on the dry western fringes of the grain belt where soil
is poorer, and since these new and expanded farmers
were the ones who had borrowed money and paid up to

get into the farming game, this left the western wheat farmer as the most vulnerable player of all. It was in the western Grain Belt therefore that farm foreclosure seemed to be hanging over the most heads.

Many beleaguered Westerners found it hard to accept the fact that the tough spot they were in was dictated solely by economics and geography. It was more palatable to the farmer's mind to just update the prairie populism of the nineteenth century. That was when the farmer had cut his teeth politically. Battles were fought from the 1830s onward against flesh and blood enemies, the price fixing railroads, grain elevators, and wheat millers. Those were fights farmers could understand and gear up for. Problem was, even with human enemies, and even when the farmer won the legal battles, prices remained low.

This was because the world settled and planted hundreds of millions of new acres during the nineteenth century, and production grew faster than demand from the late 1860s until things balanced out in the parity years. Add to that the combination of psychological isolation and the existence of some very real enemies, and it generated a sort of paranoia, an ongoing search for the culprit behind the chronic low prices.

Since such a culprit could never quite be found, farm politics gradually evolved into something more satisfying. Thought and energy were diverted into the search for a different system wherein every farmer received a fair price each year for the grain he produced. This search became the central theme of farm rhetoric.

The search for utopia through economics was a common thread in the nineteenth century. Communes of the early 1800s were succeeded by the writings of men like Karl Marx. "From each according to his abilities, to each according to his needs" sounded as fine and reasonable as "a fair and just price for every farmer."

Both ignored everything essential to economics and
human nature, and yet both were to put down very
deep roots.

Utopian Marxism and its search for a classless
society became the official dogma behind the Russian
Revolution, and the Soviet society that followed it. The
search for a utopian (fair) grain market was to become
the official goal of the farm policy of the United States.
Both systems were equally inhospitable for their
respective fine-sounding ideals, but both were hammered at for decade after decade to try and make them
fit the rhetoric.

In any case, by the mid-twenties most farmers realized that there would be no political solution from
Washington any time soon. They started rallying instead around a number of self-help plans. The earliest
of these centered on the related concept of voluntary
controls on production and planted acreage.

A cutback in acreage was the only logical tack to take
under the circumstances. No matter what your
philosophy happened to be, it was pretty obvious that
the American farmer was producing more grain than
the world wanted.

Farm groups concluded that it was possible for them
to organize farmers and get them to agree to plant
fewer acres. But the idea of voluntary reductions was
utopian too. The job was far beyond the resources of
any private farm organization. They had no power to
enforce compliance, and it was hard to convince an
individual farmer that he should plant less out of the
goodness of his heart while his neighbors continued
planting right up to the tree line. Come spring, every
farmer's most powerful instinct is to grow as large a
crop as possible. It's like birds flying south in the fall.

Voluntary acreage reduction also violated some of
the laws of economics, and it just so happened that
these laws were operating in particular force during

margins thin on each bushel, then the farmer needs to bring in the biggest possible crop each year to stretch those thin profits into a decent income. Ergo, an even bigger surplus.

Two other self-help themes rounded out the menu of major proposals made by the farm organizations in the 1920s: cooperative marketing and crop withholding. Both were just what they sound like.

Crop withholding advocates held the theory that farmers could command the higher prices they wanted by simply organizing, and refusing to sell their crops until prices rose. This tended to have a lot of the same problems as voluntary acreage reductions. How do you get farmers to comply, to actually refuse to sell their crops day in, day out, month in, month out? Human beings don't tend to be that disciplined, and the farmer of the 1920s was no exception.

Of course that farmer also had a big financial hurdle standing in the way of crop withholding. If you decide to hold onto an inventory of grain, or anything else for that matter, you need capital. This hurdle is easy enough to overcome when the farmer in question has no debt and therefore owns his grain free and clear, but when you consider that the would-be withholder of the 1920s was often the weakest and least capitalized of farmers, there was a built-in contradiction. That farmer's banker wanted mortgage payments, on schedule and in cash, something the farmer could not accomplish without selling his crops. The withholding plan therefore never had a chance; farmers had to risk foreclosure to stick it out.

Crop withholding also had little appeal among those who were not particularly militant, who were not in any immediate danger of losing their farms and who were still able to sell their grain at a profit in the depressed markets of the twenties. This was still quite true of the vast majority of farmers, east and west.

Solvent farmers simply wanted to be left alone to sell

true of the vast majority of farmers, east and west.

Solvent farmers simply wanted to be left alone to sell their crops as best they could each year, and to get on with the job of producing the next one. Spiro Agnew might have called this group the "silent majority." They may have given lip service to plans and schemes intended to give everybody a bigger price per bushel, but they did not need the scheme to survive, so they were not there in the pinch.

At any rate, all attempts at crop withholding failed before they began. In the end, it was the blood-brother to crop withholding, cooperative marketing, that proved to be the plan with staying power. Its premise was that large marketing associations of farmers could pool their grain and sell it only when prices were favorable. This was supposed to convert the small farmer into a big player who could then strike a better deal with the giant middlemen—the grain companies and processors.

It had a certain logic to it, and with nothing better waiting in the wings cooperative marketing lived on to become the proposal of choice among farm organizations. In fact it became the basis for the first national price support program in peacetime. (More on that in the next chapter.)

Until that happened, and as the decade wore on, there just didn't seem to be a clear solution. Frankly, it's tough to come up with one, even in hindsight, that could have cut through the layers of often conflicting problems faced by the farmer. There were just too many farms, too many workers on those farms, and too much productivity per farm. One of those categories had to drop in a free market to get supply and demand in rough balance. There was no peaceful way to make it be productivity. The only solution that the market could put to bear was lower prices.

The basic farm numbers in the United States were still enormous at the beginning of the 1920s. Farm of the total U.S. population. By the Roaring Twenties, however, the country no longer needed to have one-third of its population engaged in the job of feeding the other two-thirds. Some sort of shakeout was bound to come, with or without the First World War.

The number of farms had peaked at over 6.5 million in 1920, and despite the publicity over farm failures this number still stood at about that same level in 1929. The key was that those farms were able to operate with a smaller work force. Thus out of all the possible variables, it was the farm population that took the hit. It fell by about 2.0 million, or more than 6 percent between 1916 and 1929. When we consider that there was still a fairly high farm birthrate during the decade, it seems likely that the number of people who actually moved off farms and went to a town or city was much higher.

Those farm workers were men and women who were needed elsewhere in the dynamic non-farm economy. It was expanding; it needed labor, and it was willing to pay attractive wages to get that underutilized and underpaid labor force transferred to where the jobs were.

Many of those who left the farm in the 1920s were escapees, not refugees. They were only too happy to have alternative employment that paid them more than they could ever make on their father's farm and which did not include bailing hay, milking cows, and all the rest. Often these were people who looked at the lay of the land on the farms where they lived and saw little chance of ever owning one of their own, much less turning a decent profit. They chose to leave.

The refugees were far fewer in number. These were the farm families that may have wanted very much to stay in the business but didn't have the capital, or the business skills, or good enough land, or a large and healthy enough family to make their own farm a go.

The beginning of the farm shakeout in the twenties

healthy enough family to make their own farm a go.

The beginning of the farm shakeout in the twenties all seems like pretty healthy stuff in retrospect. It whittled down the numbers a bit, but still left millions of those same ordinary farm folks, the backbone of America, out there doing their own farm labor on land they owned. Farming in the late 1920s was, on balance, still the same very healthy contributor to the social equation in America that it had been for three hundred years (in the north).

Farm prices for most major crops bounced well off their lows after 1924, and most of the farm economy was again operating in the black by 1929. It was hardly the best of times, but neither was it the worst. Of course, that was 1929.

5

A NEW DEAL

The recovery in cash wheat prices in the second half of the 1920s took the market in Chicago from just above $1 per bushel in mid-1924, to well over $2 on two separate occasions—in 1925 and early 1928. After the second peak, however, they went on a protracted slide that lasted all the way through 1928 and 1929, until wheat prices were once again approaching $1.

Corn prices fared better. They bounced rather smartly off their big lows of about 40 cents a bushel in 1921 (the levels at which farmers had burned corn in Nebraska), and they never came even close to that big low again during the rest of the decade. They managed to bounce as high as $1.35 in late 1924 to early 1925 and then finished out the 1920s trading in a narrow range of about 80 cents to $1.15 a bushel at Chicago. The fact that the corn market was so successful in staying off its low of 1921 was probably a reflection of

its increasingly favorable economic position versus
wheat as the Roaring Twenties roared on.

Still, relentless pressure for federal help from farm
groups (especially wheat growers) continued, and it
finally paid off under President Herbert Hoover in
1929 as the farm recession went into its tenth year.
The Congress passed the Agricultural Marketing Act
that year which established the Federal Farm Board.

The Farm Board in turn was based on the basic
policy proposal that had proved most enduring of all
those that were run up the flag pole by farm groups
and economists over the course of the decade, that of
cooperative marketing by farmer organizations.

Cooperative marketing had emerged from the pack
for a couple of reasons. It was very popular with the
major farm organizations because it satisfied a gut
feeling on their part: Big grain companies were reap-
ing profits because they were big, and possibly in
kahoots. Farmers thought that if they were sufficient-
ly organized and funded, they could do the same. It
was clear, however, that it was only possible with the
backing of the federal government. Probably the
second greatest strength that it had over other
proposals was that, while extremely optimistic, the
basic concept did not deny the fundamental laws of
commerce and human nature.

The 1929 plan consisted of funding the Farm Board
with needed capital in the form of a $500 million
revolving fund. That fund was to be lent out to cooperative associations and "stabilization corporations" with
the goal of allowing them to purchase grain when
prices were low, and hold it off the market until prices
rose. (That's why they needed so much money.)

The Farm Board was the first major peacetime farm
program, and it established a number of important
precedents that would be repeated in one form or
another by farm programs clear through the 1980s.
Perhaps the most obvious was its reliance on credit,

the idea of adding to the debt of the farm economy to achieve the basic policy goals. If parity was Flawed Building Block Number One, then this surely had to be Number Two.

Next in importance was the premise that the U.S. farm economy could remove its own supplies from the free market in the midst of a world glut, and that this unilateral action could tighten the world's supply enough to support prices within a much larger world marketplace.

In the backs of planners' minds I'm sure was the success that the government enjoyed during World War I in supporting prices in local areas by buying grain. This sopped up surplus supplies during the height of the harvest when incoming supplies over-whelmed local transport and storage. The problem with trying to recreate this system during the 1920s, though, came after the grain was in hand.

During World War I, the federal government had been able to turn around and sell the grain it had acquired into a hot spot in the domestic marketplace where prices were exploding, or they could turn around and export it to millions of hungry Europeans who were willing, even eager, to pay up. In 1929, however, there were no hot spots domestically and everybody and his brother was competing for the European business at discount prices, including the Europeans themselves. Not only that, but once you got past the winter wheat harvest glut in June and July, you were well on your way to the fall harvest glut of corn which was frequently followed by a February glut in a variety of crops which in turn gave way to the pre-planting glut in the spring and on to the next round of harvest gluts. Gluts were not occasional things in isolated locations.

Surplus grain taken off the market at one low point, was often grain that could not be gotten rid of. If that grain had to be carried into the next crop year because

prices stayed depressed, two things were likely to
happen. The association's cost would grow because
they were forced to pay the added cost of holding that
grain in storage, and farmers would be encouraged by
any slight improvement in prices, even one caused by
an artificial shortage, to plant more acres than the
market needed. That in turn meant that prices could
stay depressed, and the surplus could get rolled forward into yet another crop year. Depriving the market
of supply was Flawed Building Block Number Three.

It's likely that this natural course of events would
have unfolded and sabotaged the Farm Board over
time in any case, but it had a much bigger problem
waiting in the wings: the stock market crash of October 1929. This in some ways represents the last
important precedent set by the Federal Farm Board—
very bad timing.

The crash turned out to be every bit as big a disaster
for the American farmer as it was for Wall Street, and
that's saying a lot since it came on the heels of the
depressed farm economy of the 1920s. One reason was
that the booming stock market that preceded the crash
had generated huge pools of paper wealth, and by 1929
speculation was competing hotly with baseball as the
true national pastime. The growing pools of speculative capital in turn needed more outlets, more games
to play. Some of that capital found its way into the
freewheeling agricultural futures pits at the Chicago
Board of Trade.

The presence of speculators usually makes a market
go up, or at least stops it from going down as much as
it otherwise would, and such was the case with the
grain markets in the years leading up to the crash.
Without the infusion of speculative capital, they
probably wouldn't have held above the lows of the first
half of the decade.

After the stock market started to plummet in October, great chunks of the paper wealth it created on

the way up simply disappeared. The agricultural futures broke in sympathy, and they continued to break, in part because a substantial portion of the world's capital base had simply gone away, and in part because what was left was often urgently needed by its owners elsewhere.

Once this broad base of speculative support in the grain markets dried up, there was nothing left that could halt, or even slow the declines that followed. Prices fell well into the 1930s and the farmer who had been operating on razor-thin profit margins in the 1920s found his thin profits had turned into big fat losses. By the time agricultural prices finally bottomed out in 1932, total net farm income in the United States had fallen to only *one-third* of its levels in 1929 (when the farmer thought he was already in a depression).

The crash generated a great deflation in the prices of most other goods and services too, and for the farmer, the two to three years that followed it must have seemed like a contest to see which would drop faster— the cost of the fuel, equipment, seed, and credit that went into producing each bushel, or the price of the bushel itself. Unfortunately, the bushel won.

Or lost, depending on your point of view. At any rate, the price of that bushel dropped faster and further than the cost of the things needed to produce it. Between 1929 and the subsequent big lows of 1932, the price of farm products dropped by a whopping 50 percent, while the cost of the goods that the farmer needed to produce his crops dropped by only 32 percent. Many thousands of farmers and farm workers who had managed to grind their way through the 1920s were therefore ruined by this second farm crash.

The new Federal Farm Board also fell victim after it turned out that it had the wrong plan for the wrong times. The bottom line dilemma for any lender is of course whether the value of the collateral will cover the principal of the loan when the loan comes due.

Since the collateral for Farm Board loans was the
grain itself and since the value of that grain kept going
down the longer one held on to it, it was rarely worth
enough to cover the loans in the end.

As if that wasn't enough, the Farm Board was also
done in by its basic purpose for existence: the Board
was to lend money so that grain could be taken off the
market when prices went down, and this need accelerated the more the market went down. With each
round of new lows, the needy constituency expanded,
and so it was compelled by its job description to dish
out still more loans that could never be repaid simply
because the price was still going down. I think that's
called a catch-22.

By the time farm prices hit bottom in 1932, the Farm
Board's $500 million was long gone, it had ceased to
function and the country's first peacetime farm program was defunct.

A Second Try and a New Deal

If there was a silver lining for the farmer in the
post-1929 crash, it was that the farm crisis was viewed
by the country at large with a great deal more urgency,
than it had been after the first farm crash in 1920–21.
This was partly because it was a lot worse, but it was
also because the economic crisis was now shared by the
rest of the citizenry. There was no longer the perceived
safety net of a booming non-farm economy to absorb
those who had been streaming off the farms in the
1920s.

The fact that urban centers were no longer an outlet
for the surplus farm population during the Depression
was graphically illustrated by an aberration in the big
new demographic trends of the twentieth century. The
farm population reversed its decline of the 1920s, and
rose by nearly two million from 1930 to 1934—very
nearly reaching back up to its all-time high of 1916.
The number of farms rose too, and that basic number

went on to set a brand new record high at over 6.8 million farms in 1935.

The reasons were simple. People with nowhere to go and no formal job that could provide a cash income took shelter on the land and subsisted. When other forms of economic activity fail, either for an individual or a society, they can only turn to the foundation of all economic activity—the production of food.

In any case, the towns and cities were no longer able to provide a decent life for all of the people who were already there, and they could ill afford the threat of a new wave of refugees from the countryside. The last thing an urban manufacturing worker needed in the 1930s was more competition.

The severity of the Depression therefore had the effect of keeping the farm crisis on more of a front burner. It would not be another nine years before the next farm program rolled around.

The slide in agricultural prices continued through the waning days of the Hoover administration, and this fact no doubt contributed to the Roosevelt victory in the presidential election of 1932. On the way down, the price of wheat at Chicago first broke below the lows of 1923 near $1 a bushel, then below the lows of the prewar parity years near 80 cents, then below the lows of 1906–07, and finally below the lows of 1894–95, to bottom out just above 40 cents per bushel.

Corn prices traveled a similar path, although corn's downtrend actually looks even steeper on the price chart because it sat at a relatively higher level before the crash. It went through its old lows as well on the way down to close out the very tough year of 1932 just above 20 cents per bushel in the Chicago cash market. It would have been cold comfort to the corn producer of 1932, but unlike wheat, the Chicago corn market managed to hold slightly above its big lows of the 1890s.

Since the farm electorate was still so large in 1932,

the fact that the agricultural markets were sitting
down at the big lows around election time no doubt
contributed to the completeness of the Roosevelt victory over Mr. Hoover, and to the Democratic base of
power in the House and Senate.

The one-sidedness of the election in turn brought
about a quantum leap in the level of involvement by
the federal government in the farm economy. Mr.
Roosevelt later stated that in the face of a crisis one
ought to "do something," and if that failed, to "do
something else."

This philosophy dramatically spilled over into farm
matters, and 1933 became a sort of "big bang" for farm
policy. The "return to normalcy" mind-set that had
thwarted farm policy proposals in the twenties was out
the window (along with billions in lost equity). The
pendulum now swung just as far in the other direction.
Now both Congress and the Roosevelt administration
couldn't do enough.

Desire was one thing, but the new farm policy "something" needed to take on form and substance. It needed
a long list of programs, and it needed some sort of
common mind-set to tie it all together. The farm community was ready with all of these things. Decades of
farm rhetoric, organizing, and economic planning were
already under the farmer's belt by 1933, and this
became the center of gravity. The rush of farm policy—
the big bang—therefore sprang largely from the tradition of farmer populism and militancy.

When the Roosevelt administration took office, it put
forth a new piece of farm legislation called the Agricultural Adjustment Act of 1933. Its basic goals were to
control the surplus, reduce planted acreage, and control crop disease. It also introduced a concept that
we've only anticipated in the story thus far: parity. The
stated goal of parity and this first big New Deal farm
bill was to restore the purchasing power that agricultural commodities had had in the prosperous and

balanced years just before World War I.

Secretary of Agriculture Henry A. Wallace's advisors, in outlining this goal, declared that the 1909–14 period (later changed to 1910–14) was, "one of considerable agricultural and industrial stability . . . with equilibrium between the purchasing power of city and country." They also stated that these years were "the most recent period when economic conditions, as a whole, were in a state of dynamic equilibrium." Flawed Building Block Number One was chiseled into stone.

To achieve parity, the USDA developed an index which could be used to calculate what the value of a bushel of wheat or corn needed to be in current dollars in order for it to generate the same purchasing power that it had in the parity years. That index was eventually updated on a monthly basis, and it continues to be updated today. Thus the goal of agricultural policy in a given year was to get farm prices close to the parity index.

The secretary of agriculture was given a variety of weapons to accomplish this. The most important was an authorization to reduce plantings through voluntary and paid acreage reduction programs. He also was authorized to regulate the marketing of basic crops through agreements with associations of farmers as well as processors and other middlemen who handled agricultural products. He also was instructed to license middlemen to eliminate unfair trading practices, to decide on a level at which processors of raw farm commodities were to be taxed, and to use the proceeds of those taxes to achieve the basic goals of the bill.

This bill was followed and augmented by a bill passed in October 1933 that established another key player in the farm policy—the Commodity Credit Corporation, or CCC. The CCC was authorized to make loans to individual farmers that would enable them to hold onto their crops instead of selling them at depressed prices. The loan terms were stated in cents per bushel, and the loan in corn was put at 45 cents a bushel, substantially higher than the farm price of the early thirties.

The theory was basically the same one that had empowered the Farm Board of 1929—that the prices would eventually rise if supplies could be taken off the market, and that the farmer could eventually sell the crops in question at the higher price and pay back the loan. The government called it "modified price-fixing." The difference between it and the Farm Board was that the Farm Board confined its loans to cooperative associations and the New Deal made them available to of individual farmers.

These loans were viewed at the time as a temporary measure, but in fact they simply reinforced a precedent, and a farm policy precedent once reinforced is something that never dies. Crop loans have remained at the core of the price support system through the end of the 1980s.

Other programs were passed that were designed to plow under cotton and tobacco acres, to buy up and liquidate hogs and pigs before they were ready for market, to establish import quotas, to buy and distribute meat to unemployed families, and put in place production and marketing controls for rice and peanuts, everything from soup to nuts, you might say.

The new thread running through the array of farm provisions placed on the table in 1933, however, was the desire to reduce overall production by reducing planted acreage. To achieve this, farmers were assigned a set allotment based on their farm's average production over the years 1928–32. They were then paid by the government to stop planting on a set percentage of that allotted acreage, and the funds to do so came from the new tax on processors.

Wheat farmers who agreed to limit planted acreage

in the upcoming 1934 and 1935 crop years received an adjustment payment up front. The USDA was so eager to boost farmer participation, that they also paid this adjustment on the crop that was still in the ground in the spring of 1933 when the first farm bills were being formulated. This payment amounted to around 30 cents per bushel paid to the average participant over the next three years, and it was pretty attractive stuff to a wheat farmer that had been looking at a total wheat price of just over 40 cents a bushel just a few short months before the sign-up started. Participation was very heavy.

As a matter of fact, the process of trying to reduce acreage was so aggressive in the spring of 1933 that a dramatic proposal was made to even pay wheat farmers to plow up acres that were growing at the time. Such was the mood of the time that the idea might just have flown, if not for a major new ingredient that entered the farm picture in 1933.

That ingredient was the Dust Bowl. By some reckonings this didn't officially begin until 1934, but in the southern Great Plains, the wheat crop of 1933 was already so greatly affected by drought that the national average yield fell to its lowest level in well over two decades. The total wheat crop dropped by over one third from the previous year. Corn yields fell too that first year, but less drastically.

This was an ironic coincidence if there ever was one. The United States had no sooner begun to implement what was probably the most aggressive attempt at acreage reduction in the history of agriculture, and it managed to do so in the first year of the Dust Bowl. With this remarkable coincidence, the USDA had already begun to enforce its propensity for very bad timing.

The Dust Bowl drought started in the southwestern Grain Belt (especially Oklahoma) where wheat production is concentrated and the climate is drier to

begin with. By 1934, the effects of it gripped nearly all
of the Wheat Belt of the Great Plains on up into the
Dakotas, and dry, hot weather ranged far to the east,
into the major corn producing regions of the central
Midwest.

Yields dropped sharply for corn that second year, to
15.8 bushels an acre versus an average corn yield in
the 1920s of nearly 27 bushels. To find a yield that was
lower, one almost has to go back to years that were
pre-tractor. Acreage was down too by then because of
the new farm programs and the heavy farmer participation in the acreage reduction programs, so the
total corn crop dropped to its lowest levels since the
nineteenth century.

The carryover (surplus) of corn dropped from a high
of 327 million bushels, down to 61 million bushels at
the end of the first official Dust Bowl crop marketing
year. The wheat surplus disappeared, and the United
States was put in the somewhat embarrassing position
of being a net importer of wheat in 1934, 1935, and
1936, a time when it was paying farmers to not plant.

There was a weather reprieve for much of the Corn
Belt in 1935 and yields bounced back to about 24
bushels per acre, but wheat yields barely recovered at
all. The drought had simply retreated back to its core
in central Oklahoma and the southern Great Plains in
general. It was this area for which the term Dust Bowl
was coined.

In some locations there was little or no rain for four
years. Topsoil moisture was depleted, then subsoil
moisture, and soon even the hardiest of dryland gras-
ses couldn't put down roots deep enough to find the
water to survive. They disappeared from the surface,
leaving only a layer of fine dust. The wind then lifted
great clouds of the dust into the air, gathered it
together into dense storms that could be a mile high,
and then marched those clouds back and forth across
the southern plains.

Overfarming and overgrazing on the edges of the Grain Belt greatly contributed to the dust storms. Planted acreage had expanded with the boom of the late war years, and this had pushed grain farming farther west onto the Great Plains, into regions that were a bit too dry and with soil that was a bit too thin and erodible to be able to withstand the stress caused by modern grain production—just like the sub-Saharan Africa today.

Some of the last patches of virgin prairie had been planted or grazed during the war boom expansion, and along with it went the vegetation that was ideally suited to protecting fragile soil from erosion and to conserving the precious moisture under the surface in times of drought. Trees had been felled too in the rush to expand—trees dividing fields that had cut down wind erosion in the past, and the trees on the edges of streams and ponds. Very little of the lost vegetation had been replaced during the bust years, so there was less of everything left growing in the 1930s to help hold down the dust.

The drought spread out one more time in the summer of 1936 from its base in the southern plains to again slash yields in the Corn Belt to the east, and they fell back down to 16.2 bushels an acre. Wheat yields just stayed at their lows for a fourth straight year.

Another irony to the start-up phase of farm policy was that prices of wheat and corn had already begun to rally by the time the first farm bills were being debated in early 1933—another symptom of chronic poor timing. In fact, the markets started to positively streak higher immediately after poor Mr. Hoover's electoral defeat in 1932.

The initial stage of the rally may have been based on sheer bounce. Nowadays they would say that the market was extremely oversold. More fuel was added by the prospect of acreage reductions as the legislative process began in early 1933, and then still more came from the drought itself. Cash wheat prices in Chicago surged from their big low just above 40 cents a bushel, to nearly $1.20 during the second half of 1933. Corn did even better in terms of its percentage gain as it leapt from its big low at just over 20 cents, to about 65 cents a bushel over about the same time span.

Both markets continued to rally all the way through the spring of 1937, when wheat topped out at about $1.50 per bushel, and corn at about $1.40 (Chicago cash market). This represented a four- year percentage gain of about 370 percent in wheat and about 620 percent for corn! If you want to wipe out a food surplus and raise prices, weather and war are the variables that will do it for you everytime.

The Dust Bowl ended with 1936, but it wasn't until spring 1937 that the market realized that there would be a return of near normal weather and precipitation across the Grain Belt. In the case of winter wheat this came just in time to stimulate growth as the crop came out of its winter dormancy, and to boost yields back into the normal range before the crop was harvested in June–July.

In the case of corn, the improved soil moisture was in place by planting time in April and May, and rainfall continued to be ample right on through the growing season. The national corn yield in 1937 hit 28.3 bushels an acre, and that was just two bushels shy of the all-time record. The market had been braced for another year of Dust Bowl when it was at the spring highs, and instead it got a good chunk of the surplus back in that one good growing season.

Prices plunged. Wheat went on a slide that lasted through the end of 1938, and in the process it fell all the way back to about 60 cents at Chicago. Corn's descent was more dizzying, just as its rise had been. It fell from the peak of just under $1.40 a bushel, down to about 53 cents in seven months during 1937. Then it spent all of 1938 slowly working its way lower still, down to about 40 cents a bushel. It finally hit bottom at about the same time as wheat.

The wheat crop was not just bigger in 1937 because of weather. The Supreme Court threw a major monkey wrench into the Roosevelt farm policies the year before by declaring most of its acreage reduction provisions unconstitutional, along with the processing taxes that helped to pay for them. In the case of wheat, more than fifteen million additional acres that were sidelined by the paid reduction program had been replanted in the fall of 1936, just in time to receive the improved snow and rains of winter and spring of 1937. This added to the size of the crop, and that added to the weight of the market as it went into its slide after the big spring high. It was a one-two punch that carried forward into the next fall when another six million acres found their way into the harvested acreage column.

(This was incidentally one of the Supreme Court decisions that so angered President Roosevelt that he subsequently tried to pack the court by passing a constitutional amendment that raised its membership from nine to twelve, in order to tilt it in his favor.)

In taking stock of all this toward the end of the 1930s, it was clear that the New Deal had been a very mixed bag in the area of farm policy. On the negative side was the fact that by the end of 1938, despite the worst series of droughts in recorded American history, and the biggest government induced acreage reduction in world history, the surplus was nearly as big as it had ever been, and prices were back down near the lows they had hit when poor Herbert Hoover was defeated in late 1932.

On the plus side, farm income had risen sharply over the first three years of the New Deal. However, about half of this was the result of government payments and half the result of higher drought prices. In any case, the government payments were eventually curtailed by the Supreme Court's decision in January 1936 to eliminate the processing taxes which had paid the farmer a good percentage of that government income. Farm income went on another serious slide after peaking in 1935.

Not surprisingly, farm numbers started dropping again too, just as they had in the 1920s. The total number of farms fell from Depression-inflated highs of over 6.8 million in 1935, to just under 6.3 million in 1941. The farm population dropped too—from about 32.4 million in 1933, to 30.1 million in 1931. This could no longer be explained as an exodus into the booming non-farm economy because that was now depressed.

More pluses included the fact that the USDA brought electricity to many depressed sections of rural America, and it began the large-scale purchase of surplus food which was distributed to those in need. The New Deal also responded fairly quickly to the Dust Bowl with the Soil Conservation and Domestic Allotment Act of 1936. This was an attempt to combine the promotion of soil conservation and the planting of soil-conserving crops, with the attempt to keep planted acreage down. The act failed at the latter, but laid a foundation for successful conservation policies that were enacted in the 1940s and 1950s.

So what conclusion can we draw from the foundation-laying decade? I think that we can cut through the minor successes and failures and judge the policy framework in light of its own stated goals. The goal was to reestablish the basic equilibrium between farm and city of the years before World War I, and at the same time to raise crop prices to the point where they equaled the buying power farmers experienced in those five parity years.

This wasn't achieved. If we judge success or failure of the basic goal by the index that the USDA had developed to measure parity, then wheat needed to be up around $1.30 at the end of the decade. In fact, it was only bouncing along between 60 and 80 cents per bushel at Chicago during 1938–39. Corn only traded at about 40–50 cents a bushel. Both were even lower in the country.

The goal of farm policy was also to manipulate the free market so that it would deliver to the farmer a "fair" price. There was an illusion of success in this regard during the middle of the decade when prices were on a four-year rally, but I think it's clear in retrospect that it was the drought that supported the market, not farm policy. When we look at the tailspin prices ended up in with some decent weather at the end of the decade, it's hard to give price-support policies any credit at all. I think it's fair to say that prices would have revisited the low end of the range a number of times during the middle of the decade, if weather had been anywhere near normal.

One critical part of the new farm policy never got a clear test during the Dust Bowl, however. The "emergency" loan provisions of the CCC were designed for a very depressed market wherein farmers would take out a government loan, and hold their crop off the market until prices rose. Since the market stayed above the loan levels during most of the Dust Bowl, this wasn't initially tested under the conditions for which it was designed—namely, a prolonged glut.

If grain prices had stayed depressed for the entire decade, maybe the whole idea of trying to recreate the "dynamic equilibrium" of the parity years would have died an early death. Perhaps the idea of supporting prices by loaning the farmer money to keep his crops off the market would have died one of those early deaths too if low prices had forced the government (CCC) to make a lot of grain loans that never got paid back, like the old Farm Board loans.

The depressed markets of 1938 onward seemed destined to put the loan policies to a more clear test since the United States was clearly headed for another glut at that point. Only another extraordinary outside

event would take prices higher, and give the whole
system a reprieve. Unfortunately such an extraordinary event was in the works. The Europeans were
starting to slaughter one another again by late 1939.
Like terrible droughts, world wars support food prices.

As all this was unfolding, a new trend starting getting underway. The size of the average farm started
going up—from about 150 acres per farm in 1933, to
about 175 in 1940. Farm assets were starting to concentrate themselves, as land has always tended to do
over time. Various flukes of American history had kept
this process at bay in the United States until the
1930s, but no longer. This would be another trend with
a very long life.

The end of the 1930s was another good time to compare the lot of the American farmer to his counterparts
elsewhere. There was still a lot to be thankful for. Most
of the world's farmers were still far poorer. Germany
and Italy had turned to fascism and were starting to
make war. Spain had spent most of the decade
embroiled in a bloody civil war. In China, where farm
life had never been easy, the great farming regions of
the northeast were by then in the process of being
brutally overrun by the Japanese.

The USSR, though, had once again reserved the
worst fate of all for its farmers. Josef Stalin had
decided with the five-year plan of 1928–32 to reverse
the relatively free (NEP) agricultural policies that
Lenin had instituted in 1921. The vast majority of all
Soviet farmland was seized from peasants who bitterly
resisted, and it was organized into huge state-owned
farms called collectives. In the early stages of the
process, farmers in the Ukraine were given unreach-
able food quotas, and the state tried to collect those
quotas whether or not there was enough food left over
for the peasant family to survive.

Resisters were sent on thousand-mile marches to
Siberia, shot, or became the victims of state-sponsored

riots against "rich" peasants. Between eight and ten million Ukrainian farmers and their family members were either starved to death or killed in the process.

It was a different and much tougher world backdrop than the one the American farmer had faced with the benign parity years just before World War I, but there was still no doubt that his lot was best.

6

A SECOND WORLD WAR

In September 1939 Hitler unleashed his blitzkrieg, or lightning war, against Poland. This time around the Soviet Union had established a nonaggression pact with the Germans before the hostilities even began. The Germans invaded Poland from the west on the 1st, and the Soviets invaded from the east on the 17th, so it was little Poland who faced a war on two fronts this time.

Clearly the situation could not last. Polish resistance was very quickly crushed, and by winter, Germany and the USSR partitioned Poland, as agreed in advance. There was no true "eastern front" at the start of this war.

There was no real western front either. There, instead of a blitzkrieg there was *sitz*krieg. Britain and France didn't attack Germany at first, although they had both declared war against it after the invasion of

Poland, and Germany didn't attack France. Both sides mostly just sat.

In May of 1940, Germany upped the scale by over-running Holland and Belgium. It then sliced through a gap in the French Maginot Line, and by June 22, it had taken Paris and signed an armistice that divided and neutralized France for the next four years. The net result of all of this for the European farm economies was a lot less disruption than had occurred in the first year of the First World War. The harvests of fall 1939, the spring plantings of 1940, and even the harvests of fall 1940 were able to proceed with less interference.

On the seas around Europe, both sides fell immediately back into the old roles. Britain attempted a naval blockade of Germany, a war of attrition with which it hoped to wear the Germans down by depriving them of basic commodities necessary for an extended war effort, such as rubber and petroleum. Germany again deployed its submarine fleet to harass the shipping lanes leading to and from Britain, and to loosen the blockade. Neither side, however, was in a position to even think that it could starve the other out of the war.

The Americans fell back into an habitual role, too. Both Congress and the American people were again determined to remain isolated from the fraternal conflict in Europe, just as they had when its ancestor began in 1914. Americans were even less interested in becoming involved in Japan's attempted takeover of China.

The United States fell immediately back into its role as the neutral supplier of war materials—again primarily for the Allies, and this in turn gave another enormous boost to the U.S. manufacturing sector. The U.S. role of world granary of last resort was reassumed as well, but with no real urgency.

Since the farming economy of Europe was less disrupted this time around, and since European and world food stocks were relatively high when the war started in 1939–40, the United States experienced only a modest increase in export demand as a result of the first year of the war. Prices started moving higher in the Chicago market in an orderly advance.

Corn prices left their big post–Dust Bowl lows above 40 cents a bushel behind, and started marching slowly and steadily on up to 80 cents a bushel by summer of 1940. Since there were still no great European shortages at that point, the market took stock of itself and proceeded to fall back to about 60 cents right after the 1940 fall corn harvest—a typical "harvest break."

This initial rally and correction still left the market well below the highs of even the mid-to-late 1920s and of the Dust Bowl, which for corn were up in the $1.20–$1.40 range. At the harvest-break low of 60 cents a bushel, the price of corn was only a fraction of the all-time highs of the price shock highs of 1917 (near $2.40).

At the beginning of the First World War there were windfall profits for the American farmer. Not so at the start of World War II. As late as 1939, direct government payments to U.S. farmers still amounted to 35 percent of the total net farm income received from the sale of crops and livestock. This figure stood at 30 percent in 1940, and 13 percent in 1941. Therefore it was not until 1941–42 that the financially weakest farmers even started losing their dependency on a government check, and became able to return to profitability based on the free-market prices.

The modesty of this initial advance was certainly no fluke. The market was well aware that the war's disruption of agriculture was localized and that the United States and the other major grain and livestock exporters like Canada, Australia, and Argentina could easily boost their production and overwhelm the modest up-front increase in wartime demand if they were stimulated to do so. Since the market knew this, it was not about to provide that stimulus in the form of sharply higher prices. That is, unless something far more drastic happened to alter the food supply and demand equation.

Something did happen, of course. In June of 1941, Adolph Hitler decided to invade the Soviet Union, with the goals (at least according to Albert Speer) of testing the mettle of the German people against that of the Russian people and obtaining for the German people some *lebensraum* (living room). On a more practical level he sought greater access to the food and raw material resources that were contained within the USSR, which the Third Reich sorely needed to supply its armed forces and fuel the voracious pace of German expansion.

The invasion itself was a spectacular success initially, as so many of the historic invasions of Mother Russia have been. Since it was so successful, and since it occurred right in the middle of the summer grain growing season, it meant a vast disruption of Soviet agriculture.

German armies advanced eastward all through that 1941 growing season, and on into fall harvest, annexing hundreds of thousands of square kilometers of the USSR and Soviet-occupied Poland, territory that contained millions of the most important food-producing acres in Europe. The foodstuffs that the Germans didn't destroy or confiscate in the conquered regions often were either carted off or destroyed by the retreating Soviet armies and by Russian peasants committed to an official Soviet policy of scorched earth.

This was the first widespread destruction of the basic means of production in European agriculture, and in combination with the huge losses of existing stocks of foodstuffs it also generated the first great food shortage of the Second World War outside of the Nazi death and labor camps. This shortage was so profound that by the winter of 1941–42 there was already widespread starvation in the USSR, including a par-

ticularly notable and severe pocket in the besieged city
of Leningrad.

The events of 1941 stimulated the American corn
market to march itself on up another notch, but when
all was said and done, the market took this acceleration of the crisis well in stride, and it stopped just short
of 90 cents a bushel at Chicago. It even proceeded to
stage another quick little post–harvest break at year
end, just as it had in 1940.

All this orderliness and normalcy in the midst of a
growing world food crisis could be explained in large
part by the technological capacity of the peaceful part
of the world food chain to expand its production and
meet the need. However, it was also due to the fact
that the American food supply simply couldn't be con-
nected to much of the new Soviet food demand, especially that part represented by those millions now
behind German lines.

The United States remained technically neutral
through the German invasion of the USSR, but it was
hardly "neutral in thought and deed," as President
Wilson had urged Americans to remain in the early
part of the first war. In March of 1941, for instance, the
United States committed itself more directly to the
Allied cause with the passage of the Lend-Lease Bill.
Lend-Lease sent critical war material to Britain under
the guise of *lending* it since Britain was clearly unable
to afford the cost of all of the arms needed for its own
defense. Lend-Lease also included foodstuffs, and it
was extended to the Soviet government in November
of that same year.

On December 7, 1941, the other shoe dropped when
the Airforce of the Imperial Navy of Japan attacked
the U.S. Pacific Fleet at Pearl Harbor, Hawaii. The
United States declared war on all three Axis powers,
and so made its participation in the world war official,
just as it eventually had in 1917. It then accelerated
its efforts to supply its official Allies in the USSR and

Great Britain, and it began the process of mobilizing its own armed forces. This included the vast preparations needed to supply and feed them thousands of miles from home.

All of which added a good deal more urgency to the price equation, and the market's upward momentum accelerated. Corn moved past $1.10 a bushel by the end of 1942, and then a little further still to near $1.25 by mid-1943. This was now right under the highs of the mid-1920s and the Dust Bowl, but the market still couldn't quite break through them and it was certainly still far below the all-time highs of 1917–20.

The orderly nature of the price advance was aided in these middle war years because the USDA still possessed some food assets that were a remarkably lucky legacy of unsuccessful New Deal policies. During the period of low prices after the end of the Dust Bowl (late 1937 to 1940), the CCC had acquired large stocks of wheat, cotton, and corn through defaulted farmer loans. The CCC made loans available to farmers as an alternative to simply dumping their crops on the market at a loss. Since these loans were often above the free market price to begin with, they were often still above the free market price when the loans came due. The farmer was therefore unable to raise enough money by selling the crop to pay off both interest and principal, so he defaulted on the loan and kept the money. The federal government (CCC) was left holding title to the grain (and cotton), which started to pile up after 1937.

With the advent of the war, this very sticky and growing political and economic problem disappeared. These unwanted stocks were transformed into a valuable emergency wartime asset of food and fiber that increased a bit in value each year that the war progressed. Debates that had raged over arcane and complicated things such as whether a farmer marketing quota should be based on an "actual" or "normal"

allotment (and what exactly did that mean anyway?),
were swept aside by concern over how to raise production to meet the growing wartime needs.

(On the one hand you might say, thank God for the
fact that the country and the Western Alliance had
these assets waiting in the wings when it needed them.
On the other hand, if your basic price support system
doesn't work in the first place, and it leaves the government with growing stocks of grain that it can't unload,
what does one do when there isn't a world war ready
to bail out the flawed system?)

In any case, during the war the USDA was entrusted
with the job of boosting production—a job at which the
USDA could excel. As early as December 1940, it had
begun by asking farmers to have at least as many sows
farrowing (female hogs impregnated) over the next
year as they had the last. Following the passage of
Lend-Lease Act on March 11, 1941 the USDA announced a price support program for hogs, dairy
products, chickens, and eggs—all above free-market
prices.

They concentrated at first on boosting these con-
sumer-type products instead of the grain that went
into them, in part because these items were a value-
added part of the economy, and in part because they
had come to represent a substantial portion of the
American diet since the early 1920s. They also were
able to concentrate on the product end at first because
there was still an ample supply of the grain that was
needed to feed all those extra chickens, hogs, and dairy
cows.

This was augmented in May 1941 (just a month
before the German invasion of the USSR), when Congress passed a joint resolution raising the loan rates
on cotton, corn, wheat, rice, and that other famous
staple, tobacco. They did so not because supplies of
these basics were getting especially tight, but to ensure that the farmer who produced them shared in the

profits that the war was bringing to the economy as a whole. Although popular in the farm community, this resolution had to stick a bit in the craw of older farmers who remembered their glory years before and during the first war. Now they were a weak sister that had to be helped along.

After Pearl Harbor, Congress and the Roosevelt administration believed it was finally time to directly stimulate the production of all basic grain and food commodities. They extended the new higher loan rates all the way through the 1946 crop year, so farmers would not fear getting lured into expanding one year, only to be left holding the bag if the market collapsed the next. They also extended the life of the CCC which was the agency that made the crop loans to farmers, and stipulated that loans should not fall below 90 percent of the parity index for all of those same basics, (plus peanuts) until 1946. (The parity index rose with inflation, so this meant gradually higher loan levels.)

Congress also added many "non-basic" commodities to the list receiving 90 percent of parity value: manufacturing milk, butterfat, eggs, chickens, turkeys, hogs, dry peas, dry beans, soybeans for oil, flaxseed for oil, peanuts for oil, Egyptian cotton, Irish potatoes, and sweet potatoes. By the mid-1940s, over a hundred commodities were being supported.

Stimulating production in the second war was again just half the battle, however. Getting the food (and war materials) to the customers who would use up the stuff was the other half, just as it had been in the first war. The Allies once again deployed the anti-submarine convoy system that had been so successful in the first war, and it was successful again. This time, the most critical supply line for the Allies (in the Atlantic at least) was probably not the one from the United States to Great Britain, but rather the other supply route from the United States and Great Britain, to the USSR.

Germany controlled all sea access to the Soviet
Union through the Baltic and Black seas, as well as
any land access through Hitler's Festung Europa
(Fortress Europe). The only alternatives were to either
go completely around the world in the other direction
and land supplies in Vladivostok and then rail them
all the way across Asia, or to skirt the coast of Norway
and travel up through the Arctic Ocean to Murmansk.
The route to Murmansk was the logical choice, and it
soon became one of the most heavily traveled sea lanes
in history.

Although the Germans were able to harass this and
other shipping lanes and sink millions of tons of Allied
shipping, the supply line to the USSR was never
seriously threatened. Neither were the sea lanes from
the United States to Britain and from the United
States to the Mediterranean Sea later in the war. The
mere fact that this war was so spread out worked
against the basic objective of the submarine warfare
which was to sink ships faster than the Allies could
build and load them. As a result, supplies got through
in enormous quantities, and the Germans never came
close to starving out Great Britain, as they almost had
in 1917.

The supply route to the USSR was always kept open,
but it could not handle all of the goods that were
needed by the Soviet government and its people. Food
was clearly of secondary importance to the mix of
supplies in comparison to tanks, munitions, and
trucks. The existence of this difficult priority meant
that many Soviets working and fighting behind their
own lines were forced to fight on substandard diets.
For the millions of Soviet citizens trapped behind the
German lines, food from the West was not even an
issue, and millions of ethnic Russians and Ukrainians
continued to face starvation into 1943 and 1944, just
as they had in 1917 and 1920 and again during the
collectivization process in the early 1930s.

The point of all this is that as late as 1943 and 1944, the U.S. farm economy still wasn't being forced to extend its role of "world granary of last resort" to all of the hungry people in the world. It wasn't yet even forced to extend it to all of the citizens of its needier Allies. Since most of the potential demand was out of reach, it stayed pretty much out of the price equation as well.

Therefore, even by early 1943 there was still no runaway price rally or "price shock" in the Chicago grain markets. As I have already mentioned, the price of corn had only made it to the $1.25 level by spring of that year. This was still just below the highs that had been hit on the recovery of the mid-1920s, and on two occasions during the Dust Bowl. (In fact corn had even traded higher during the aftermath of the American Civil War.)

Although it was still a modest rally by all historical standards, the federal government suspended trading in various commodity futures contracts at the Chicago Board of Trade and elsewhere in 1943. How long the trading stayed suspended depended on the commodity. In the case of corn it lasted from early 1943 to late 1944.

The government feared that since the war was causing more and more food disruptions each year it continued, the market was bound to vault up to another price shock high eventually, unless wartime speculation was eliminated altogether.

The war in Europe continued until May of 1945, and it continued in the Pacific until the following year. For the duration, the American farmer pretty well met all of the production goals that were set by the government, and he received profitable prices to do so. Control of most sea lanes in both the Atlantic and the Pacific passed to the Allies after 1943, and so food was delivered with greater dispatch to the Allied armed forces.

The civilian supply situation, however, got worse as the war went on. The problem was that as the Allied armies advanced on Germany and Japan, they liberated more and more of the people who had food deficits. Territory that the Allies liberated (or conquered) contained hundreds of millions of people who lacked the ability to adequately feed themselves.

Even the Germans had come to rely increasingly on food that was produced in conquered sections of the USSR, Poland, and elsewhere during the war. As the Soviet Red Army moved west and forced the Germans out of those areas, that food was of course kept instead by the populations that produced it, or else it was "liberated" by the Red Army. In many cases it even was gathered and sent back to Soviet-controlled territory far to the rear which continued to run a basic food shortage for the duration of the war.

On top of all this dislocation, was the enormous destruction of the productive capacity of the farm economies of Europe—losses that mounted rapidly in the later years of the war. The process first started in earnest as the invading Germans swept eastward into the USSR in 1941 and 1942. The brutal nature of the German occupation did not allow for much rebuilding of farm economies in the areas they conquered, and so the lost productive capacity stayed lost.

Then, while the farming economy of Eastern Europe was still in this weakened condition, the production problem was aggravated when the Soviets turned the tables and in turn began to drive the Nazis westward—back toward Germany across those same important farming regions of Russia, the Ukraine, and Poland. Farms and equipment were again simply destroyed in the fighting, as were more stocks of foodstuffs and many of the people who were capable of producing more food if things could ever just settle down.

The destructive process then began in earnest in

western Europe with the Allied invasion of southern
Italy in 1943. The Allies worked their way up the
Italian Peninsula all through 1944 against bitter German resistance, causing great destruction of the farm
and non-farm economies alike. This destructive phase
accelerated with the big D-day invasion of France in
June of 1944, after which major battles raged from
west to east across Normandy, northern France, and
Belgium through the end of that year. Hitler's
counteroffensive Battle of the Bulge intensified the
destruction a bit in Belgium in December and January
of 1944–45, and then the battle lines all surged east
again and converged with onrushing Soviet forces to
create one final orgy of destruction on German territory and on German farmlands through May of 1945.

World War II in Europe therefore ended much differently than it began, with its blockades and
sitzkrieg. After the slow start, it had managed very
well to catch up with and even surpass the total
destruction that had occurred in World War I. It had
ravaged even more of Europe's farm economy than had
the first war, and it did this in a shorter span of time,
in 1941 and then 1944–45.

The Allies and the Western food markets were therefore once again presented at the end of hostilities with
the responsibility of feeding a huge new hungry
market, a market that was even bigger and more
needy than the one faced by the Western food markets
at the end of the First World War.

So in the first years of peace the full effect of the
wartime food problem hit the American grain markets.
Likewise the problem did not influence grain prices
until after the war, as trading suspensions were lifted
in all of the (grain and soybean) futures markets, and
price ceilings got lifted in the cash grain market.

As the markets were freed from their wartime con-
straints, it became clear that price volatility had merely been postponed. The corn market regained its

freedom in 1946, and it quickly vaulted to about $2.30 per bushel—just under the all-time (price shock) high. Corn yields were expected to be excellent that year, however, (36.7 bushels per acre) and the market suddenly panicked to find itself at such a rarefied level. It proceeded to take an enormous tumble in price as the favorable growing season developed. The tumble lasted right on through the harvest, and into January 1947, falling down to nearly $1.30 a bushel.

This was just the overture though; 1947 turned out to be the biggest single year for the corn market since 1917. The market started to rally from $1.30 a bushel, and the 1947 growing season provided it with even more fuel. Corn yields fell to 28.6 bushels an acre, down 22 percent from the big yields of 1946. This was enough to take the market to a new all-time price high of nearly $3.00 per bushel, well above the 1917 high of about $2.35. It was another price shock for corn—the second of the twentieth century.

In some ways perhaps this second price shock was not all that shocking. The market had already trod this shortage path before, and everybody already knew that big new highs were a very real possibility after a world war. Most people were also well aware that, despite the enormity of the problem, a big postwar market could be very short lived.

And perhaps this second price shock was not so big a surprise to the farm economy because not every major market made a new all-time high. For instance, wheat, a former barometer of the world food demand, stopped well short of its big highs of $3.50 that were hit in 1919–29. In 1947, the cash wheat market in Chicago peaked at just over $3.20 per bushel.

The failure to make a new high also showed that wheat farmers still had plenty of latent capacity to expand left over from the Depression and the acreage expansion that had occurred in World War I. Therefore, it didn't take big new highs to induce them to replant some of those acres. Just as important, it also showed how wheat's role as the central ingredient in the diet of Western countries had diminished. Corn, as well as all of the animal-related food products that it helped to put on the American plate, was now more critical.

The Second World War didn't start any major new farm trends of its own, but it had a powerful impact on the existing trends that were started during and after World War I—trends toward fewer farms, bigger farms, and a smaller farm population.

In fact, the basic farm numbers starting dropping like a rock. The farm population first fell slowly from its temporary high of 32.4 million in 1933 as the non-farm economy recovered a bit in the second half of that decade. It still stood at over 30.5 million in 1940, but by 1945 it had dropped all the way to 24.4 million—a loss of 20 percent from the high. Some of this was due to the fact that the military draft had pulled great numbers off the farm on a temporary basis, but the postwar bounce only got as high as 25.8 million (in 1947), and by 1948 the farm population number had fallen to another new low.

The total number of farms had peaked in 1935 at over 6.8 million. This fell to about 6.35 million in 1940, and to just under 6.0 million in 1945, but for the total number of farms there was no postwar bounce. The number slid gradually down to about 5.7 million in 1949.

Few of those returning from the war were in a financial position to start up a new operation or buy an existing farm; this was getting to be an expensive proposition. For one thing, the trend toward bigger American farms was in full cry during the war years, and by 1945 the size of an average U.S. farm was close to 200 acres, up from only 150 acres on average in 1933.

The value of each one of those acres was on the rise

too. Land prices had bottomed out in the mid-1930s, and they took a big jump in 1943–46. When you threw in the fact that the war years had also seen a big increase in the expensive use of commercial fertilizers and in the level of mechanization on the American farm, it put the business of farming beyond the means of the average American citizen. This was a first in American history.

Most important from a farm policy standpoint, the war generated another high-priced environment that not only reprieved many of the farm policies of the New Deal, but it locked them in. Those policies had brought a very mixed bag of results when they were instituted in the 1930s, and then the war turned the equation upside down.

In some ways the equation stayed upside down. The farm programs put in place by the New Deal and fleshed out during the Second World War, were programs that seemed to work a whole lot better in the years that followed war—in a world system that put the United States and its food surplus firmly at center stage.

7

THE TOP OF THE HEAP

As soon as the war ended, the United States had to perform some fancy footwork.

The world's (non-U.S.) industrialized economies emerged from the Second World War every bit as battered as they had from the first, and this time the physical devastation was spread over far more of the planet's surface. More people were crowded into the world's cities, a smaller percentage of them had land they could return to, and more people were refugees. It all added up to a world that was even less able to feed itself than the world of 1918–19.

Again, the situation was worst in the defeated countries. In Germany and Japan, the prewar order had been smashed, resulting in both hunger and a political vacuum. The lessons of recent history were pretty clear on this score; violent and undesirable forms of government tended to emerge out of hunger and chaos.

If that weren't enough, there was the USSR. It was adding to the worries of the Western democracies after this war, just as it had after the first, this time by busying itself in support of a guerrilla movement in Greece, making territorial demands on Turkey and with the aggressive consolidation of its hold over Eastern Europe.

Western Europe's 400-year dominance of the world, and the order it brought, was battered by the first war and basically ended by the second. Britain and its navy had been the glue that held much of the world economy together during the nineteenth and very early twentieth centuries, but now Britain was broke. In the late forties it was shedding much of its colonial empire to conserve dwindling resources. The ball was in America's court.

The United States was the only power in a position to take up the mantle of Britain and Western Europe after the war ended, since its armed forces were in direct control of a larger portion of the globe than even those of the USSR. It simply had to choose whether to stay heavily armed and hold onto the positions where it sat as of V-E and V-J days, or to largely disarm itself as it had traditionally done after wars, and retreat back into the Western Hemisphere.

It chose the former.

When you got right down to it, the United States had a very strong hand to play. It had the world's most powerful fleet, the most powerful airforce, and the Bomb. It also had the lion's share of the world's surplus capital, a GNP approaching half of the non-communist world's total, and a big technological lead in just about every economic sector.

If the goal had been simply to continue the hostilities or to rule the areas the United States had conquered, that hand was more than adequate. It was not quite enough, though, if the goal was to quickly establish peace and reprogram a big portion of the world along American-style economic and political lines.

The only way to jump start *that* kind of a process in a hungry world, was to start adequately feeding those under Allied control at the end of the war who were quite unable to feed themselves.

It was on this score that the United States was able to play the trump card to end all trump cards: the huge American food surplus. The USSR didn't even have this card in its deck and could not conjure or acquire it no matter what they did. The violence of the war, piled on top of Stalin's brutal drive to "collectivize" Soviet agriculture in the early 1930s, had eliminated the USSR from the ranks of major grain and food exporters, a list they had dominated before World War I.

The United States played the food card for all it was worth. It not only sold the food surplus aggressively, but it decided that if the hungry part of the world under Allied control needed to be fed for free to accomplish its goals, so be it. In many cases, free was precisely what the food aid needed to be.

It was also needed in enormous quantities. Events surrounding Germany were a case in point. The Soviet Union (Stalin) had agreed before the war ended to continue shipping food from the predominantly agricultural German lands it occupied in the east, to the more heavily populated and industrialized German lands occupied by Britain, France, and the United States in the West after the war ended.

He was apparently just kidding because the USSR almost immediately commenced stripping eastern Germany of its food surplus, (along with much of its movable industrial capacity), and sent it all packing back east into the USSR. The more than fifty million hungry Germans waiting among the ruins of the industrial west for what they probably thought of as "German" food, were left facing an even bigger food deficit than the one expected by the Allies when they took over in early 1945.

Japan was equally problematic. It had long had difficulty in feeding itself, and like Germany, it became accustomed during the war to solving its big deficit with food produced in its conquered territories. As the Japanese were forced to quit northern China and Southeast Asia, this source of food was no longer available. As with the Germans, the Japanese needed a large alternative source of food toute de suite.

Douglas MacArthur, who was the military governor of Japan after their surrender, used wheat as the solution. He started to import it and other American foodstuffs to bridge the food gap. The Japanese liked the wheat products, and with time they were weaned off an exclusively rice and noodle diet and introduced to more and more American-style foods.

The United States, committed to filling food gaps in central Europe and eastern Asia, drew its own food reserves in the United States to dangerously low levels. In 1945–47 this helped set off what I've called the second great price shock of the century. Combined with the poor corn harvest of 1947, this took corn in Chicago up to that new all-time high, near $3 a bushel.

During those rather dicey years, the American consumer was therefore forced to compete rather aggressively with his own government for the domestic food supply. This set off a round of worrisome inflation, and if the corn crop had failed for a second year in a row in 1948, some part of the newly designed postwar world might have been relinquished.

The American government placed its bets on the farm, however, confident that it could outproduce the food crisis. The American consumer was willing to go along and make the sacrifices asked of him, and so the country stuck with its aid and export policy. It turned out the government bet right. In 1948, yields returned to normal, and the potential for a serious domestic food shortage evaporated with that one good corn harvest.

The emotional climax of the postwar food diplomacy, and one of the biggest tests of America's resolve in playing its hand, came just after the price shock, in 1948–49, with the Berlin Airlift. In 1947, the Allies moved to officially create the independent state of West Germany. The Soviets were bitterly opposed to a strong and unified German state (as they apparently still are). They responded by cutting all surface travel and communication with West Berlin. It was left completely surrounded by Soviet-held territory, and apparently at the Soviets' mercy.

Mercy, however, was not what the Soviets had in mind. The city's two million people had no means to feed themselves, and the Soviets figured that their hunger card could beat the American food card, at least in this one small case. They thought that West Berlin would be forced to capitulate. East and West Berlin would then be under Soviet control, and this would greatly dismay and weaken the new German state in the West.

As power plays go, this was a pretty sound plan. Hungry people crowded together in a small space are usually willing to do most anything in order to eat. What the Soviets didn't know was that a food card beats a hunger card, and the United States was determined to keep on playing. Britain and the United States commenced an airborne convoy, not unlike the sea convoys that rescued Britain in 1917.

It flew food and fuel, day and night along a narrow corridor of free airspace between Allied-occupied West Germany, and the beleaguered city. At various points during the airlift the city's food stocks could be counted as only a matter of days' worth, and it all made for some very high drama. The press painted a graphic image of hungry Berliners waiting on the edges of Templehof Airport for the planes to land with their next meal, and that image was quite legitimate. Both sides held out through mid-1949 when the Soviets finally relented and reopened the highway to the west.

It was a thrilling rescue event by any standard, and I'm not sure that there has been anything quite like it before or since. It was only fourteen years later that President Kennedy traveled to West Berlin in the aftermath of another Berlin/Soviet Crisis, the newly constructed Berlin Wall. When he declared in his famous speech, "Ich bin ein Berliner," the quarter million West Berliners listening responded with the greatest ovation that any American President has ever received.

Those words represented far more to that audience than just a very good line from a very charismatic man. They were bankable words with intrinsic worth. For all the tragedy that surrounded the building of the Berlin Wall, it was the second time that the Soviets had been forced to give up. Both sides knew the Soviets couldn't take the western half of the city short of declaring war. West Berliners knew this too, and they could believe the president's speech; they remembered the airlift.

In the beginning the United States performed such acts with high, almost altruistic motives. The American government and citizens were willing to make substantial sacrifices and put the American food supply at some risk, if necessary. They were resolved to maintain peace and prevent the spread of Soviet power.

Altruism was still the order of the day when Secretary of State George Marshall announced the Marshall Plan in 1947. It added the goal of aggressive economic (industrial) development to those of simply feeding people, maintaining order, and keeping the Soviet Union out of places like Greece and Turkey.

Aid was offered to all of Europe, but the USSR quickly declined to accept it and was kind enough to decline the offer on behalf of all areas of Eastern Europe that were under its control. (What a bitter memory this must be today for those Eastern Europeans who are even aware that this offer was made.)

The Marshall Plan proved to be a springboard that assured the rapid economic recovery of Western Europe, along with its middle and working classes. Within four years, the industrial production of the countries that accepted Marshall Plan aid had jumped by 64 percent over the levels of 1947, and by 41 percent over prewar levels. This success, coupled with a less burdensome debt load than the one the Europeans had carried after the first war, set the continent on a much gentler and more prosperous course than the one onto which it had careened in the 1920s.

At some point over this stretch, the American altruism was undoubtedly joined by additional motives, at least in the area of food policy. It gradually dawned on the planners in Washington that the events of the postwar era were starting to work very nicely in favor of the American farm economy. It gradually became clear as well that with some careful planning, the forces that were naturally working for the benefit of the United States could be given a healthy boost.

The introduction of wheat and bread products into the Far East was a case in point. Wheat was still the cheapest way for the United States to feed large numbers of hungry people in the big cities of Asia, just like it had been the cheapest and most efficient way to feed soldiers and civilians in the more rustic dietary world of World War I.

In the process, it created a chronic dependency on the American wheat farmer, because there was no way that Japan could begin to produce all of the wheat that it suddenly wanted to eat. Since the United States produced a wheat surplus that it hadn't been able to market successfully in peacetime for more than thirty years, it was a tailor-made setup. Japan became a long-term customer for imported U.S., Canadian, and Australian wheat.

As other Asian economies recovered and became even more industrial in nature, their cities grew too. Cities always grow in a developing country, and the existence of this variable in the natural order of things helped the Asian wheat dependency start to feed on itself. The United States supported this new trend with an aggressive program of introducing more and more wheat products to Japanese school children and consumers.

Soon the Japanese were not only accustomed to American-style wheat products, but they graduated to meat and dairy just as Americans had. This made them even more dependent on the American farm, and today Japan is the biggest single customer for U.S. agricultural products.

Back in Europe, the population was being introduced to a more American-style diet as well. In part this came with the original food aid which included meat and dairy products. In part it came through liberal credit terms and the Marshall Plan. It was all backed up, however, by the walking, talking advertisement provided by the American armed forces. Europeans were able to see an American-style diet firsthand, and most of them considered it an exceedingly good idea. As the European economies rebuilt and prospered, they were able to afford to buy some of that same diet from the United States.

It took grain to feed the animals that were needed to satisfy the growing European appetite for meat. More to the point, it took feedgrains, leaving a sizable opening for American corn exports. (American corn constitutes the world's biggest feedgrain crop by far.) Europe could produce fairly large quantities of feedgrains, but it fell far short of being able to produce enough. Europe became locked into a new dependency.

With a little bit of planning, a few nips and tucks, it all seemed to hang together. Europe was firmly steered onto a path of industrialization and middle classdom by the Marshall Plan. That sent more Europeans flocking to the prospering cities of Germany and the northeast, where they could join the prospering middle and working classes. That was the sort of European customer that had sopped up the American wheat surplus in the parity years before the first war. This one was sopping up a surplus of corn, soybeans, and beef. There were no "battles of the wheat" this time.

Anything short of this combination would have almost certainly crashed the American grain market in the late forties, just as it had crashed in 1920. If there'd been no Marshall Plan, and only food aid and tough credit terms, the customer wouldn't have been able to upgrade his diet as fast as the U.S. surplus was increasing. If the United States had not aggressively developed the market, the Japanese and Europeans might well have retreated into their old dietary habits when the crisis passed.

A crashing postwar market would have shaken the price support system, busted the USDA budget, and been a drag on the U.S. economy. Farmers, especially the poorer ones, would have been unable to market their crops at a profit. They would have taken out expensive government loan/subsidies on their crops, instead of selling them. In all likelihood they would not have been able to repay those loans because they were set at such high levels during the war.

The grain that backed those government-to-farmer loans would therefore have been defaulted to the Federal Government (CCC), just like it was after the support system was first installed in the 1930s. Once again the CCC would not have known what to with it all, except to give it away.

Far better to think of as many ways as possible to

push the stuff out of the country in the first place, instead of making the grain wend its way through the complicated support system beforehand. The market trends set in motion by these policy decisions made the United States the linchpin of the world food system for a generation. (It's still our role to lose today, despite all of the erosion.)

And yet. Having a sound marketing strategy and a world economic equation that worked beautifully for the United States did not make the world of farming perfect. You might say that the show ended up playing a lot better on the road than it did at home.

No matter how great a share of the world market one nation manages to nail down, there's always that nagging other side to the coin. You should only produce as much as your markets can absorb and maybe just a bit more to give away, and keep the competition at bay. If production exceeds demand by too much, prices are going to sag in response. If overproduction turns into a trend, the surplus will grow into a glut, and boom goes bust no matter how hard you hustle the merchandise overseas.

For the United States, it was the supply side of the coin that contained all the flies in the ointment after the late 1940s. Productivity, always such a mixed bag for farmers, seemed to get a big second wind from the price stimulation of the war. After the war ended, it broke into a sprint.

It was the same old story. For one thing, the equipment improved. Farm implement and tractor dealers began introducing a whole new generation of bigger and better farm machinery in the 1940s and 1950s that greatly expanded the number of acres one grain farmer could handle—this time by 25–50 percent. That was for starters. This also happened to be the period of time when the American farmer waded into the chemical age, or perhaps it was the chemical industry that waded into farming.

Along with the war effort had come an aggressive effort to boost yields. The chemical industry complied with the development of commercial fertilizers that were easier to apply and they worked hand in hand with the USDA to encourage usage and stimulate production. When the war ended, the chemical industry was much bigger and more productive than it had been at the start. It had new products on the market and a whole lot more waiting in the pipeline, including more and better insecticides and weed killers.

Like other American industries, it followed the government's cue on market development and aggressively began to open up new markets and widen its presence in the old ones. (The chemical industry liked to claim, "Without chemistry, life itself is impossible.")

Agriculture proved to be a chemical sponge. Fertilizer and chemical salesmen became a part of the rural landscape, just as farm implement dealers had by the parity years and World War I. The war effort had helped position them to market directly to individual farmers, and to show those farmers how these wonder drugs for the soil could cure what ailed their crops, and greatly boost yields.

All of what the company salesmen said was true, and as usage spread farmers could see for themselves that those who adopted the modern farming methods were getting impressive yields. The national average corn yield rose from over 37 bushels an acre in 1946, to over 47 bushels in 1956 and nearly 74 in the summer of 1965. The choice was to join in the rush or sit and watch as everyone else's yields doubled, and yours didn't.

When farmers introduce commercial fertilizers they see their dreams coming true. First they see a big leap in yields. Then, up to a point, bigger yields keep coming with the application of even more fertilizer and the appropriate use of even more weed killers and insecticides. These benefits cannot be denied.

But what about the price? The chemicals have since worked their way down through the shallower water tables and into deeper ground and deeper wells across the United States; drinking them puts farm and non-farm populations at much greater risk of a variety of cancers and other diseases.

One chemical bath after another since the late 1940s has tainted the groundwater on which half the population of the United States depends, according to the Environmental Protection Agency. The USDA was silent on this very dirty aspect of farming then, and it has been mostly silent on the matter ever since.

Silence can be read as assent in this case. In fact, to the extent that the USDA involved itself in the use of more chemicals by the farmer, it was to promote them. Was this an understandable ignorance surrounding an emerging industry? Is our own nice clear perspective on the matter today simply 20/20 hindsight? I think not.

Rachel Carson recognized this crisis by the late 1950s and wrote *The Silent Spring* (published in 1962). Anybody who has watched water run off a farm field or been downwind of a good chemical spraying can also tell that this is very bad stuff. It doesn't take a rocket scientist to figure out that much of it ends up in the water we drink.

Why then did agricultural policy make the conscious choice to go with the chemical flow? The catalyst was the farmer. As a businessman, he is economically and culturally driven to do whatever it takes to squeeze out as many bushels per acre as he possibly can each year. Fertilizer and chemicals were the magic elixir that made yields grow, and for that reason he has fought for the freedom to use them since they first burst onto the scene.

The role of government, however, is to restrain the self-interest of one group when it starts to do harm to

another. Government is supposed to promote virtue—
the public good.

This view of the American system may sound pretty
wishful and starry-eyed, given the need to produce
food to fulfill our brave new position in the world of the
1940s and 1950s, but we'll see that it wasn't long
before American agriculture was busily sacrificing the
environment to boost yields with one hand, and
desperately trying to reduce overall production with
the other.

The increasing productivity meant that in fits and
spurts, the supply side was bound to eventually out-
strip the demand side, no matter how much food the
United States pushed into the export markets, and no
matter how prosperous the new West German and
Japanese consumer became.

As the supply gradually started to outweigh demand,
grain prices did what they seem to do most naturally;
they started going down. The inevitable rolling over
started for the corn market after the big price shock in
1947. Corn spent most of 1948 working its way down
from just under $3.00, to $2.20–$2.30. In 1949 it
plunged to a dismaying low of about $1.10.

Then, all of those wonderful new variables on the
demand side of the equation kicked in, and the market
staged a brilliant, albeit temporary, recovery. It
vaulted back over $2.40 by late 1950, and by the
summer of 1952 it was all the way back up to about
$2.90, only 10 cents a bushel from the all-time high.
This was to be the last big surge of the postwar years,
though. After 1952, productivity flexed its muscles but
good, and it was no longer a contest. Grain prices
headed consistently lower for the next decade.

As the big new variables were making themselves
felt in the market, the USDA and Congress were left
with the job of deciding how the domestic end of farm
policy needed to be redesigned in light of them. In the
end, they punted. The New Deal programs that had

been reprieved by World War II got patched up and extended. Most people seemed to forget that these programs had failed before the war.

Such as it was, the debate over farm policy began as soon as the war ended. It basically broke down between those who favored a continuation of the high price supports (loans) of the war years, and those who favored flexible price supports at lower levels.

Not surprisingly, the farmer favored continuation of high wartime supports which in most cases had been set at 90 percent of the parity index.

Those who favored flexible supports at lower levels tended to be urban congressmen, and the bureaucrats at the USDA. They were strongly supported by a consensus of most economists who felt that flexible support levels were the way to both control prices and reestablish parity. In essence they were saying that they could gauge the growth of the surplus in advance and reduce subsidies on some sort of schedule that would compensate. That's quite a bold claim.

They had apparently forgotten about wars and weather, about how unforeseeable events, like the Dust Bowl and the attack on Pearl Harbor, could alter the supply/demand equation more drastically than any farm program or fiddling with loan levels could ever do. They also forgot how farm production outstripped demand even after farm profits were sliced in the early 1920s, and then sliced to the bone in 1929-32.

The cheerleaders for high support had problems that were equally acute. They failed to spell out exactly how they planned to dispose of the huge surpluses that were bound to come if the farm economy continued to get stimulated by the government in the way it had been during the war years.

Both positions failed to even address the soaring yields per acre that were just coming from the modern farmer with his fertilizers and chemicals.

The debate continued until 1948, when the first major new peacetime farm bill was passed. It was a compromise between the two positions. The high World War II subsidies were to be maintained until 1950, followed by a gradual decline. By the next year, however, the farm lobby pressured Congress into extending wartime supports for most commodities for still another year. Policy momentum was in the hands of the farmer.

So much so that 1951 *still* didn't mark the end of fixed supports at 90 percent of parity. The Korean War began in June 1950, and the secretary of agriculture used his power within the existing legislation to extend the high wartime loans all over again. Then another piece of legislation locked in that extension until April 1953, and high supports were then extended for the last time to include the entire 1953 and 1954 crop years. Keep in mind that World War II had ended nine years earlier.

Why did U.S. farm policy continue down the same path after the war? Inertia was probably the biggest reason. Congress is always reluctant to open a can of its own worms if it can be avoided, and farm policy was already getting to be one heckuva can of worms. Evidently, the decision to lower the wartime supports took all the energy they had to exert on behalf of the American farm. There was no energy left for reform.

However, there was also an active ingredient at work: the farmers and their powerful lobby. These were their programs, and they had waited an awfully long time to get in the federal subsidy door. Farmers liked the programs. They liked having the loan levels at 90 percent of parity. Given their druthers, they wanted to *add* to the federal farm policy menu, not subtract or rebuild. They were determined to go to the mat on every point.

In the 1950s, the rest of the political system was not especially inclined to resist. For one thing, the farm depression and the Dust Bowl and all of the other events of the twenties and thirties were very recent history. This image, burned into the consciousness of the American public, was hard to dislodge. If pressed, most non-farmers probably thought every farmer was just a hop, skip, and a jump from Henry Fonda loading up the truck in *The Grapes of Wrath*.

On top of all that, the country was experiencing an unprecedented prosperity, and in an expansive mood. Since it was willing and able to share its plenty with former enemies in Japan and Germany, the idea of leaving poor Henry Fonda at the mercy of the markets and weather was an idea that would not fly. All of which left the momentum with the farm lobby.

The farmers had learned to play the political game very well. Unlike big labor and blacks, they carefully and wisely avoided allying themselves exclusively with either political party. They established a tradition of actively supporting candidates on both sides of the fence and quickly punishing those few who strayed.

Farmers earned a well-deserved reputation as the one major socioeconomic group that truly voted "independent." This left them with a committed bloc of votes on both sides of both aisles on Capitol Hill.

Although the farm population had dropped long and hard before the early 1950s, the basic numbers were still plenty big enough to do the job. There were over 20 million people still living on farms in the United States (four times the number living on farms at the end of the 1980s). There were still a lot of kids on those farms, but that left at least three times the number of farm voters as today, and those adults voted in relatively heavy numbers. Their organization and independence made them a potential swing vote in congressional elections in a score of states including electoral vote rich industrial states such as Illinois and Ohio.

It added up to a power bloc few were interested in crossing. National parties could still lose a close presidential election, if the farm vote were truly riled by one side or the other. Individual senators in less populated farm states might as well kiss their political careers goodbye if they fought against a popular new farm program, or the old high loan levels.

Even most non-farm congressmen and senators had little to gain by harping on farm expenditures because most of the nation's voters were vaguely in the farmers' corner as well.

Ergo, nine years of high wartime subsidies, and no change in the basic structure of farm supports as designed during the Depression. This was just another reprieve on top of the one that came with the advent of the Second World War.

As productivity picked up and prices started sliding from their summertime peak of 1952, the process started to generate another round of winners and losers. Those with the better land and the capital to introduce the expensive new fertilizers and equipment got the jump on those who could not, or who did so more slowly. They farmed more acres and got higher yields and that meant more income to buy more land and use more fertilizer.

In 1950, the farm population had stood at just over 23 million—15 percent of the total U.S. population at that point. The number of U.S. farms stood at 5.647 million. Both numbers slid right on through the end of the decade until in 1959 there were only 4.097 million farms and about 16.6 million people living on them—a mere 9.4 percent of the U.S. population. This was a remarkable drop from one-third of the total population in 1916.

This loss was generally reported as great progress. Any time the subject of declining farm numbers came up in the mass media, it was played up as a very good thing. "In 1930," a public relations blurb might intone, "each American farmer fed only X number of his fellow citizens, but today that number has risen all the way to Y."

As farm numbers dropped, however, the amount of land being farmed didn't. Productivity not only meant bigger yields, it meant that a single farmer could plant and harvest more acres, and so the size of the average farm grew rapidly. When the New Deal began in 1933, the average farm was around 150 acres. By 1940, this number had cruised on up to about 175 acres. In 1948 it passed 200, and by 1958 it was all the way up to about 280. This also struck most Americans as a very good thing. Bigger was clearly better.

Farm assets were now concentrating themselves into fewer and fewer hands at a rapid pace. So fast that by the late 1950s, a basic element of the social equation in America was being altered, reversing a plan that the country had very carefully started to put into place more than a century earlier.

As early as 1820, the United States pointedly veered from a system of selling land to speculators and persons of wealth. Public land thereafter could be sold in plots as small as 80 acres for as little as $1.25 per acre. In 1830, squatters were given the right to register ownership, pay the minimum cost, and gain title to the land they were living on. In 1862 the door was flung wide open. The Homestead Act of May 20, offered 160-acre farm homesteads to settlers free of charge.

The plan to settle the land quickly had been successful. The wide dispersal of land also went according to plan. Intended to preempt the extreme concentration of ownership that existed in Europe, the American system of land ownership would not be based purely on cash and competition. From the perspective of the 1800s, the European system left the majority disadvantaged and forever poor. In the United States, a stake in the land gave everyone a chance.

It had been a very solid plan, and it had helped

ensure emergence of a big, stabilizing American middle class. But in the middle of the twentieth century it was unraveling.

8

THE PACE QUICKENS

As the surplus started to grow, Congress first tried to stem the tide by organizing and firing up the export side of the equation with a 1954 bill called Public Law 480 (PL480).

PL480, the first formal peacetime program related to exports, was basically designed to enhance the export policies that had evolved piecemeal after the war. Under it, farm products were to be exchanged for foreign currencies, instead of the dollars that were scarce for most potential customers, and for strategic materials. It also made farm products regularly available for food relief.

This could not compensate, however, for rising productivity, and by 1956 the smell of glut was unmistakable. By then it was also clear to most that simply cutting back farm subsidies a little at a time was a joke. It wouldn't eliminate the growing glut, or even put a dent in it.

Yet if subsidies didn't decline in some fashion, production would get stimulated even further. Both the glut and the USDA budget would almost certainly explode, and the slide in free market grain prices could get on a real roll.

A wave of Depression-style farm foreclosure and rural poverty was not going to be acceptable to the American government and public (not to mention the politically adroit farmer) at this stage in the history of farm policy. The country considered itself well able to afford an alternative, and so the obvious answer was to drag out the idea of a paid acreage reduction like the one that had proved so popular in the year that the Dust Bowl began.

And so in 1956 Congress enacted its second big acreage reduction program and called it the Soil Bank.

Farm programs had expanded in every way since the 1930s, and the Soil Bank fit nicely with the trend. It was big. It was a two-part program that again boiled down to paying farmers to take acreage out of production and put it into conservation uses of one sort or another. This time there were no attempts at creative financing, like the processor taxes that the Supreme Court had declared unconstitutional in the 1930s. The federal government would bear the cost.

Participation was again very high, and why not? Prices were low. The farmer would be paid cash in exchange for *not* planting, and he would save on the rising cost of putting a crop in the ground during the chemical age.

The short-term half attracted a whopping 21.4 million acres in 1957. As has been the case with such programs before and since, however, these acres were the poorest and least productive ones on the participating farms. Too often in fact, the land enrolled was on the bottom of a pond or a drainage ditch, and it therefore didn't represent a real decrease in planted acreage anyway.

This was also right smack in the middle of that stretch where yields were truly taking off, especially for corn. Farmers compensated for the lost acreage by coaxing a bigger crop from the acres still in production. They did so with better seed and more fertilizers. The money the farmer saved by not having to plant, harvest, and fertilize the idle program acres could be used to apply more of all that to the rest of the farm.

In any case, production didn't drop at all despite the huge number of acres involved. The short-term half of the program was quickly perceived to be a boondoggle and a failure, and it was abandoned in 1958.

The longer term half of the Soil Bank required farmers to contract with the USDA to idle specific acres for up to ten years. It too was a big success in terms of acreage enrolled which hit a high of 28.6 million acres in 1960. (After that the contracts gradually expired until the last land came out of the Soil Bank in 1972.)

Success in getting acres out of production for the long haul, however, again didn't translate into success in reducing the surplus. On the contrary, 1960 was not only the peak in Soil Bank enrollment, but it was also the year that postwar surpluses peaked. Farm programs were starting to drive Washington crazy.

When the Kennedy administration took office in January 1961 it faced a farm formula that was obviously not working. Farm prices and farm income had both been in a downtrend since summer of 1952. The average price a farmer received for a bushel of corn in 1960 was only about $1.00, the lowest level since 1942. The average wheat price was in pretty much the same shape at $1.74 a bushel—the lowest since 1945.

The markets and programs were reminiscent of the last years of the Depression. As prices ground their way lower, all of the support programs kicked in. The farmer who participated in the basic subsidy program took out a price support loan that was higher than the price he could get in the free market.

He was rarely able to recover the principal plus interest from the free market when the loan came due, so a substantial part of the record large stocks of corn and wheat were again getting defaulted to the federal government. In the case of wheat, this amounted to nearly all of the record 1.4 billion bushels that were left unsold at the beginning of the harvest of 1960. The only reason that corn and wheat were not being dumped in rivers and burned for fuel was that the government was taking final ownership of the unwanted surplus and either paying to store it or giving it away through PL480.

It all made for a much quieter and less messy farm crisis than that of the 1920s and 1930s, but it was a farm crisis nonetheless. Congressmen who weren't beholden to the farm voting bloc began to balk at the rising cost of carrying all those bushels of wheat and corn, at the forgiving of all those unpayable farm loans, and at the record of expensive failures like the Soil Bank.

The Kennedy administration entered the fray determined to shake things up. They decided that the surplus would continue to grow and grow unless there were even more cutbacks in planted acreage, and they instituted another program to pay the farmer to reduce planted acreage (for corn and sorghum since it was those yields that were rising fastest).

Their acreage program added an important new twist to farm policy. Instead of paying the farmer not to plant with dollars, they paid him with government grain—a so-called "payment in kind." Given the problems facing the USDA, it was really a clever way out. Paying the farmer with grain killed a couple of very big birds. It reduced both production and bulging federal inventories. The languishing surplus was pushed back in the farmer's hands, and onto the free market. On top of that, it all tended to keep a lid on the USDA budget, since there was no need for a cash outlay.

The payment in kind turned out to be the last new wrinkle of note in the national farm policy. With it, all of the building blocks were essentially in place— flawed and otherwise.

There would be endless fiddling with details over the next twenty-five years, but certain things about the grain programs did not change.

1. The goal was to outthink the market—to manipulate the supply in such a way that kept prices above certain support levels.

2. Farmers had to sign up in advance and meet basic requirements to be eligible for subsidies.

3. The on-going subsidies were based on debt. A loan rate was available for each crop. It fluctuated from one farm bill to the next, and sometimes from one crop year to the next.

4. Crop loans were theoretically to be repaid, but the government would accept the grain as collateral in default instead.

5. Overproduction was to be controlled through a variety of acreage reduction programs that paid the farmer not to plant.

The overriding goal was to support farm income, and thereby help the family farmer.

Despite all of the programs and money, however, there wasn't much progress on that basic goal. The United States continued to lose farms and farmers at a rapid clip, nearly as fast as it had when some twelve million men and women were packed off to the armed forces during World War II, and it lost them much faster than it had during the darkest days of the Depression.

This occurred through attrition, through friendly buyouts by larger and wealthier farmers who could afford the capital outlays required of modern farming, and through an exodus by others who were drawn as always to the nation's powerful urban magnets. The 1960s, for example, were the decade of the great farm exodus by poor blacks who moved from the farms of the south, to the cities of the north).

For most, farming was survivable during this entire stretch, but for smaller and poorer farmers the low prices meant a standard of living that was not at all up to the middle-class lifestyle they saw in the more prosperous towns of the Midwest where they shopped, and in places like the Ward and June Cleaver household on TV. Thin profit margins on a small farm equaled a thin income, just as it had in the far more troubled 1920s and 1930s. A thin profit margin on a larger farm, however, might well mean a decent income, plus the capital to expand and upgrade.

A small percentage of the lost farmers went down kicking, but most simply chose to not live in what looked to them like poverty. They folded their tents, liquidated, and got "regular" jobs.

What was left over each year always looked pretty spiffy, however. When Nikita Khrushchev made his famous visit to Iowa in the middle of this long postwar era, he was clearly stunned by the fact that every farm seemed neat and prosperous, and that every farmer seemed to operate a gleaming array of brand new equipment that outclassed anything in the USSR.

This was the image that most Americans carried, too. Each summer, when they packed up the family and drove from Chicago to St. Louis or from Fargo to Kansas City, Americans saw progress and prosperity stretching across the Grain Belt. What was on display each year, however, were the winners of the race. Each new wave of equipment represented an upgrade that some farmers could afford, and others could not. Those

that had made it from one summer to the next looked
good, but they were always fewer in number than the
year before. If Khrushchev were still alive today, he
might look back and take comfort from the fact that
the American farm economy was in decline, just like
the one back in Russia. You just couldn't see it very
easily beneath that shiny surface.

Prices flattened out during the sixties, and this was
largely the result of farm policies. If supplies grew too
much, subsidies could be lowered a bit, the government could sweeten the incentive to set aside acres,
and the international food aid spigot could be opened
a little wider. If free market supplies shrank and
prices rose, government controlled supplies were
released onto the market via a preset formula, and the
rally would stop.

Since the United States had the majority of the world
marketable surplus of grains and soybeans, its mixture of subsidies and incentives finally seemed to
work. They exerted an enormous influence over world
and domestic prices which tended to stop going down
when they were supposed to stop going down. In the
end, that was all anybody really wanted from farm
policy.

Traders at the Chicago Board of Trade who were
there during the flat sixties sometimes refer to that
decade as the time they all worked for the government.
From the perspective of today's freewheeling futures
traders, prices barely moved. The image we have of
shouting, shoving traders packed into the Chicago
Board of Trade's soybean pit was about the last thing
one would encounter on a typical day during those
slow years.

What old traders remember about the 1960s is days
spent just sitting on the edge of the trading pits,
reading the paper and doing crossword puzzles until
the occasional runner wandered up with an order.

The program decade ended with just a bit over ten

million persons living on farms. It began with over sixteen million. That, by the way, is a drop of more than 37 percent. The number of farms dropped by more than a quarter. This didn't seem to bother people much.

On top of the flawed programs were sins of omission that were laying the groundwork for even bigger problems. Bigger farms and bigger equipment meant that smaller fields were being combined into larger fields. That meant a loss of the trees and hedges that separated them which sheltered the soil from the wind. As was the custom in the United States, the large open expanses were often plowed in the fall and left bare to wind erosion all through the winter. Farmers did this so that, come spring, they could get in the field to plant as soon as the weather broke. As a result, topsoil was eroding faster than nature could replace it, but farm policy remained silent.

Losing topsoil was a lot like losing farmers. People knew it was happening, but the land got planted each year, and a bigger crop seemed to jump off it in the fall, and food was cheap. Why worry?

Another sin of omission surfaced in the 1960s that has since come back to haunt the country. Not only was the new farm economy in the process of poisoning the well, it was also in the early stages of pumping it dry. Commercial-scale irrigation equipment was becoming readily available.

Bigger and more successful farms were better able to afford powerful new pumps, so they could bring water to the surface even faster. Rain makes grain, and so does irrigation. Thirsty fields that get watered are fields that will produce more grain. That higher yield skews even more wealth to farms that can afford to irrigate.

Eventually, this also puts smaller farmers and neighboring non-farmers into a race for the area's groundwater supply. If this gets taken to its logical extreme (and it has been), a simple non-farming homeowner who happens to live in the vicinity of a big commercial farm needs to compete for well water by drilling deeper and deeper.

To the extent that this was even acknowledged by the federal government, it was encouraged—just like the use of chemicals. During the sixties and seventies, huge water projects, the very essence of what we call pork barrel, were built like mad in the western Grain Belt, where rainfall is less reliable. The water from them was delivered to farms at heavily subsidized rates, and so production of irrigated corn grew rapidly in dry places like Nebraska, at the exact same time that the USDA was jumping through hoops trying to reduce the supply of corn with paid set-asides. To say that this was a conflict would be charitable.

Despite their incredible detail, farm policies virtually ignored this loss of and damage to the only two natural resources that are essential to producing a crop—soil and water. (There were conservation provisions for the 10–30 million acres in set- aside programs at a given time, but not for the 300–400 million acres that were cultivated each and every year.) It was a disaster on two fronts. They largely ignored the erosion of the human resource as well.

Farmers were silent on all of these fundamental issues. They were free to choose the priorities of their own farm policies. They lobbied long and hard for higher loan rates, subsidized exports, and limits on production, but not at all for the preservation of the basic assets.

However, whether the nation's policies of the 1950s and 1960s were good, bad, or just incomplete, would soon to be irrelevant. The American grip on the world's farm technology was loosening in the 1960s, and its ability to use its huge surplus to dictate price was ending, as all such abnormalities eventually end.

If anyone thought that the race the farmer was in

could slow down once the number of runners in the United States lessened after the war, he was in for a rude shock. The technology that had boosted American production into its enormous lead was gaining momentum in the 1960s.

On top of that, the number of competitors had not been whittled down at all. It was starting to grow. Millions of acres were being planted to soybeans in Brazil, and the "green revolution" was soon to take the giant population of India off the world's food relief rolls.

Farmers and farm economies around the world were studying and adopting American farming methods. The pace was picking up, and the runners would soon be forced to break from their trot into a gallop.

This was not at all what the planners saw in 1970, however. The American farm economy had huge, seemingly insurmountable leads in every important category, just like the auto industry. That's what most people saw. The United States was number one in productivity, in the size of its food surplus, in its export market share, available farm capital, applied technology, transportation, processing and refining, storage capacity. . . . It was at least third in total production of calories for human consumption behind only China, which had more than four times the U.S. population, and India with three times its population.

American farm policy didn't need to be perfect. It didn't even need to be especially close.

"Where does a 500-pound gorilla sleep?" the riddle asks. As we know, the answer is, "anywhere it wants." Apparently that answer is just as true for the policies of agricultural giants, as it is for 500-pound gorillas. It doesn't much matter where the gorilla sleeps, as long as he doesn't fall off a cliff in the middle of the night. It also doesn't seem to matter all that much how the 500-pound farm giant manages its affairs as long as it can avoid major cataclysms like an invasion or economic collapse . . . or change.

In the gorilla riddle, as in life, temporary is the key unspoken word. The answer changes when the 500-pound gorilla grows old. At some point, it starts to matter very much where he sleeps, especially if there are some eager 300-pound youngsters also looking for turf in his part of the jungle.

9

MORE GORILLAS

If the United States was getting myopic in the 1960s, there were plenty of developments on the horizon that should have raised its sights. Come 1970, there was a lot more competition. It wasn't overwhelming yet by any means, but then neither was the competition for American automakers.

The United States had staved off competition in the noncommunist world's food economy after World War II with cheap and abundant American products like corn, wheat flour, and soybeans as the currency.

Gradually, the United States broadened the mix of food products it exported, creating niches for value-added derivatives of its basic crops, like soybean oil, and eventually even consumer packaged goods. In time, it succeeded in exporting many aspects of the American diet, and this victory for both culture and policy widened the beachhead for U.S. food exports during the 1960s and 1970s.

As the world food market grew, however, other countries started seeing opportunities to participate. One of the most attractive was in the production, processing, and export of soybeans and their products.

Soybean production in the United States did not even begin in earnest until after 1922 when the first soybean processing plant opened. Soybeans are a cheap source of both vegetable oil for human consumption and high-protein meal for feeding livestock. As the American diet changed to include more meat in the 1920's, a niche opened.

Demand for meal and oil accelerated with World War II, and so did American production of soybeans. Soybeans moved in, taking over oat acres that were abandoned by the millions from 1900 through the 1950s, as the nation's horse population declined; some corn acres that weren't needed because the corn yields were exploding; and some pasture land, no longer needed as the livestock industry converted to bigger feedlot operations out west.

By the late 1960s, forty million acres were being planted to soybeans, and they were the American farmers' number one cash crop. Worldwide red meat consumption increased dramatically in the sixties, as the American diet was exported. This used up as much soymeal as the United States could produce. Americans and everyone else were eating more processed and fast foods too, and the vegetable oil that came from the soybean proved to be the perfect generic oil for everything from salad oil and mayonnaise, to french fries. There seemed no end to the market for the miracle bean.

Others wanted to get in on the production and marketing of soybeans. The major grain companies who formed the middle of the world food chain wanted to cheapen and diversify their sources, and it was

Brazil that happened to be in the right place, at the right time.

The Brazilian government also wanted to populate its interior, and farming has traditionally been the way to get large numbers of people to spread out and become economically viable. (The United States had milked that method of economic development for all it was worth in the 1800s.)

International lending agencies were eager to lend a hand. They wanted to lend to the expanding Brazilian economy, but they wanted a stronger cash flow. Soybeans were the world's hottest cash crop. It was a marriage made in heaven, and by 1970 Brazil had emerged as the world's third largest soybean producer after the United States and China. It was the second largest exporter of soybeans.

The Brazilians, along with Japanese and Western Europeans, were also expanding their processing industries by the early 1970s, posing a serious threat to the U.S. dominance of these value-adding and job-creating industries. Brazil wanted to add that value to their own soybeans before they got shipped, thereby boosting cash flow. The Japanese and Western Europeans who were forced by climate and geography to import, wanted to buy raw materials, and turn soybeans into finished products like vegetable oil and protein meal on their home ground. By the early seventies, Brazil was challenging the U.S. position as the number one exporter of soymeal.

The "green revolution" was also taking shape in those years, and it was in the process of turning customers into potential competitors. India, which had been the basket case of the world food system for much of the twentieth century, began to modernize its farming methods in the early sixties, largely through the efforts of western organizations such as the Peace Corps. By 1972 they were on the road to self-sufficiency.

This was obviously a cause for humanitarian rejoic-
ing, since it eased the ancient sufferings of the Indian
people, but from the standpoint of the world's agricultural giant it meant losing a major safety valve. India
had given the United States a bottomless hole into
which it was able to dump wheat and other surplus
commodities for nearly a quarter century. That had
been one of the variables that kept the wheat surplus
from exploding in the 1950s and 1960s.

America's big lead in technology and farm productivity was also eroding. If a country like India could
take itself off the world's food welfare rolls, far more
advanced *paying* customers in places like Western
Europe could narrow the gap even faster. Ditto for
increasingly tough competitors in South America,
Canada, and Australia.

That realization was one of the things policymakers
had to chew on, and the Nixon administration came to
office in early 1969 with the goal of making farm policy
more "market-oriented" in response. In the end they
made very little headway against an entrenched maze
of farm programs and a farm lobby that was deeply
suspicious of fundamental policy changes. All that
happened initially was that farmers were given more
leeway in choosing crops they could plant while participating in the USDA acreage reduction programs.

Farmers also lobbied for and received higher basic
price supports, but Congress rebelled on that score.
They limited total government payments that could be
made to a single farmer to $55,000 after it was noted
that payments of as much as $1,000,000 had been
made to some of the country's wealthiest farmland
owners.

The Nixon administration may have wanted to make
farm policy more market-oriented, but this was easier
said than done. The energetic Kennedy administration
had also come into office ready to overhaul the system,
but had to settle for simply tacking the payment in

kind concept onto the old acreage programs. There was even less room to maneuver eight years later.

Since there was little hope of actually restructuring farm policy, the frustrated Nixon administration had to search among the little details for policies that could be changed by executive order. One option that seemed to fit the bill was in the area of export licensing. The administration decided in 1971 to eliminate a seemingly obscure trade provision that required grain exporting companies to report in advance sales of certain basic commodities above a certain amount.

This was a tactical error, one that proved to be the first of many. The reporting requirement had been a fairly sensible little provision that allowed the government to have a handle on the eventual whereabouts of its own food supplies, and to determine whether they would remain adequate.

Any of the countries that had been victims of starvation in the twentieth century would not have considered eliminating such a rule, but the United States had been well fed since the Civil War. It just wasn't trained to protect its food. It was trained instead to think of the surplus as the problem.

A tactical error by one party creates opportunity for another. Whether or not the Nixon administration knew it, a momentous decision was being made several thousand miles away that would take advantage of their miscue and leave the American farm economy unbalanced for over a decade—like the German decision to embark on unrestricted U-boat warfare in 1917.

In a surprise policy change of its own, the USSR decided virtually overnight to become the world's largest importer of grain.

Since the late stages of World War II, the Soviet Union had mostly been a bit player in the Western grain markets, with the exception of the mid-1960s, when they made a large bloc of wheat purchases from

Australia, Canada, and the United States to cover crop
failures of 1961–62 and 1965.

Those crop failures had scared the Soviet leadership.
They had spawned serious food shortages in the
USSR, which was not all that unusual, and the Soviet
government initially turned to the time-honored formula of exhorting the beleaguered Soviet population to
tighten its belt. They also raised food prices just to help
the belt-tightening along, and sat back to ride things
out.

In 1962, however, the rest of the story did not
proceed according to plan. Food riots broke out. The
worst one, in the city of Novocherkassk, ended with the
deaths of some seventy to eighty rioters. This caused
so great a strain within the Soviet leadership that the
USSR swallowed its considerable national pride and
bought wheat from the West to relieve the shortages.

Shortly afterward, and in part as a result of his failed
agricultural policies, the Soviet Politburo also deposed
Communist Party Chairman Nikita Khrushchev. This
stunning series of events deeply rattled the entire
Soviet hierarchy; Khrushchev's successors did not
plan to repeat it.

Unfortunately for the USSR, their agricultural
problems didn't end with the "one time only" imports
of 1963, or the exit of Mr. Khrushchev. There was yet
another crop failure in 1965, and this time the USSR
didn't hesitate to cover the deficit with another round
of purchases from the West.

The food rioters of 1962 had demanded better food,
and under Khrushchev's successor, Leonid Brezhnev,
the decision was made to try and give it to them. (It
has been reported that rioters in Novocherkassk
shouted for Khrushchev sausage.)

This meant production of more red meat, poultry,
eggs, and so on. It takes a lot more grain to produce
meat, than to simply feed grain directly to people.
There was little chance that the creaking Soviet

agricultural system could deliver the meat its citizens wanted, even without a crop failure, so this committed the USSR to a steady diet of grain imports.

Fortunately for the Soviets (and unfortunately for American exporters), Soviet weather took a turn for the better during the last half of the 1960s. To the amazement of all, they produced one bumper crop after another. The Soviets were therefore able to maintain a steady, modest course of dietary improvements with mostly domestic grain and only modest imports. Back in the United States, hope quickly faded that the USSR would be the new outlet for the chronic American grain surplus.

A bit more patience on the part of exporters was in order though. Despite modest improvements in the average diet in the USSR and Eastern Europe during the late 1960s, the Soviet diet still stood at levels that might have started riots in the United States and Western Europe. In fact, there were major areas, such as Poland, where the average diet seemed to be deteriorating by the early 1970s.

As dismal and deteriorating as the Polish diet was, it depended on heavy government subsidies. In 1970, the cash-strapped Polish government decided that it could no longer afford the high subsidies and sharply raised food prices to help balance the books about two weeks before Christmas.

The result was much the same as it had been in Novocherkassk in 1962. Bloody riots broke out first in the Polish port city of Gdansk (where else?), and spread quickly to surrounding industrial towns and the port city of Sczcezin, near the border with East Germany. (This was the genesis of the Solidarity labor movement still headquartered in the city of Gdansk.)

Polish troops were ordered in to quell the insurrection which had turned both violent and anti-Party. The army used live ammunition to do so, and scores (maybe even hundreds) of strikers died. The spectre of

Polish troops shooting Polish citizens rattled the
Polish government every bit as much as the riots of
1962 had rattled the Soviets. It rescinded the price
increases, and the Communist Party demanded the
resignation of Party Chairman and Head of State
Wladyslaw Gomulka, literally on his death bed just
days before Christmas.

To the governments of the USSR and the rest of the
Eastern Bloc, this had all the earmarks of a trend.
Food riots could become a chronic problem if the status
quo were maintained. And the fallout from these
riots—up to and including the removal of the heads of
state—created more strain than the Soviet system was
designed to accommodate.

Worse still for the Soviets, they couldn't be certain in
1972 that they could maintain the quality of their own
diet. They stood to lose the hard-won gains of the late
1960s. The string of bumper crops had only resulted in
modest improvements to begin with, allowing little or
no surplus to be carried forward in anticipation of
inevitable crop disasters. In a rather pitiful version of
America's own use of food aid to prevent the spread of
Communism after World War II, the USSR was also
committed to exporting a growing quantity of grain
each year to impoverished client states like Cuba. The
Soviet food numbers did not add up.

Fortunately, however, all of the riots had a specific
cause. Whether the locale was Poland or the USSR,
whether it was 1962 or 1970, the conflict centered on
food—period. People weren't demanding Western-
style freedoms or national independence; they were
demanding better food, more of it, and very low, subsidized prices. More to the point, they were demanding
a diet that contained a lot more red meat. Any problem
that focused is a problem that can be solved.

The Politburo could see only two realistic ways to end
this chronic threat to the stability of the Soviet state.
They could either institute sweeping economic

(capitalistic) reforms on their farms, such as allowing more private ownership of land, or they could import food. No other option solved the problem.

Since any hint of capitalist reform was considered a direct threat to the authority of the state in those pre-glasnost days, that course was unthinkable. Besides, such measures could take years to bring the desired results, and the country needed a quicker fix.

That left imports as the only workable option other than to continue putting down the occasional food riot. Swallowing its national pride, the Politburo made the obvious choice and in 1971 established a five-year plan of increased red meat production based on increased grain imports.

Once they had cleared that emotional hurdle, the Politburo realized that the decision opened up a whole new world of very constructive options. Soviet credit was extremely good, and the country produced surpluses of a variety of desirable raw materials such as crude oil, natural gas, and gold which could be sold to the West to raise enough hard currency to buy all the grain that they could realistically use at that point.

At first they moved carefully, but the events of 1972 sped things up. That was the year Soviet grain production was to suffer the long-awaited shortfall, and careful buying would not be good enough. The winter wheat yields fell sharply, and by June things looked poor for the summer crops as well. The USSR began booking ocean freight and buying grain from the export houses in unprecedented quantities starting in June. By the end of August, they had racked up total purchases of over 24 million metric tons, about 17.5 million of it from the United States, and most of it at prices that turned out to be bargain basement by year end.

The Soviet buying agency, Exportkhleb, apparently decided that the best defense was a spirited offense. Since they were being forced to import in any case, and

since the crop was poor, why not take that extra step
and buy themselves a bit of a surplus? The removal of
the USDA reporting function allowed them to sneak in
and convert ownership of the bulk of the world's food
surplus from the U.S. to the USSR. (It was the all-time
insider trade.)

In the process, they could accelerate the building up
of their domestic herds of cattle and hogs and dramatically increase the amount of red meat available to the
Soviet consumer. In that way they would not only
stave off further unrest, but they could tangibly improve the life of the Soviet consumer and thereby earn
a considerable number of political points at home.
When all was said and done, the Soviet government
had turned the proverbial sow's ear into a silk purse of
sorts.

In any case, the initial purchases in 1972 vaulted the
USSR into the position of being the largest net importer of grain and oilseeds—a distinction they've held
on and off to this day. They bought wheat, soybeans,
and soybean protein meal. They bought from Canada
and South America, but mostly they bought from their
old sparring partner in the Cold War: the United
States. In 1972, the United States was the only
country in the world that could deliver such large
quantities of grain, oil, and protein meal, and spread
them out at a rate that the Soviet infrastructure could
handle.

The Soviets made these decisions about the future of
the American food surplus without notifying the
United States itself. Contract negotiation occurred between the USSR and the private grain companies who
were going to deliver the goods.

There's still room for debate on the subject of just
who knew what and when. The CIA had detailed information about the Soviet trading activities before it hit
the news wires—information which it forwarded to the
USDA, and which the USDA later claimed to have lost

in its bureaucratic cracks. If we believe the official version, the president of the United States and the secretary of agriculture read about the "Great Grain Robbery" in the newspaper like everybody else.

Did the USDA really just *lose* vital intelligence reports from the CIA that indicated the country's grain surplus was on the verge of being eliminated? Did certain recipients of CIA reports suppress them? Did high-level officials read the CIA reports and not comprehend how big 24 million metric tons is? Did any officials with advance knowledge of the sales profit by buying grain futures? Did any government officials know in 1971 that the Soviets were on the brink of massive grain purchases, and actually plan to eliminate export licensing regulations to allow the transactions to occur in secret and on the cheap? Were they unable to do the basic arithmetic?

Any one of these questions is going to have a mighty stinky answer, but we'll probably never know because the trail dead-ended in a bureaucratic maze, and the controversy has long since cooled. Congressional hearings conducted afterward turned up incompetence and shortsightedness, and basically left it at that.

In any case, the Soviet grain, soybean, and soybean meal purchases hit the world markets like a ton of bricks. The wheat surplus that the United States had been trying to control or unload for most of the previous twenty-five years was suddenly cut by more than two-thirds. The huge cheap corn surplus that had fueled our steak and hamburger habit was gone. The soybean crop that made up an increasingly important part of the diets of both livestock and humans in the United States was also spoken for, and as it turned out, oversold.

The Soviet buying spree couldn't have come at a worse time for the hapless American consumer. It coincided with a worldwide series of droughts and crop failures that had commenced in 1971, and which

diverted even more unexpected buying to the United
States. Orders poured in for not only corn, wheat, and
soybeans, but barley, oats, rice, sorghum, and cotton.
Total grain exports of the United States—already the
world's largest agricultural exporter—nearly doubled
between the 1971 crop marketing year (which ended
on September 30, 1972), and the 1972 crop marketing
year.

At first prices reacted to this sudden elimination of
the world's grain and soybean reserves with remarkable restraint. The soybean market had been slowly
trending higher since it bottomed out in 1969 at about
$2.40 per bushel. By summer of 1972, it was up to
$3.60. At that level, it was approaching its historic
highs of about $4.40 established after the war, but
there was no urgency to the trade.

The soybean market even managed the traditional
"harvest break," falling back to about $3.25 by Oc-
tober, but then the market started catching on. Prices
started rising at an unprecedented rate, up through
the summer highs, up through the all-time highs. They
were just getting warmed up. After the first of the
year, the soybean market turned vertical, and by the
time it was finished in May–June of 1973, it had
topped out at just under $13 per bushel.

In the late stages of the rally, traders in the soybean
pit chanted, "beans in the teens!" The market never
quite made the teens, but it was still the most frenzied
food price rally in American history. In about eight
months, prices for the new basic ingredient had increased about three and a half times from their starting point, and they had nearly tripled the all-time
highs. It was the third and greatest price shock of the
century, and it turned the world agricultural markets
upside down.

The soybean price shock of 1972–73 was different
than the ones associated with the two world wars, and
in many ways it was the most severe in its effect on the

American consumer. The consumer price index for food (1967=100) advanced from 114.9 in 1970 to 141.4 in 1973—a gain of about 23 percent—the greatest U.S. inflation in food prices since the Civil War. This was no mean feat, given the fact that it was accomplished in peacetime in a country producing about 50 percent more of basic commodities like corn, wheat, and soybeans than it consumed internally.

With the surplus essentially gone, the industrialized American food chain (and with it the American consumer) was forced into the unaccustomed role of having to compete, and compete aggressively, with users around the world for the wheat that made the flour in American bread, and the corn that was fed to the cattle that produced the steak and hamburgers Americans ate. Same for the soybean oil in salad dressing and mayonnaise, and soymeal and corn that fed chicken, hogs, and more than a few students in college cafeterias across the country.

The guy at Kellogg who needed to book the corn for the Cornflakes to be packaged in coming months now had to contend for a finite supply with the guy from Exportkhleb in Moscow who wanted that same corn for cattle-on-feed in the Soviet Ukraine. American companies who had no way of knowing that their world would be turned upside down that year were stuck with long-term contracts to deliver processed products to food manufacturers. They had to pay up for the raw materials and deliver their processed goods at below cost.

A generation of business practices had been built up in the middle layers of the American food chain, and they were based on oversupply. Buyers had to relearn real fast. It now made a very big difference whether a merchandiser bought the corn and soybeans he needed in six months, today, or the day before they were needed. The price might double or be cut in half in that stretch, and a misstep could easily wipe out the company's profit on the final product. In an efficient industry with thin profit margins, a cut in profits could quickly become a cut in capital.

Most made it through the initial crunch. Thereafter they paid up when necessary and passed the cost on down the chain. The volatility gradually took a toll though. It greatly increased the need for operating capital on all fronts, and smaller and less well-capitalized firms were not always able to outlive an instance of bad timing. In an industry that was rapidly consolidating on all levels long before 1972, the shock increased the rate at which smaller firms were forced to sell, merge with a competitor, or simply disappear.

A large, diverse food industry is a rich source of jobs, new food products, domestic corporate profits, and export earnings. Very high prices boost export earnings too, but they also make it profitable for foreign competition to jump in the game.

Low food prices mean that most individuals and families can afford to feed themselves with a small percentage of their hours worked each week. This has obvious humanitarian benefits, but it also leaves a citizen able to earn money that he can spend on better housing, goods, and services, giving the economy far more of a boost in the end. Low food prices also reduce the cost of food stamps and the spin-off costs of other welfare programs.

The boost in agricultural export earnings that came with higher farm prices was therefore a placebo. It helped cover the already worrisome trade deficit that came from higher oil prices, and the influx of consumer goods from the Far East. As such, it made our trade problem seem like no big deal. Maybe a little bigger trade deficit in the 1970s would have alarmed the country enough to retool sooner.

Keep in mind too that by the mid-1970s, the American taxpayer had been paying generously for this system for about forty years. Didn't he have some sort of dividend coming? Say, affordable food prices?

Instead of dividends, it was the list of *consequences* arising from farm policy that grew. This list included the rapid loss of topsoil and a damaged water supply. Now it was eroding the consumer's bottom line. Were we starting to see these problems yet? Apparently not.

10

BONANZA!

To the farmers and the agricultural policy establishment in Washington, the events of 1972 seemed like a dream come true. Through the 1950s and 1960s, they had been conditioned to think of the food surplus as a problem and to direct their efforts toward making it go away.

Suddenly, it was gone, and export customers were lining up to pay cash money for all the surplus grain and soybeans the country could produce.

A lot of that cash was going directly to the bottom line of the farmer. Even those who sold their crops at the absolute bottom of the price troughs that followed the summer of 1972 were getting a price that was double or more the average price their crops had fetched in the 1960s. Land prices soared along with the higher return that it could generate to a farmer or investor, and many ordinary Midwestern farmers became millionaires on paper.

The USDA faced a financial turnaround that was nearly as profound as the one experienced by the farmer. Prior to 1972, American agricultural exports often depended on years of intensive and expensive market development by the USDA before the first sales were booked and even then, many needed to be subsidized with the ubiquitous PL480 export financing. In 1971, PL480 credits were involved in some 15 percent of all U.S. agricultural exports (by value), and this total had reached as high as 75 percent of the value of wheat exports (in 1959). By 1973, that total had dropped to perhaps 4 percent, and political pressure was being applied to further reduce or even eliminate all export subsidies due to growing inflation at home.

Most important to the USDA though, these higher prices brought an immediate and outright reduction in the cost of grain and soybean subsidies, and a latent reduction in the sense that they would not need to gear up for yet another round of paid acreage reductions. Farmers survived the late 1950s and all of the 1960s by participating in government programs, taking out loans when prices fell, and frequently defaulting their grain to the government if the market stayed down.

After the summer of 1972, the free-market price nearly always offered the farmer a more attractive price than the loan, so few took out loans. Crops moved directly to the market or got stored by the farmer at the farmer's expense.

In fact, the total demand for one commodity bought by the Soviets that first year—soymeal—nearly exceeded the available supply in 1973. The Soviets were in the process of discovering what the livestock industries of the United States and Western Europe already knew, that you could accelerate weight gain among cattle, hogs, and chickens if you mixed in a higher protein source like soybean meal. Since Soviet animals were all on a crash weight-gain program that year, Exportkhleb bought lots of meal.

Since the United States was not paying attention, the Americans didn't realize for some time that their own supplies would be depleted before the next soybean crop could be harvested in the fall of 1973. President Nixon declared a partial embargo of soymeal exports, canceling contracts across the board, including those made in good faith by old non–Soviet Bloc customers. This spawned more financial tremors for the industry's middlemen, who thought they were well positioned for the big market of 1973 but found that their supplies were suddenly cut off.

This sent the involved parties into international arbitration that in some cases dragged on until 1977, and it generated the first rumblings of concern over the reliability of the American export contracts. It was bad business.

The country was in the midst of all this as Congress debated a new farm bill in the spring of 1973, and the confusion and volatility of the markets no doubt added to the confusion and volatility of the agricultural policy it spawned. The height of the debate occurred when many markets were roaring toward their all-time highs at the end of May. Everybody knew that the United States had been caught off balance, pushing food out of the country with one hand and trying to hold down production with the other.

Often when we are caught off balance in one direction, we react by leaning too far in the other. The obvious answer in the minds of American policymakers was to turn existing farm policy around, and march it in the opposite direction. With this goal in mind, a new farm bill was passed in August 1973.

Officially, the bill declared that its purpose was to expand production to meet an "ever growing worldwide demand for food and fiber," and to hold down consumer prices in the United States. Secretary of Agriculture Earl Butz proclaimed that the bill represented "an historic turning point in the philosophy of farm programs in the United States." How true. Mr. Butz then went out on the stump to promote the change. He preached a gospel of expanded acreage and adoption of scientific farming methods. He believed very strongly that the future belonged to the emerging large and capital intensive farms that already accounted for nearly half of all corn and bean production by the time the 1973 bill was passed. In going out to share his vision, he was preaching to the converted.

Mr. Butz was credited with two key phrases that encapsuled the message that the capital was trying to convey to the hinterlands. Farmers were urged to: A) "plant fencerow to fencerow," in order to B) "feed the world." Fencerow to fencerow meant just that—right up to the property line and as close to the ditch as you could manage without having the tractor fall in. It meant cutting down trees that took up the suddenly valuable acreage between fields, and on the edges of streams and ponds. (This included many of the last remaining tree rows that were planted as wind-blocks after the Dust Bowl in the 1930s.)

In many cases, the pond went too. It was drained and planted both to add acres to the farm and to allow the tractors and combines to travel in the longest possible straight line; turning the tractor around wasted fuel.

The latest generation of farm equipment made the acceleration as easy as falling off a log. Powerful new tractors of up to 150 horsepower were developed and marketed by the late sixties. The planters that they pulled were in the process of growing from six to twelve rows. A farmer who could plant a little over fifty acres per day in the mid-sixties, could now plant over a hundred. With or without Mr. Butz's exhortation, this was defining the trends of modern farming.

So soil conservation took a direct hit. The USDA's modest efforts to preserve soil were overwhelmed. It had carefully crafted procedures to be used on set-aside acreage like that in the Soil Bank. It had tried to educate the farmer on the best means of terracing hilly land, and on the need to plant a runoff area to heavy grass so it didn't turn into a gully.

In the face of the big new equipment and the call to expand, these tender conservation methods didn't stand a chance. Big tractors weren't designed to mince around the little terraces and grassy culverts. They were made to bull right over and through them.

Wealthy farmers, large corporations, and foreign investors also bought and drained tracts of wetlands that were far bigger than the ones under the average family farm. Large-scale farming now plunged into the vast coastal marshlands of the southeast and the swampy lands of the Mississippi Delta, with full blessings from the USDA. All across the northern Great Plains (and into Canada) farmers began draining thousands of the "potholes," or ponds, which shelter North American waterfowl and replenish groundwater.

Fencerow to fencerow meant expanded planting on land that had been too poor or too hilly to be profitably cultivated in the low-priced years, land that often had a very fragile layer of thin topsoil that was subject to rapid wind and water erosion once its protective cover was turned under.

Fencerow to fencerow meant that the government actually encouraged the production of crops in regions that were normally too dry for those crops. A big farm outfit in the Great Plains could not only plant thirsty corn plants on thinner topsoil that was vulnerable to winter wind erosion, but it could water that corn crop to the point where yields approached those produced on better land in the heart of the Corn Belt. In some cases, this was only economically feasible because of federally sponsored water and irrigation projects.

In most cases however, the water came from the

ground and it was brought to the surface in bigger and bigger quantities by more and more powerful pumping systems that were affordable to large and midsize farm operations in the new high-priced world of the 1970s. Farms in the wetter regions east of the Great Plains pumped too. If you were already getting seventy-five bushels of corn per acre with the rain that God sent in an average year, why not shoot for eighty-five or ninety bushels per acre with irrigation? Water tables that had been dropping in spots for years starting dropping more dramatically and over a much broader area.

The blast of intensive farming and more planted acreage that came after the price shock was generated by market forces. All humans tend to suffer the same faults when large sums of money are involved; we become greedy. If there is potential for a bigger income, most of us will do our best to get our share. If you happen to be a farmer, and that means engaging in business practices that are not in the best interests of either the environment or your fellow citizens, odds are you'll plunge ahead anyway.

Unfortunately, left to their own devices, some will go to great extremes in the pursuit of gain before good sense and good citizenship intervene, unless something or someone restrains them.

The purpose of government is to identify those activities that are destructive to society and restrict or eliminate them. In 1973, our political leaders looked at some dangerous trends that were overheating and chose to pour even more fuel on them, instead of a little cold water. They encouraged destructive practices so that they, the USDA, and the farmer could cash in on the boom.

Apparently, the policymaking machine saw the boom not only as a golden goose, but as a reality that was here to stay. Framers of the new farm bill were confident enough to go so far as to lower the cap on payments to an individual farmer from $55,000, to $20,000. This was to cut costs, but it meant that if a grain surplus and low prices returned, the losses incurred on even a midsize farm might no longer be covered by federal subsidies. The new bill was an act of faith that there would not be another string of low-priced years.

Policymakers also felt confident enough about higher prices to raise basic supports (loans), and institute a concept called "target prices" for cotton, corn, and wheat. Target prices were set well above the old loan levels and if prices fell below the targets, participating farmers would be paid an amount as high as the difference between the two.

The higher levels for loans and the even higher target prices would make the USDA budget explode if the prices went down as production grew. Congress was taking a calculated gamble with these changes, though. It was going on record with an extravagant promise to a still-powerful farm bloc and assuming that promise would never come due.

The bill set specific targets for 1974, slightly higher ones for 1975, and established a new formula for setting those of 1976 and 1977, an index of the cost of gasoline, fertilizer, interest rates, taxes, and so on. These were of course rising at a brisk clip in the mid-1970s, so the targets were scheduled to do the same. As they rose, so did the theoretical budget expense they represented. All of this would come back to haunt farmers and congressmen.

Actually the higher targets were doing damage to those who were at the lower end of the farm business, long before they did any to the USDA budget. They represented a guaranteed theoretical income with no strings attached for the participating farmer. Unlike the old underlying loan subsidies that might have to be paid back and required that crops be kept off the market, the targets locked in a profit for each bushel of corn and wheat that the farmer produced. Lending agencies, which were becoming more aggressive on all fronts in the 1970s took note, and they used this along with the advent of higher prices to justify endless strings of new loans for expansion and new equipment.

After all, if the farmer was locked into the programs and the index that set the target was going up along with inflation and interest rates, how could the new loans fail? Most lenders no longer cared that the newest and fastest growing operations were rolling over and increasing their debt year by year. Even more than the lender euphoria that came with the price shock, it was the rising targets that spurred the accumulation of farm debt.

All of this occurred against a backdrop of an international financial system with billions of petrodollars to recirculate. The huge increase in oil prices in 1973, and the big one that followed in 1978 created dollars that mostly stayed in the Western banks where their Arab and non-Arab owners earned interest. Of course, that interest could only be paid if the banks loaned those billions to others who in turn made interest payments to the banks, and so on.

This process concentrated huge sums of capital into the hands of money center banks that were eager to channel them through Midwestern lenders and quasi-government farm credit agencies that could distribute all of those dollars in the form of loans to the fine folks who were so eagerly waiting to borrow out in the rock-solid American farm belt. All those eager borrowers had to do, of course, was put up all of their land and equipment as collateral.

By the mid-1980s the total farm debt had grown to a monster weighing well over $200 billion—more than double the staggering sums owed by either Brazil or Mexico at the time.

The newly volatile world marketplace had more surprises in store for the American farm economy. In

October of 1973, Syria and Egypt launched a surprise
attack against Israel, inflicting alarming early rever-
sals against the Israeli army, and throwing it into
retreat. Golda Meir, fearing that her country was in
danger of being overrun, appealed to President Nixon
for immediate and massive military aid, and he
delivered.

The Israelis eventually prevailed, but angry Arab oil
producers began a six-month boycott of sales of their
crude oil to those who had helped Israel in the war.
This generated an *apparent* shortage of petroleum-
based products called the "Oil Crisis," and it was accompanied by a giant run-up in oil prices.

The success that the Arab producers had in generating shortages and higher prices energized a moribund
oil cartel called the Organization of Petroleum Exporting Countries (OPEC). Producers agreed to quadruple
the organization's benchmark price for crude, and they
made the price increase stick.

The American farm had long since become addicted
to a variety of petroleum-based products, and the more
intensive farming efforts of the post-1972 years only
served to increase the level of dependence. Bigger
tractors and combines were needed on the ever bigger
farms. The price of fuel needed to operate these gas
guzzlers shot up along with the world price of crude,
and that took the first bite out of the newly expanded
profit margin.

The modern and expanding American farm was also
spreading more chemical fertilizers, insecticides, and
pesticides on each one of those acres than ever before
in search of higher yields and greater profits. Since a
substantial portion of these ingredients were
petroleum-based, they too shot up in price and took a
bigger bite out of the farmer's big new profit margin.

In the rush to enjoy higher and higher yields in the
1950s and 1960s, the dangers to the ecology from
chemical pollution were completely ignored. Also ig-

nored in the modernization rush was the fact that at
the time, the country was overproducing, and it didn't
need dramatically higher yields.

Then along came the 1970s, and the aftermath of the
latest price shocks by both the USSR and OPEC. The
price of fertilizers and chemicals was soaring, and the
American farmer was addicted. Many had gotten rid of
the livestock that provided manure for natural fertilizers before the 1950s and 1960s. There would be a
lot of time and expense involved in building up a new
herd and switching back. In fact, the growing size of
the average farm conspired against the organic
method. (The more land you farm, the more animals
you need to generate enough manure.)

Besides, by then the livestock industry had heavily
concentrated itself into big feedlot operations, and the
slaughterhouses had moved west to accommodate
them. Even if they wanted to, smaller farmers would
have had a hard time competing. Few wanted to, and
those who were tempted feared that the chemical
users would blow them out of the grain market with
even bigger yields on down the road.

Furthermore, much of the American soil was addicted. Herbicides like Roundup solved annoying (and
yield-reducing) weed problems, but many left a
residue that committed the field to the same crop and
herbicide the following year. This often ruled out crop
rotation, which was a time-honored method of resting
the soil and replenishing it. (Soybeans for instance put
back the nitrogen that corn takes out.)

In any case, depending on petroleum-based chemicals made the already costly business of being an
average modern farmer even more expensive. To add
to the other expenses, productive land in the heart of
the Corn Belt quadrupled in price during the 1970s.
That of course presented more equity (a new word for
the farmer) against which to borrow. Come to think of
it, that sounds a lot like all those wonderful new home

equity loans that the banking industry has been ped-
dling in the late 1980s.

Other costs rose too. The cost of a single large and
basic piece of equipment such as a 100 horsepower
tractor cost perhaps $7,000 in 1970, but by 1978 it shot
up to over $20,000. And the equipment a farmer at-
tached to the back of that tractor also became much
more expensive and sophisticated. Combines for har-
vesting the crop went up at least as fast as tractors. A
first-rate combine cost perhaps $20,000 in the early
1970s, and in the late 1980s the top of the line has
reached $100,000. Like the more intensive use of
chemicals, all of this new and improved equipment
increased productivity which in turn increased the
potential profit on a big farm, but it was uneconomical
for the smaller farm.

If a farmer already owned enough good land to keep
him busy during planting and harvest season and
carried little or no long-term debt, he probably earned
year after year of big profits throughout the 1970s, just
as the policymakers hoped. If he only needed to borrow
for planting expenses in the spring, most years this
could easily be repaid when the crop was marketed,
and there was still profit to spare.

However, if he was just starting out in the suddenly
hot and expensive farming business and he needed to
finance start-up costs, or if he wanted to emulate the
big glamorous commercial farming enterprises by borrowing to expand, he developed a troublesome balance
sheet. Debt was rolled over from one season to the
next. These players borrowed in the lower-priced years
to cover expenses and interest. They borrowed in the
good years to expand.

Lenders and borrowers both became comfortable
with long-term debt loads many times heavier than
those carried by an average farm operation a few short
years earlier. All parties took comfort from the fact
that land prices and USDA targets were rising. The

common wisdom—often repeated, and virtually un-questioned—was that the price of farmland always rose. The new farmer needed to do whatever was necessary to break into this upward spiral.

For this rapidly growing slice of the American farm population, an operating profit was an occasional thing, and in many cases, it never really happened. Debt fueled the upward spiral in land values which spawned more debt. One look at the USDA's own chart of land values since the parity years might have dis-pelled some of this enthusiasm. Land values had peaked in 1916 with the boom that accompanied World War I. After that they fell nearly every year for the next eighteen! Even the most casual observer of price history could see this dramatic precedent.

The new higher prices reinforced important trends already underway outside the United States, too. The soybean producer in Brazil was stimulated to increase his production every bit as much as the soybean producer in Illinois, and his government was right behind him with policies designed to expand commer-cial farming by any and all means possible.

Aided by the international lenders with petrodollars to burn, Brazil opened up its interior with new roads and towns, and they cleared millions of new acres which could then be planted with soybeans for a frac-tion of the cost of buying and planting a new acre of farmland in the United States.

As American farmland prices rose, the Brazilian cost advantage widened. The Brazilian government ac-celerated development of their soybean processing in-dustry so that they could create jobs and add value to the crop before it was loaded on a ship. Port facilities were enlarged and modernized, and by the mid-1970s, ten or more years of concerted effort to make Brazil a major player in the soybean business had paid off. The United States had a tough competitor in the world market for the miracle bean, a competitor that actual-

ly exported more soymeal and about the same amount
of soyoil, despite the fact that its crop was only about
one-third the size.

Different versions of the same story were being
played out around the world. Longtime competitors
like Canada and Australia were also jolted by the price
shock, and they too attacked the growing world
market in wheat and feedgrains with dollar signs in
their eyes.

It was Western Europe, however, that had the most
dramatic and negative effect in the post-1972 era. That
part of the world had been a net importer of food since
the early 1800s; in fact it *was* the world market until
the twentieth century. American food policy had
helped develop and expand the Western European
import market after World War II. In 1972, they were
still the largest single destination for food exports.

When the Soviets burst on the scene, the European
processing industry did its best to be positioned between the United States and its new customer. They
negotiated direct sales of soymeal with Exportkhleb;
bought the beans from the United States, Brazil, or
Argentina; and processed them in crushing plants
such as those near the great harbor at Rotterdam.

The Western Europeans' response was not limited to
their role as middlemen. With higher world prices
came a much higher European food import bill, and
this was an important stimulus to increase production,
even for countries that were well able to afford the
higher cost of imported food. Lucky for the Western
Europeans, the European Economic Community (EC)
already had in place a pervasive subsidy system that
was designed to stimulate both production and exports. It was also designed to protect its farmers from
tough foreign competition, and to boost their income
without shoveling them more debt.

The Common Agricultural Policy (CAP) of the EC
was instituted by the original six members in 1962 to

break down agricultural trade barriers between them, and to guarantee European farmers prices that were well above prevailing world prices. (The United States supported CAP in the interests of European unity and the common defense. Today, Europe with its CAP is the most dangerous and relentless of all the competitors.) CAP not only supported feedgrains and wheat at levels that were much higher than the world price, it erected tariffs and levies on the imports that raised them to the much higher levels that their own subsidies paid the European farmer.

The tariffs, or levies, that the CAP garnered were then applied to the expense of paying those high subsidies to the farmers. It was a neat little system that was made possible by the fact that they were such large producers and importers. (This is a bit like the Export Debenture proposal in the U.S. in the 1920s.)

CAP sheltered European farmers from much of the competition and farm consolidation that was being experienced in the United States in the 1960s. As a result, the farm population in the EC remained much larger than that of the United States. (It is four times larger today.)

CAP consistently stimulated production, so it had the EC leaning in the right direction when the pivotal year of 1972 arrived, unlike the United States, which was suppressing production. When the market took off, world prices quickly caught up with the high CAP price guarantees, and this gave the EC some rather attractive choices. It could drive for a reduced budget like the USDA by leaving price guarantees at pre-1972 levels, or it could keep bumping its own subsidy margin over the higher world prices. In so doing, it could boost domestic grain production even more.

If CAP stimulated production enough, it could start to whittle down its food import bill (at the expense of the U.S.). That import bill was sure to rise because there was more competition after 1972 for the

American crops. It could also start snagging some of the growing world market in wheat, where it was getting close to producing a surplus, along with a share of the market for soymeal needed in Eastern Europe.

The EC therefore kept tariffs on imported corn and aggressively subsidized its small export business at a time when the United States was reducing export subsidies. The EC could afford this politically because it hadn't had its food surplus wiped out by secret Soviet purchases. The guaranteed prices were set so high that the much smaller European farms remained profitable enough to support a family. Farmers did not need to expand and rip down protective windbreaks at anything like the rate of American farmers.

Farms in Europe were able to make a technological leap of sorts as a result of the fat support prices. They doused themselves in a chemical and fertilizer bath even more intense that that of the Americans, and in the process generated yields far above those being fetched on even the most productive farms in the United States. (Their report card therefore should contain an F for the environment, but As in competitiveness and keeping land ownership in the hands of the many.)

Europe, especially France, started producing an exportable surplus of wheat that grew and grew. They combined that surplus with timing and relentless export subsidies to seize markets from the United States, particularly in North Africa and the Middle East. In 1977, the EC's imports and exports of wheat roughly balanced out, but by 1984 they were a net exporter of over 15 million metric tons. In 1976, the EC was a net importer of over 20 million metric tons of the feedgrains needed to fuel Europe's livestock industries. By 1984 they were a small net exporter. This combined net gain of over thirty-five million metric tons on the grain balance sheet created or preserved agriculturally related jobs at all levels, and it was made almost entirely at the expense of the United States.

I'm getting a little ahead of our story, but it's worth pointing out that some systems have had all sorts of dividends, in contrast to those of the United States.

There are plenty of examples of how higher prices generated wave after wave of competition for the always off-balance United States, but perhaps the most remarkable is Malaysia. Malaysia, a tropical country in Southeast Asia, is the world's largest producer and exporter of palm oil, a vegetable oil that competes directly with soybean oil for a variety of product uses.

In 1972, Malaysia produced about 730,000 metric tons of it, and exported nearly 700,000 of those tons, mainly to India, Europe, and the United States. Palm oil was a respectable factor in world vegetable oil trade at the time, but it was a distant second in terms of total volume behind soyoil,the product of the miracle bean.

The Malaysian government made a commitment following the price shock to go head-to-head with soyoil and with the United States. They vastly expanded planted area, developed institutes for plant genetics and general research, and started to expand their own processing industry so that they could turn out a more finished and profitable product.

They succeeded on all levels, and total production soared from that original 730,000 metric tons in 1972, to 4.75 *million* tons in 1988—an increase of over 650 percent! Palm oil has in the process bumped soyoil from its number one market share among the world's vegetable oils. It did this in spite of the fact that palm oil is a less stable product than soyoil, and vastly inferior to it in terms health benefits. (Palm oil has far more saturated fat than lard.)

So the world got a little tougher for the American farmer in the 1970s, you say. How is that the fault of farm policy? It's not, but let me remind you that the basic goal of policy was to manipulate the markets so that they went up. Remember too, that their means of doing this was to unilaterally remove supplies from the market if prices went down.

Our scheme in the face of all this competition was to refuse to sell our merchandise.

Let's say for the sake of argument that the policy planners were in the habit of presenting their ideas about farm policy to an American public that was in the habit of listening. I like to think of it in business terms. Let's say that there is a large chain of retail stores that has controlled its markets for years. Suddenly it encounters aggressive new competition from discounters like K mart and Venture.

It asks its marketing experts to develop a strategy in the face of tougher competition and price wars. Unbeknownst to the retailer, however, the people in the marketing department have taken complete leave of their senses.

On presentation day, they gather in the boardroom, and the marketing folks present their plan. They suggest that the company immediately begin pulling merchandise off the shelves every time the competition starts selling it for less. They suggest putting the merchandise in storage, borrowing money to finance keeping it there, and laying off employees until the customers cry "uncle" and are willing to come back to their stores and start paying the higher prices.

No doubt there would be a few mouths hanging open and an embarrassed silence until someone had the presence to ask, "Do you have any other ideas?"

When this scene gets played out in the realm of farm policy, however, nobody is actually listening. And darned if the crazy plan doesn't get the OK.

11

THE ROLLER COASTER

As the 1970s rolled on, the American farmer continued to expand amidst the joys and sorrows of the greatest price roller coaster in farm history. The first rally began in October 1972 as the scale of the Soviet purchases became known. The big grain companies that had made those sales started buying cash grain in the country from farmers who were starting to bring their crops in from the field.

Instead of moving lower, as futures prices usually do when the harvest is in full swing, they had turned higher and entered the rarefied atmosphere of new all-time highs. Soybeans were already the American glamour crop in the 1960s, and they positively stole the show on the great price rally.

The other side of the coin unfortunately was that after the soybean market hit that big high of about

$12.90 a bushel, it headed south at a rate that was perhaps even more breathtaking. By the time that summer's first soybeans were being harvested in September–October 1973, the CBOT futures price had plunged to only about $5.20, a drop of 60 percent in just five months. (55 percent of the break came in just five weeks!) President Nixon's hasty soymeal embargo in the summer of 1973 no doubt added to the swiftness of the decline.

Imagine the stock market staging a 390 percent rally in eight months, then breaking by 60 percent. If the stock crash of 1987 had taken 60 percent off its all-time high of that year, the Dow would have dropped from over 2,700, to about 1,090; 1972–73 therefore contained both the biggest rally and biggest crash in the history of American agriculture. Both took place within about one year. Both records still stand.

The rally in winter wheat prices had more staying power than the one in soybeans, partly because the Soviets remained in the wheat market longer, partly because there was no embargo of wheat sales, and partly because the next crop was already being planted in the fall when the rally began. With the crop already in the ground, farmers weren't able to react to the big new highs of winter and spring 1973 by planting more acres. They could, however, plant more beans.

In any case, the 1973 wheat crop was still too small to meet the demands of the new export market. In July 1972, while the Soviets were still in the middle of their secret buying campaign, wheat prices had started rising before beans. They started at $1.40 and made it up to about $3.05 in May–June 1973 when soybeans peaked. They broke in sympathy with beans, but only by about 50 cents over four weeks. They then came roaring back to a new all-time high of nearly $5.50 by the beginning of October. After another brief correction, they outdid even that. In February 1974 they hit the record futures price that still stands—$6.45 a bushel.

As is usually the case, however, it was the big corn crop that had the greatest staying power. The American corn crop is such a behemoth that when it finally turns and starts to gain momentum in a new direction, it resembles a locomotive. It takes a long time to stop.

Corn futures began their run at about the same time as wheat and peaked just after beans at a new record of $3.90. They fell nearly as hard through November, but then commenced a new rally that lasted until October of 1974 and peaked at $4.00.

Timing is the name of the game in futures trading, and it's also the name of the game when a farmer pulls the trigger and sells his own crop. The farmer who sold beans right out of the field in the early stages of the rally in 1972 got a price that seemed stupendous at the time—$3.50 to $4.00 per bushel—but he probably wanted to shoot himself come May when the price was more than four times higher.

On the other hand, the small minority of farmers who held out and marketed their crops near the highs reaped profits of truly windfall proportions. A farmer in central Illinois who had a (larger than average) crop of 15,000 bushels of beans to sell that year, and who managed to do so near the highs, made well in excess of $9 per bushel ($135,000) on his crop, and that alone was enough to buy another small farm containing some of the most productive farm land in the world.

Most of the crop was marketed closer to the lows than it was to the highs that year, as is the case most years. In the case of soybeans the bulk of it fetched from four to six dollars. Whether a farmer marketed at the highs or the lows, however, soybeans, corn, and wheat all returned a handsome profit. Net farm income posted a big new record of $34.4 billion, a figure that was not exceeded until 1986.

For the vast majority of farmers, the market continued to return a decent profit per bushel through the
mid-1970s no matter how ill timed their marketing.
For the growing minority who fell into the farm debt
spiral, however, the timing issue loomed larger and
larger.

A farmer with an average size corn and soybean
operation in Illinois or Iowa who owned his land free
and clear could sell at the lows every year, and be well
into the black. The guy who borrowed to expand his
holdings a bit in the early years could probably make
a profit if he managed to sell in 10–15 percent off the
lows in the bad years, and he was still almost guaranteed a profit at any price in a good year like 1975.

The guy who expanded his holdings by 25–50 percent, bought the big new more efficient equipment to
handle the added land, and borrowed to finance it all,
needed to market his crops more along the lines of
40–50 percent off the lows in the bad years, and even
a bit off the lows in the higher-priced years like 1975
in order to write his bottom line in black ink.

The brand new farmer, who had to finance the purchase of all his base acres and all new equipment plus
all of the short-term planting expenses for which many
farmers need to borrow each spring, was in the
toughest spot of all. He might be alright if he sold only
10–15 percent off the highs in a good year like 1975. A
low-priced year like 1976, however, might leave him
with no chance whatsoever of a profit, even if he sold
his crops on the very top. His timing had to be perfect
every year. But who has perpetually perfect timing?

This was especially true for those who entered at the
end of the decade when land values and interest rates
were at their peaks. The later they started, the higher
the land prices and the higher the interest rate. Since
the volatile new markets only traded at their big highs
for a grand total of a couple of weeks every other year
or so, the odds of the heavily leveraged farmer turning

a profit were pretty slim.

The problem was initially masked by the small numbers involved. Even after the numbers started to grow in 1976, however, there was a curious lack of concern (aside from those who carried the debt). For its part, the USDA was basking in the glow of lower budget outlays. Direct government payments to farmers fell to just $530 billion in 1974, the lowest total since 1955.

National leaders outside the farm establishment saw the financial contribution that increased farm exports were making to the trade balance. The higher prices they were fetching were a blessed counterbalance to the soaring oil import bill, and they weren't inclined to look for dark linings in the silver cloud. The lender was the absolute last one who was asking any questions. He was awash in pools of dollars that needed to be lent, and agriculture was proving to be as big a sponge for debt as it had been for chemicals in the two decades after the war. The whole thing was backed by higher land values anyway, so why worry?

Something I read about the mid-to-late seventies in a USDA publication caught my eye. The publication, *History of Agricultural Price Support and Adjustment Programs, 1933–84,* was an overview of farm policy between 1933 and 1984, and it was published in December of that year. It described the conditions and problems that surrounded the post-Soviet boom, and it made this statement: "There were clouds on the horizon, however. High farm prices set off a scramble for farmland that drove land values up, and left many farmers overcapitalized." Overcapitalized?!

Every time I read that line, it stops me dead in my tracks. It was written in 1984, long after the farm crisis was full blown. Farm foreclosures and tractor-cades and distraught farmers losing land that had been in the family for generations were on the front pages. So was the underlying problem of farm debt. In looking back on all of this, at the late date of December

1984, the USDA thought that the cloud on the horizon was that farmers were overcapitalized. Perish the thought that anyone would have a valuable asset that wasn't balanced out by debt.

Some of the biggest new borrowers were no doubt taken aback by the huge dollar figures on their credit sheet, but they too were buoyed by higher land prices. On top of that (this too is stunning), most farmers and their lenders had only the vaguest idea of what it cost them to produce a bushel of beans, corn, or wheat.

I can remember doing hedging and marketing seminars for farmers as late as the early 1980s. The starting point was always *cost of production*, and it had to be hammered home. I'm talking about a simple analysis that added the cost of seed, plus fertilizer, plus chemicals, plus fuel, plus interest on debt, and so on, and then subtracting all that from the price the crop fetched when it was finally marketed. People who were a half million in debt often operated with only a vague idea of what the price of corn "ought" to be. Same with the lenders. The "ought" price often was based on farm rhetoric, or the parity index, or the last good year they had.

Words like "ought" and "fair price" meant nothing to the viciously competitive world agricultural markets that were just gaining steam in the mid-to-late seventies. These farmers were the people that the USDA had pushed into the hairy world of high finance and international competition.

At any rate, if there were still concerns on the part of borrower or lender, the rising USDA target prices provided an illusion of long-term cash flow for those unwilling to rely on land equity and paper assets alone to justify more debt. In most minds, the targets represented a minimum price that the farmer could receive each year, come what may.

Remember that if prices fell below the targets, the government guaranteed the farmer the difference between the market price and the target (for corn and wheat). However, the payment could not exceed the difference between the targets, and the considerably lower loan rates. All parties seemed convinced that prices would never drop all the way below the loan. Ergo, a guaranteed cash flow. (Just don't crunch those numbers too hard.)

After the rally of 1975, all of the major farm commodity markets cooled off at the same time. Soybean futures dropped from that year's high of about $9.50 per bushel, to less than $5.00 at harvest. Corn dropped from its all-time high of nearly $4.00, to $2.60 at harvest. Corn then showed the same stamina on the downside that it had on the upside. Prices continued to decline for three straight years.

Wheat prices were into an even longer downtrend, beginning with the all-time peak in 1974 and continuing along with the downtrend in corn until very late 1977.

Sagging prices left farmers with the frustration of unrealized expectations. Since farmers are a well-organized, outspoken, and pretty darned volatile lot historically, it didn't take too long for the growing minority of farmers, who were bathing in red ink in the midst of the biggest, greatest farm boom of all time, to start putting their heads together and develop an agenda.

They saw their problems as being a lack of income (fair enough), lower than expected prices, and an inability to justify needed borrowing given their lack of profitability. Farm populist rhetoric of the nineteenth century and 1920s came rushing back to the surface as this minority called for "parity, not charity."

What also reemerged was the darker aspects of farm populism, the suspicion that some sort of a conspiracy existed to take away part of their fair share and give it to someone else, like one of the big grain companies, or a speculator in Chicago.

Since the more militant farmers went back to the
century old wellspring of farm thought, they emerged
with the same ideas that farm populism had coughed
up in the first place. The consensus favored still higher
government price supports (targets and loans), to
boost farm income—all things that were pouring fuel
on the debt spiral to begin with.

This fixation on price supports was the flip side of the
one planners had in the late 1940s and early 1950s. At
that time most thought that gradually lower supports
would reduce surpluses and support prices. They ignored the effect of exploding yields per acre that were
the result of better seed and more chemicals. The idea
that lower supports could slow this process down was
a joke.

In the late 1970s, the belief had emerged that *higher*
supports would cure the spiraling cost of production
for the indebted minority. Policymakers, lenders, and
farmers were all betting that prices would spiral
higher indefinitely. This too was a joke.

Once again there was barely a peep from the vast
majority of farmers in the mid-to-late 1970s who were
still able to market all of their crops at a decent profit
each and every year. Somehow, nobody was stealing a
part of their fair share of the price of each bushel sold,
and they were selling those crops to the same elevators
at the same prices as their indebted neighbors.

This was the atmosphere that led up to the critical
year of 1977 when two major farm bills were scheduled
to expire. Most important was the 1973 bill that invented targets and stimulated the fencerow to fencerow expansion in the first place. This was Congress'
first chance to respond to the fallout of the volatile new
world farm economy. Debate began in earnest in the
winter of 1976–77, and it continued on through the
planting and growing season for corn and beans.

As if things weren't complicated enough, the proceed-
ings were punctuated by yet another big price rally in

the peripatetic soybean market. It started in late 1976 and peaked in spring 1977.

It seems that the export houses had once again over-sold the American crop. Or rather, the USDA (which should have known better by now) had once again allowed exporters to sell more soybeans than the country had to spare. As market analysts in Chicago crunched their supply/demand numbers over the winter, it became apparent that the market would run out of soybeans before the next crop was harvested in the fall.

This time there was no need for an embargo. Soybean futures surged to nearly $10.80 per bushel by April, and this served the economic function of "rationing" out many users who hadn't locked in a supply at lower levels, and who were unable or unwilling to pay up. The sharply higher prices eliminated enough demand to balance the projected supply/demand equation for the rest of the crop year. The newly harvested South American soybean crop started moving onto the world market at about the same time and so the shortage disappeared.

Of course as it did, so did the value of a bushel of American soybeans. As is so often the case with this volatile market, it again turned lower with a ferocity that exceeded that of the big rally. Prices plunged from the spring high, to nearly $5.00 by September, a drop of well over 50 percent in just five months.

I'm not sure how all of this affected the policy debate, but it certainly gave the old pot one more stir and probably confused some of the issues that were not viewed with much clarity in the first place.

In any case, what policy momentum there was came from the small, but increasingly vocal minority that saw trouble in their bottom line. It was a bit like asking the uncle who's a chronic gambler to handle the family finances.

12

THE DIE IS CAST

Spring of 1977 also happens to be the time that I stumbled into the agriculture industry, fresh from counting socks at Marshall Fields department store. The details of retailing certainly didn't interest me, and frankly it was a bit of a mystery how my departments got stocked and organized.

Anyway, a young man who worked for me in the afternoon and was a runner on the floor of the Chicago Board of Trade in the morning seemed to think the CBOT was the place to be. On his advice, I went down to the "Board" to start looking for work in the sizzling futures markets.

My game plan was two pronged. First I did my market research. I asked the guard in the lobby which floor he thought was the best place to start filling out applications. He gave me a number, and I went with it. When I got off the elevator, I spied another guy who was just emerging from the men's room, and I asked him where *he* thought I should start knocking on doors. He said, "I'm your man," and ushered me into the splendid offices of his boss, who happened to be a former chairman of the exchange. We exchanged pleasantries, and the man offered me a job.

Plan A had worked so well that I went straight to plan B, which was equally sophisticated. I went down to the trading floor and walked up to one of the guards at the entrance and asked him if he thought anybody in there might want to hire me.

The guard too seemed to think this was a reasonable question, and he paged Joe Dugan of Reynolds Securities to the door for me. Joe was about five feet, four inches tall, maybe 60 years old, and had a face that belonged on a travel poster for the Republic of Ireland. He also seemed to be a very nice man, and darned if he didn't offer me a job too. This job was as a runner on the trading floor, and that's the one I took.

The job of runner is just what the name implies. One runs from the company desk where brokers from around the country phone in their orders, to the trading pit. You hope to end up in the right pit with the right broker because (as in the bean rally of 1977) if you don't, those brokers will scream at you at the top of their lungs.

After I had been running for about two weeks, someone pointed out to me that we were in the midst of an historic rally in soybeans (soon to be an historic break), a fact that was news to me since it was still all I could do to remember who was taking the buy orders in November soybeans that day.

Lucky for me the world of agriculture and futures was still so unsophisticated. The futures industry was nearly unregulated at the time. Big agricultural markets were generating boom times and lots of new jobs on LaSalle Street. Apparently somebody like me could literally walk in off the street, not know up from down, and be on his way to becoming a grain analyst for a major clearing house in a year or two.

At any rate, there was that new farm bill to write in 1977. The support aspects of farm policy had only been needed occasionally after the price shock, and people again seemed to forget about its inherent flaws. Prices had generally stayed above the basic loan levels, so the farmer continued selling his crops into the free market, instead of taking out a government loan and putting his crops in storage.

The last time the loan system had been used extensively, in the sleepy world markets of the 1950s and 1960s, it seemed to work well enough. Its major defect was playing hard to get with the merchandise, and that was covered by the aggressive use of export subsidies (PL480), and the fact that the competition was much weaker. By 1977, however, competing exporters produced much bigger crops. They were also more technologically advanced, more vertically integrated, and better financed.

With the exception of Western Europe, the competition also could deliver its crops to the world marketplace every bit as cheaply as the most efficient and least indebted American farmer. Therefore, by 1977 when prices declined and the support system again started taking bushels off the market, the Brazilians were right there with even cheaper bushels of soybeans. The Europeans were there with heavily subsidized bushels of wheat. All parties were glad to sell, at even lower prices too.

If the United States wasn't careful, the potential clearly existed for it to give away a big chunk of its customer base if prices ever fell below the loan level, and the process of removal commenced in earnest. This hadn't been a critical problem from 1973–1977 since prices were relatively high, but a flaw is a flaw. The logical way to approach the new farm bill in 1977 was clearly to tailor it so that it was more aggressive in keeping American supplies flowing onto the market at a competitive price no matter how low the world prices got.

It was also pretty logical to start helping the farmers who were troubled by excessive debt in a way that either reduced current debts, or slowed the rate of future debt growth. It seemed especially important to zero in on the higher cost and indebted farmers because the vast majority of grain and soybean farmers were operating with a decent profit margin even at the very lowest prices of the 1970s.

However, logic was about the last thing to be applied in 1977. Early on, it became clear that structural changes were not even being considered. The debate centered instead on how much the supports should be raised. This is what the loudest voices demanded. The Carter administration led off the process by playing it safe. It proposed slightly higher loan and target levels. The House submitted its proposed bill with rates that were slightly higher still, and the Senate weighed in with increases in all supports that were well above even those of the House.

Why would the Senate of all people be the ones on the high end? The answer was demographics. A declining farm population had greatly diluted the farm lobby's power in the House, but farmers could still make or break a hefty percentage of senatorial careers between the Mississippi River and the Rockies. It was in those states that the voices in favor of loan and target increases were again the strongest. That's because it was generally in the west that farmers were again having the toughest time.

No wonder. The western Grain Belt was where the nation had added the biggest chunks of new acreage after the price shock in 1972 because that's where the most empty land was. (Same as World War I.) Farmers there found that they needed to irrigate to match the yields of their counterparts in a place like Illinois. That

increased costs along with the simple fact that these
farms had established themselves when it was very
expensive to do so, and borrowing was all the rage.
Combine those higher costs with the native prairie
populism, and you get demands for higher supports.

In any case that was what induced the Senate to
aggressively up the ante. A compromise was hammered out, but it was hammered out between the
House and Senate—the two proposals with the highest
loans and targets. President Carter's bill was brushed
aside in part because of the influence of the farm lobby,
and in part because he had already begun to alienate
his own congressional leadership with the outsider
mentality he brought from Georgia. There were no
other voices around that weighed in on the side of the
laws of commerce and lower supports, much less the
idea of building a better mousetrap.

Wheat and corn target prices, for example, were
raised 17.5 percent in 1978, the first year that the new
bill covered. As with the 1973 bill, the rates were
scheduled to increase in subsequent years as well, in
this case to what was called a "fair and reasonable
level." This was an acceleration of the basic problem.
As if that weren't enough, the bill took a giant step
further and added a new dimension to the galaxy of
programs that had accumulated since the early 1930s,
the Farmer Owned Reserve (FOR).

The 1977 bill directed the secretary of agriculture to
administer a Reserve Program for wheat, and (at his
discretion) feedgrains such as corn. Under the Reserve
system, new loans were written with an *extended* term
of three to five years. The grain that was collateral for
the Reserve loans was to be removed from the market
as before, and if prices failed to rise it was to be kept
off the market until the loan matured at the end of that
time.

Under the old loan system, loans were due much
sooner. Those loans got defaulted on much more quick-

ly, putting the grain into government (CCC) hands that much faster where it could be pushed onto the world market through some sort of subsidized credit or outright gift—a convoluted system to be sure, but one that had preserved markets in the end.

The new Reserve Program, on the other hand, raised the possibility of taking grain off the market and keeping it there ad infinitum if prices kept trending lower. It combined this with sharply raising the prices at which this process began.

What did Congress expect the low-cost producers in South America and the aggressively subsidized exporters of Western Europe to do? Did it think they would also start taking their supplies off the market out of respect for the U.S. policy, even though most could still earn a substantial profit at even lower prices yet? Or did Congress just not think?

Congress seemed to understand that there was some danger. It set a limit on the amount of grain that would be allowed into the Reserve for those three- to five-year stretches, but then it said that this limit could be adjusted upward. The secretary was also given the option of extending old regular loans which were technically due after nine months. I guess the farm community and its policymakers had become convinced that protracted gluts were a thing of the past even though they had represented the norm since World War I. The awesome new Reserve was apparently not expected to kick in any time soon.

Congress went even further. It wanted to induce a big farmer participation in the Farmer Owned Reserve (FOR), so that as many farmers as possible could be "protected" by this ultimate insurance policy. The one thing that might have stood in the way of a big sign-up was the simple fact that it was based on issuance of still more debt. Even in 1977 there was a reluctance among farmers to tack another loan, with yet another annual interest payment, onto the pile of loans that

they already carried. To overcome this healthy reluctance the secretary of agriculture was permitted to
adjust or even waive the interest due on the Reserve
loans if "conditions merited."

There was also the rather obvious drawback of
having to pay to store your grain for three to five years
without any income (other than the principal on your
loan) to cover the cost of doing so. Congress covered
this by authorizing sizable storage payments that
varied according to the crop.

You say you're a farmer and you want to sign up for
the new Reserve Program, and you'd like to store the
grain and earn that storage payment yourself, but you
don't have enough space available. No problem! The
bill also required that the USDA make storage loans
available to farmers to construct advanced new and
very expensive silos on their own farms. This proposed
new layer of loans had terms of up to ten years, and it
attracted a very large client base that also tended to be
concentrated among those who were already hooked
on a diet of private and program debt, and therefore
needed to buy into the farm programs in a big way.

The Food and Agriculture Act of 1977 was passed on
September 29 of that year. By that time, the big
demand-driven soybean rally that peaked in May was
a distant memory. High prices at planting time had
caused a vast expansion of soybean acreage, and the
excellent crop weather that followed did the rest.

Prices plunged from the peak of about $10.50, to an
early harvest low of $5.00. The corn yield did well too,
but corn prices were already in a three-year
downtrend, so the market was tired of going down.
Prices bottomed out at a four-year low of $1.80 a
bushel that summer. Things were about the same for
wheat. Before the bill was even passed, these low
prices pressured the Carter administration to go one
misguided step further. It expanded its commitment to
an emergency food and feedgrain reserve. This meant

that an additional 30–35 million metric tons of U.S. grains were to be taken off the market. (This, by the way, was more than the Soviet Union had bought from the United States during the Great Grain Robbery of 1972–73.)

There was an edge of panic to all this, but it was all a false alarm. The downtrend was over, and the big lows were put in while the ink was still wet on the 1977 farm bill. The drastic steps it took to pull supplies off the market were therefore taken when the "danger" was already past.

Prices recovered in all of the agricultural markets in late 1977, buoyed by the fact that most of the weaker players in the futures market had been washed out by the plunge in soybeans and the fact that most of the weaker farmers had finished dumping their grain. Perhaps an element of support was also added by the threat that the farm bill would deplete the free supply if prices broke any further.

To the extent that the new supports contributed to the bounce in prices that year, it was an unfortunate success. It encouraged the farm lobby and legislators to think that American programs did in fact have the power to support the world price in the volatile new grain age. If they did so in 1977, the thinking went, they would do it again in the future. Policy framers didn't need this sort of encouragement.

The farm lobby had known a long string of deceptive "successes" in the twentieth century. The first price shock in 1917 and the lobby's success in hanging onto the high price supports after the Second World War were a couple. Getting a free rein in the use of yield-boosting fertilizers and chemicals in the 1950s and 1960s was another. The farmer kept getting what he wanted, but in the end each triumph was the worst thing that could have happened.

Turning the markets higher at this juncture was a case in point. Higher prices created more financial incentive for the foreign competition that was already expanding its acreage and technology. If prices had continued to drop, it might have slowed their advance.

There were many individual success stories that were were very real in the Farm Belt, however. The majority had huge assets on paper, little or no long-term debt, and an income that was sufficient to consistently upgrade farm operations and gradually buy more land.

Those among this group who raised only grain (no livestock) also had the considerable luxury of owning a business that could support them with perhaps four to five months of actual farm-related work, tops. Continued rapid improvements in farm equipment contributed to this shrinking work year for the average grain only farmer, and it made the remaining work hours a lot less demanding.

The 1970s were the era during which air-conditioned tractors and combines became commonplace. TV and stereo radio followed right behind. Huge numbers of the "haves" bought or shared condos in Florida, where it has become common for ordinary Midwestern farm couples to spend several months each year vacationing. Farming was becoming a very desirable vocation for many, and for a lot more reasons than just nice clean air and friendly neighbors.

There was still another apparent success in the late 1970s. Total farm numbers in the United States stabilized at about 2.4 to 2.5 million, halting a decline that had been underway since 1935. It was made possible by relatively high prices and freewheeling lenders, and there were large numbers of those farms that were technically bankrupt all the while.

The farm population, however, continued to slide. A change in the way the Census Bureau counts the farm population distorts the numbers a bit, but the loss was something along the lines of two million people during the 1970s, a good 20 percent. On the surface, this wave of farm refugees was the least painful to date. It was mostly farm children who left. They went to college in droves, got good jobs, and moved to the city.

(A disproportionate share were young women who decided against a farm marriage. They added to the growing armies of career women in business suits and running shoes seen marching to work in the nation's cities in the eighties. This incidentally has added slightly to the imbalance of men and women in the big cities.)

Since it was the children who left, there were more demographic twists to the number changes in the 1970s. Not only was the size of the farm population shrinking, but the size of the average farm family dropped sharply as well. As it did, the age of the average farmer rose well above the average age in the population at large. Not only did the tiny remaining farm population have to hold the line against the economic forces that had shrunk it for decades, now it also had to fight a rapidly growing rate of attrition through retirement and death.

On the surface, however, things seemed to settle down. The all-out victory won by the more militant farmers stilled their voices for awhile. The fact that prices slowly trended higher brought hope to the hopeless. The extreme volatility which had turned out to be such a mixed blessing in the past, was absent.

Over it all brooded the ubiquitous USDA with its enormous web of farm programs. In a sense, it had changed along with the average farmer. It had long been imperfect, but its influence had been mixed before 1977. Events outside the control of policymakers had been the farmer's worst enemy. After 1977, however, it was the variables injected into the farm equation by the USDA itself that wreaked the most havoc.

Farm policy was like having a dangerous giant in the house. He might be eager to please and protect, but instead he manages to hurt someone or smash something every time he moves.

After coughing up the 1977 farm bill, the policy giant took a nap. He roused himself briefly in 1978 to raise wheat targets even more—from $3.05 a bushel to a robust $3.40—and to take away a few of the remaining restraints on higher targets in other commodities. He also raised the borrowing authority of the CCC from $14.5 to $25 billion so that agency could purchase more of the grain that was getting dumped into it from defaulted loans and hold onto it that much longer.

A little bit more grain could now be taken off the market. It could be locked a bit more firmly out of the reach of potential customers. Low prices are bad. High prices are good, thought the farm policy giant. Confident in a job well done, he rolled over to sleep for a couple more years.

13

THOSE FLAWED BUILDING BLOCKS

Prices slowly trended higher in all the major agricultural futures markets after 1977, but this rally had none of the pop of the first great rallies of the decade.

The first half of this rally was probably more bounce than anything else, but in the spring, summer, and fall of 1979 the USSR again came to the farmers' aid with a genuine surge of fresh demand. The always capricious Soviet weather had battered the winter wheat crop over the winter and spring of 1978–79 with drought and hot, dry winds called *sukhoveys* in Russian ("thirsty wind"), and production dropped sharply all around.

The Soviets booked huge quantities of American corn and wheat to make up these losses, with the heaviest buying coming in the summer months of 1979. By year

end, total sales of American grain and soybeans to the
USSR reached over 25 million metric tons, more than
40 percent above the total booked during the Great
Grain Robbery of 1972. During the growing season,
this unprecedented buying pace took futures prices
substantially higher—to over $3.20 in the case of corn
and about $8.15 for soybeans—the best prices in years.

This filled most farmers with hope, but as the summer progressed it was clear that the U.S. corn, wheat,
and soybean crops were going to be huge—record large
in fact. As estimated yields climbed in July and
August, and grain analysts around the world crunched
their supply/demand numbers for the coming marketing year, it was clear that the 1979 crops could satisfy
Moscow with room to spare. The surpluses would actually grow.

Prices took a quick dive in late July and early August
and continued to wander lower for most of the rest of
the year. Corn staged a nice little bounce in December,
but it could only finish the year at about $2.90. Beans
did not recover, and they finished the year at $6.40.
This was letdown enough for farmers and futures
traders in general, but it had the faint ring of the death
knell in it for the layer of high-cost farmers who now
truly *needed* $8 or $9 beans to turn a profit. If the
unprecedented new demand of 1979 couldn't sop up
the surplus and give the farmer the price he needed, or
thought he needed, what could?

As frustrating as things seemed that December, they
were about to get a whole lot worse. The Soviet's
summer buying spree hadn't been a true shock to the
markets this time around, but there was going to be a
Soviet shock before that marketing year ended nonetheless.

It started on December 27. That was the day that the
Soviets engineered a coup against the disintegrating
Communist government of neighboring Afghanistan, a
government they had helped install in 1978. Over the

following week, they began airlifting a large military force to shore up the new government which was just as beleaguered as the first.

The move apparently surprised Western intelligence in general and President Carter in particular. The president seemed to feel that he had demonstrated good faith in reaching out to the Soviets during his three years in office, and that they had betrayed his trust. He was plainly angry.

The Soviets knew that they would lose all hope of getting the SALT II Treaty ratified after the invasion, but they had largely given that up for lost already. They were a bit nervous that the United States would cut off further grain sales, however, and in just one day that week they added another 2.7 million metric tons of corn and 400,000 tons of wheat to their already huge American purchases of that year.

President Carter monitored the situation during the first week of January and issued a series of statements that made it clear the United States would vigorously retaliate for the invasion. He recommended that the Western Alliance prepare to do the same, and most of them began mouthing an appropriate level of concern.

Late in the week President Carter announced that measures were being considered, and that the exact package would be announced by Friday evening, January 4. The markets in Chicago started getting very nervous as the week wore on. The United States engages in very little trade and commerce with the Soviet Union, and it engaged in even less in 1979–80. Grain traders are not necessarily geniuses, but under the circumstances it didn't take a genius to figure out that the 25 million tons in grain export sales to the USSR were the only big card that the president had to play.

The Chicago Board of Trade was advised to close its agricultural futures markets for two days after the announcement. Sure enough, on Friday night the

President announced an embargo of all sales and shipments to the USSR of grain, soybeans, and soy
products beyond the 8 million tons that the U.S. was
obligated to deliver under a long-term purchase agreement between the two countries.

That long-term agreement required the Soviets to
buy at least 6 million tons of American grain each
marketing year, to be about evenly divided between
wheat and corn. They were permitted to buy another 2
million tons for a total of 8 million without the approval of the U.S. government, and with its approval
they could buy just about all they wanted.

President Carter allowed exporters to ship the 8
million tons as agreed, but the other 17 million tons
were canceled (about 4 million tons of wheat and 13
million corn). This was far and away the largest embargo or partial embargo of grain in the nation's history; it dwarfed the runner-up, the one inaugurated
against the German Empire after the United States
entered World War I in 1917.

To simply dump all of that grain onto the market
would probably have sent the already disappointing
prices plummeting back to the big lows of 1977, wiping
out nearly two and a half years of grudgingly won
financial gains in the process. This in turn would have
probably wiped out some of the smaller merchandising
houses that owned some of that grain, thinking that
they had a buyer. Most important in the minds of
policymakers, it would have stomped on the fingers of
the most indebted farmers, who were barely hanging
on to the edge of the debt cliff as it was.

To cover the considerable downside of the embargo,
President Carter and the USDA (CCC) decided to
assume ownership of all of the canceled wheat sales,
and up to 10 of the 13 million tons in canceled corn
sales. After the CCC took title, the grain was to be
either completely removed from the market and stored
(something that the government was getting mighty

good at by the way), or gradually meted out to other grain customers.

To help sop up the rest of the canceled sales as well as the rest of the surplus from the big 1979 crops, the USDA also sweetened provisions of the existing farm programs to attract more grain away from the free market, more quickly, by raising the loan and target supports further above the sagging world prices.

The USDA also raised what are called the "release" and "call" levels. These were the prices at which grain already in the reserve could be sold, or "released" if the market rallied, and at the even higher price at which it *must* be sold or "called" if the rally continued. The world's buyers would now be forced to "pay up" just that much more.

As luck would have it Secretary of Agriculture Bob Bergland had already eliminated all eligibility requirements for the loan and reserve programs in corn in October, and he quickly did the same for wheat. Farmers who missed the deadline for signing up, or who were not interested in meeting all of the stipulations the first time around could now come in and claim the benefits offered by the reserve and loan programs anyway.

Other benefits were also sweetened. Storage payments were raised 6 percent. Interest was waived on first year reserve loans (making more debt more attractive), and the USDA capped it all off by allowing farmers with grain already in the reserve to rewrite their old reserve contracts at the higher post-embargo loan levels.

The farmer was therefore being encouraged to take on even more debt, and to actually raise the dollar totals on older government debts by filling out another form down at the county office!

The reaction of the futures market prices to the embargo was rather muted as a result of all this artificial supply-tightening. (That was the goal.) When the

CBOT reopened on Wednesday the 9th, prices for nearly every contract month of every agricultural commodity fell by the daily limit. The next day soybeans opened lower and corn opened limit down again, but that's where the support measures started kicking in. Beans actually rallied sharply to close nearly 20 cents higher. Corn and wheat struggled off their lows, but still closed substantially lower. By the next day, however, all markets took heart from the performance of soybeans, and corn erased nearly all of Thursday's loss.

That was about it. The government's moves to support prices had been another success. The 17 million tons in lost sales disappeared from the balance sheet.

The Soviets seemed to be genuinely surprised by the embargo. Perhaps they trusted too much in Lenin's famous dictum that the last capitalist will sell the rope used to hang him. In any case they began to scramble. They needed to replace as much of that 17 million tons to preserve their livestock herds after the poor crops of 1979, and they needed to do that for all of the same old reasons.

They scrambled in particular down to Argentina, where it was then summer and the feedgrain crops were already planted and growing by January. They bought the lion's share of those crops up front, setting off a mini-boom in Argentine farm prices.

One of the new terms we learned that year as the Soviets scrambled to rebook grain, was *trans-shipment*. This was the other principal way that the Soviets replaced lost purchases. One of the grain companies would buy U.S. grain, load it on a non-Soviet ship supposedly bound for Europe, and then simply change ownership of the cargo and the direction it was headed once that ship was at sea. The Soviets were not able to replace all of the canceled sales, and it cost them more money to scramble around and load smaller ships in South America, but they managed to cover most of their losses in the end.

Both sides were victims of the roles they choose to play on the world stage. Seeing themselves as the leaders of an expanding list of Communist countries, the Soviets were committed by the Brezhnev Doctrine to preserving every existing one on earth. To do this they had to risk food imports needed by their people as well as by their government.

The United States, on the other hand, seeing itself as foil for all Soviet thrusts, was compelled to counter the Soviet aggression in Afghanistan, and the only logical means it had to do so was to embargo grain shipments.

In light of their respective self-images both countries saw no choice in this instance other than to play their respective roles, and shoot themselves in the foot in the process. The real kicker for the United States was that most of its allies in Western Europe, Australia, and Canada also are its major grain exporting competitors. They too were (perhaps) indignant at the Soviets, but their roles as grain exporters superseded their obligations as members of the Western Alliance. They reacted in pure self-interest and absconded with the business that the United States felt morally compelled to abandon.

The shock quickly wore off in any case, and it seems likely that the futures markets would have continued wandering lower from there in a normal growing season, but 1980 was not to be a normal summer. It was to be the first of the great drought years of the 1980s, and perhaps the first true U.S. drought in major growing areas since 1956.

It came with little warning after ample spring rains, and was focused along the periphery of the Corn Belt, especially in the western and southwestern sectors. Weather was particularly severe during the crucial two-week period in July when corn tasseling and pollination occur and the final yields are determined. As a result, the 1980 corn crop fell to only 6.6 billion bushels from the record 7.9 billion the year before.

This was to be the mildest of the droughts of the decade, but futures markets trade on expectations, and this crop was going to be as much as 1.5 billion bushels below the planting time expectations. That left only about 100 million bushels at the end of the following year if the demand were normal; 100 million bushels are not even enough to keep the "pipeline" stocked (that takes at least 500–600 million bushels). As the growing season wore on, it was clear that the market had to ration out several hundred million bushels in demand over the coming marketing year.

In theory, this could have been done with only a modest rally in price since the United States still had large surpluses from the big 1979 crops, and of course the residue of the embargo. The problem with the theory, however, was that the USDA just finished doing everything in its power after the embargo to remove supplies from the market and lock them away for years. The market not only had to rally to attract farmer selling, it had to rally even higher to the new "release" and the "call" levels before it could get at all the corn socked away in the reserve.

As a result, we grain analysts added another term to our daily lexicon that year—*free stocks*. If you took the total supply in all positions and subtracted both estimated usage and the government-held stocks, you got your free stocks. During the summer and fall of 1980, most grain analysts as well as the USDA came up with negative free stocks in corn. That meant that the market had to stay up at those release and call prices, to pull enough grain onto the market, to satisfy the expected usage.

With those assumptions in mind, the corn futures market (with soybeans tagging along behind) did something that was unprecedented after a summer "weather rally." They stayed right up near their summer highs, and in the case of corn actually made new highs right up through the tail end of the harvest in November. All this meant that the U.S. prices were trading at a big premium to competing prices overseas. Domestic users naturally paid the premium because it was still cheaper than importing. Foreign users for the most part were willing to pay up as well because American grains could be loaded and shipped more efficiently, and because quality could be better assured. Some stuck around out of sheer habit.

However, others found alternative sources that they may not have considered in the past: barley, sorghum, tapioca, millet, and low-grade wheat in place of American corn; and palm oil, coconut oil, rapeseed oil, and even butter in place of soyoil. Still others simply cut back on total purchases of grains and oilseeds until prices fell.

Corn rallied from just under $2.60 a bushel in early spring, to over $3.60 in August. It only dropped about 20 cents in September and early October before turning higher again, right into the teeth of the harvest.

Corn chugged laboriously higher for nearly two months, and by about the first of December it had made it up to $3.96 a bushel, just a few cents shy of the all-time highs of $4.00 set in late 1974.

Soybeans received timely rains in August which boosted yields a bit, and so their rally took second fiddle right from the start. It only moved from about $5.70 in April to about $8.20 in July. Like corn, soybean prices paused for breath in September, and then worked their way up to about $9.60 by the end of November—a good price, but well short of the all-time highs.

This rally was therefore different than the ones in the 1970s. The time spent at the big peaks had typically added up to only a couple of weeks at a time. This was duly noted by market participants, and a growing number of them drew the conclusion that prices weren't in the process of topping out at all. They were

simply gathering steam for another burst to the upside. This analytical conclusion was also based on the
belief that prices had to rise in order to pull needed
supplies away from the government programs.

Small and large speculators lined up to participate in
the expected boom in futures prices when the market
finally took off. Open interest at the Chicago Board of
Trade (the number of futures contracts being held by
all participants) rose to record high levels that still
stand today. By December 1, 1980 everybody who
wanted to be on board was in, and the train started
pulling out of the station.

Unfortunately, when everyone who wants to be in a
financial happening is already in, there's nobody left
for them to sell to at a profit. In fact, there's only one
direction that prices can take. The train pulled out of
the station and headed south. Starting after December
1, the futures market started a plunge that lasted ten
trading days and slaughtered most of those small and
large traders who had made up that huge open interest. The price of soybeans dropped about $2.20 over
those ten days, and even the more sturdy and sensible
corn market lost over 60 cents.

Small and midsize speculators liquidated their positions to pay their margin calls. Many left the field
severely injured and stayed away for years.

Although this drop was small potatoes compared to
the price plunges of 1973, 1974, and 1977, this one was
more important. It served notice that the gig was up
for the farmer and the go-go grain futures markets of
the 1970s. For one thing, it showed that demand which
was thought to belong permanently to the United
States could literally disappear at higher prices. The
world no longer had to pay what American farm policy
dictated.

In the meantime, the competition had received
another timely and massive shot in the arm. While
they lasted, higher U.S. prices had shagged a bit more

business into other, cheaper hands. The rally had extended into fall when the South American corn and soybean crops were being planted, and that in turn increased their incentive to plant more acres. By this time, the Brazilian crushing industry was perfectly capable of turning those added bushels of soybeans into meal and oil, and pushing it all onto the world market.

By artificially raising the price of American grain and soybeans, the system had worked as hoped for a couple of months. As a matter of fact, it even worked after the December crash was over. Basic U.S. commodities continued to be the world's most expensive, and they were going to stay that way for most of the 1980s.

By diverting business to the competition, the USDA had also diverted additional revenue, and in many cases that was available for just those last improvements and modernizations needed in the basic agricultural economy of a country like Brazil. That in turn would make the competition in general even stronger on the next go-around.

Corn prices bounced off the lows of the big December break, and they tried to hold up through the 1981 spring planting season on the continued illusion that the world needed to retrieve those government stocks. All this did, though, was prolong the effects that relatively higher prices have on demand. It rationed more out and diverted more to the competition. By the time the corn crop was planted in mid-May, it was clear that carryover stocks of corn would be double the estimates of the previous fall.

At the time, American soybean farmers were planting the second largest number of acres in history, and corn farmers had already weighed in with near record acreage. Once again there was ample spring moisture to get the summer crops started, and as May flowed into June, temperatures and moisture continued to be beneficial to growing conditions. There would be no drought in 1981.

By early July, the government's crop bulletins described the corn crop as being in mostly good-to-excellent condition. By late July, this became irreversible, and the market was forced to add another big piece of bearish news to the already considerable list that had accumulated over the past year or two: the United States was going to produce more corn than it could hope to sell or use in the coming year. Any hope of stemming the slide in prices went out the window.

Soybean prices fared a little better at first since their critical weather period of August was less favorable than July had been for corn, but it was all academic. There were more beans than the market needed too, and wheat, and soyoil, and soymeal. Prices for all markets slid right through the end of the year. Bean and corn prices flattened out and staged an anemic little bounce into early 1982, but there were to be no great rallies this time around, and everyone knew it.

In Chicago, the great floor speculators started deserting the soybean and corn pits for the greener pastures (and greater volatility) of T-bonds and Ginnie Maes. That left the indebted farmer to carry his grain alone, clinging to a flawed subsidy system that was a reed in the wind if there ever was one.

For some the end came very soon after the summer of 1981. The downtrend in farm numbers and farm population resumed with a vengeance. This time it was not to be the sort of gentle downtrend that had occurred in the fifties, sixties, and seventies, when the numbers dropped due to attrition, urban expansion, and people leaving the farm to do something they wanted to do instead. This time it was to be more like the 1920s and 1930s. Foreclosure and poverty.

By 1981, it was time for another big farm bill, and so another one was cranked out. It had its myriad details like the others, but they only amounted to minor adjustments of a "done deal."

Suffice it to say that the target and loan rates were put on a new schedule of annual increases that would in turn take grain off the market at slightly higher levels each year over the life of the bill, further widening the grain price disadvantage the United States suffered, and boosting the competition in South America, Europe, Canada, Australia, Malaysia. . . .

It was crop production that became the big new story. It just grew and grew. Corn crops rose from the 1980 drought-year low of 6.6 billion bushels in 1980, to over 8.1 billion in 1981 and 8.2 billion in 1982. The bullishly low carryover stocks of just 500 million bushels that were expected in the bullish fall of 1980, turned into actual stocks of 1.034 billion by the end of that crop year (October 1, 1981). This rose to 2.174 billion the next year and 3.120 billion the year after that. Most of it found its way into the government loan and reserve programs, where it sat.

This was accompanied by a long steady slide in prices that left traders in Chicago and farmers in the country with a feeling of helplessness that was almost palpable. Prices bounced along near their lows until spring 1983. Volume and open interest dried up in the agricultural futures pits, and many of the futures clearing houses began to shed personnel (and analysts) in the traditional grain markets.

The sinking feeling that came with sinking markets brought with it another surge of the farmer populism which had bubbled below the surface since 1976. This one, however, was more quiet than the protests and tractorcades of the late 1970s.

Perhaps a bit of the quiet desperation had been in evidence all along. My one and only experience with a organized farm protest came in 1979. One day a genuine tractorcade came to the intersection of Lasalle and Jackson in front of the exchange to "shut the place down." Several pieces of farm equipment that had somehow made it all the way downtown were parked by the farmers at that intersection, and some of the farmers dismounted to picket outside or troop on up to the fourth floor to confront the big bad Chicago grain speculators.

At that point I was only a phone clerk on the trading floor, and therefore somewhat peripheral to the protest. Yet I vividly remember that day. I went out to the fourth floor elevator lobby with some of the traders who seemed to appoint themselves as more or less official ambassadors of the CBOT. We were instructed by an exchange announcement to treat the farmers with sympathy (kid gloves), and that advice was heeded.

So there we all were, standing around making uncomfortable small talk. We wound up talking about the day's market news, how interesting it was to work on the floor, etc. Some of the members took farmers onto the floor for a tour, and that was about it.

There was no serious discussion or debate because there was nothing to say. None of the traders wanted a confrontation, and that went for me as well, but the sense of anticlimax was almost too much. I left with a very sad impression. Here were a bunch of men who had literally driven their tractors and combines all the way into the center of the city of Chicago. They came to the epicenter of the world grain trade looking for the conspiracy that was causing their problems, and couldn't find it when they got there.

As I look back, I'm not so sure that there wasn't a conspiracy of sorts after all, a conspiracy of silence. Those of us at the exchange feared the power that the farm lobby had over the Congress, which in turn had the power to interfere with the freedom that our markets enjoyed. We walked on egg shells, careful not to offend farmers who really could have used some straight talk or meaningful dialogue.

The press tended to play the role of farm advocate. Out of ignorance, they simply rehashed much of what the farm protesters said. Suffering farmers were a group with obvious appeal who said they just needed a fair shake. A fair shake meant higher support prices. In the eyes of the press, that was the message. Those in the Congress probably saw the tangled web as well as anyone, and yet they too chose to react with soothing words and proposals for still higher loans and target rates.

Last but not least, the conspiracy of silence extended to the majority of farmers themselves, the ones who were still quite solvent. They again failed to speak up and make it known that most of them could still earn a profit at the low free-market prices of late 1981, 1982, and early 1983. Farmers could have helped themselves and the agricultural support system by helping the rest of us see that the farm problems were concentrated among those with the highest production costs, and that production costs basically rose for one reason: too much debt. Even in the early 1980s, the government's solutions were all tied to inducing still more farm debt.

Fear of the farm lobby on the part of we few was immersed in the ignorance of the many. The slim possibility of meaningful reform or rebuilding of the flawed foundation was left in the hands of the political establishment that had helped author and preserve the problems in the first place, and farmers like those I met at the Chicago Board of Trade in 1979.

14

PIK

After the last of the big 1982 corn crop was in from the fields, and grain elevators everywhere were bursting at the seams, one thing was clear. There would not be enough room to store the next year's corn, wheat, and soybean crops if yields were good again. The surplus had become a glut.

It was also apparent that this glut would push another couple of billion bushels of corn and wheat into government support programs by the mid-1980s, which in turn would devastate the groaning USDA budget that was paying to carry all that grain. It would also widen the spread between American grain prices and those of the competition, lose more export market share, greatly add to the farm debt with government loans, etc. All that could go wrong with the basic system was doing so.

The obvious answer was the usual one—a massive

paid acreage reduction program to trim the 1983 crops. Pay the farmer not to plant several millions of acres, and the storage problem might just go away. The problem was that a paid set-aside big enough to get rid of the glut would cost billions. This huge expense would have to be layered on top of the already soaring cost of the price support system, it would bust the USDA budget. Neither Congress nor the Reagan administration was in any mood for that in 1982. Yet if something didn't change, the budget would bust later, rather than sooner, as loan and reserve stocks exploded.

I believe this is called "the horns of a dilemma." The USDA, and farm economy as a whole, had backed itself into a rather tight little corner with its years of bad habits. It was visibly losing markets because it refused to market its grain. Yet it couldn't stop pulling grain off the market let alone dump what it owned because this would greatly depress prices. The reason it could no longer risk depressing prices was that this would drive many thousands of farmers out of business because they would be forced to sell their 1982 crops at a loss.

This was the legacy of the farm economy's years of addiction to debt, and to expensive chemical farming, and land speculation, and the latest equipment needed on the bigger farms, and so on. This had irrevocably raised many farmers' cost of production above the world price.

In the past, of course, many farmers had claimed it was impossible for them to make a profit without heavy federal subsidies. This was nonsense for the vast majority in the seventies, but it was getting to be true for perhaps a third of the nation's grain farmers by 1982. What on earth could the USDA do?

Perhaps you can guess. There was already a pretested quick fix scheme on the farm policy menu that seemed tailor made for 1982–83. The decision was made in November to bring out a program first used on a large scale by the Kennedy administration in 1960: the Payment in Kind, or PIK.

The new PIK was designed to start with the USDA soliciting "bids" from producers of wheat, corn, and other feedgrain farmers. The farmers bid that portion of their acreage that they wanted to set aside in 1983. They could bid the whole farm if they wanted, and it was up to the USDA to accept or reject the bid. The USDA based its ultimate decision on a review of all the bids in aggregate. It wouldn't do for example to idle all of the corn acres in one county, and shut down all the local businesses.

The bait was of course the fact that the farmer would be *paid* to set that acreage aside, only this time he would be paid with a generous allotment of that particular crop, and not with money. The payment was to be based on his past yields. The grain in question would be taken from government stocks. Ergo, a payment in kind.

The beauty of the plan was the same as it had been in 1961. It killed a number of very big birds with one stone. American corn and wheat production could be substantially reduced to a level that would enable the country to physically store all the 1983 crops. That was probably the USDA's top priority since the subsidy system simply couldn't function as designed if crops could not be stored ad infinitum. Most important to the hardest-pressed farmer was his ability to save a lot of money and still earn farm income. He could bid to enroll a high number of acres, and thereby eliminate the cost of seed, fuel, fertilizers, chemical, and any borrowing he needed to get through planting time.

On top of that, the farmer would still have a crop to market because he was to be paid in grain. It was fervently hoped that he could sell it at a higher price to boot, since market prices were likely to get a big boost from the smaller 1983 planted acreage. Best of

all, the plan reversed the inane process of taking more
and more grain off the market and paying to store it
while Europe and South America raided the U.S. customer base at lower prices. At least it reversed the
process for one year.

In many respects, it was a very good plan. Like all
good farm policy ideas, however, it was not implemented to its best advantage. Basic dogma insists that
all new farm policies (and all quick fixes) have to be
modified until they fit the basic goals and objectives of
farm policy. To put it another way, snags had to be
purposely built into PIK.

The rub came with the realization that releasing PIK
payments onto the free market would also depress free
market prices. Dogma 101 teaches that the goal of all
farm policy is to manipulate the free market so that it
delivers a *higher* fair price to the farmer, not a lower
one. The answer was delay.

The initial decision to go with PIK was made in the
fall of 1982. The farmer was to make his bids by late
winter. The government would accept or reject them in
time for the 1983 planting season. However, the PIK
grain itself would not actually be released to the
farmer (and thence onto the free market) until the next
year's crops were being harvested in the fall—nearly a
full year later.

Even then, it would only come at a dribble, and the
bulk would actually be released well into 1984, a year
and a half after the PIK plan was decided and a year
and a half after the crisis came to a head. Clearly the
idea of recapturing lost markets was an also ran
among the USDA's priorities.

In the meantime the USDA actually intended to go
full speed ahead with the old flawed system. That
winter (1982–83) it took grain off the market and put
it into the loan and reserve programs as fast as ever.
Why?

A) There was the basic old goal of supporting prices,

and B) the USDA needed to pull in as much grain as possible that winter in order to be sure it had the hundreds of millions of bushels that would be needed to make all the PIK payments in the spring.

Thus the USDA would issue more government debt to the farmer to facilitate those loan and reserve entries, and it would deprive more customers of cheap grain. It would lose more market share over the winter as it pulled grain off the market. It would lose more in the summer growing months by refusing to release the PIK grain when cheap South American supplies flood the market. It would lose more the following year, when there was a smaller crop available because of reduced acres.

The depressed futures markets responded to the PIK Program with a fair degree of enthusiasm. Corn did especially well. When the PIK details were announced in November 1982, corn futures were in the process of coming off four-year lows of about $2.15 per bushel.

Whether it was on rumors of PIK or just the fact that the market was oversold, it's hard to say, but they turned on a dime, and they proceeded to march higher through the entire winter and on into the 1983 planting season. By the time the 1983 corn crop was in the ground, prices had rallied to nearly $3.25, an increase of nearly 50 percent from the lows! To the USDA and the farm lobby, this was the very essence of a policy success.

Beans also rallied over most of this stretch, but far more modestly than corn since the PIK Program didn't include soybean acreage. The soybean market was also held back because carryover stocks from the old (1982) crop were expected to be record large. Bean prices rallied from a low near $5.20 in the fall, to just over $6.50 in April.

Prices then headed lower after planting got underway in May, and they continued heading lower through the end of June. By then the "bears" were firmly in control of the market again. They believed that even an average yield would easily generate more new crop soybeans than the market could hope to use over the course of the next marketing year. All obvious signs pointed to new lows.

However, there was a catch. When something is as convoluted as PIK, there's always a catch—little twists that the market can't see up front. It turned out that there was a very big twist in the case of soybeans.

The program was designed to be so lucrative that farmers were stimulated to load every acre they could into their corn and wheat set-aside bids. Although these were supposed to be acres that in the past had been devoted exclusively to corn and wheat, farmers pushed millions of soybean acres into the corn and wheat category, and put them into their bids. (Farmers have a long history of great liberality in their interpretation of acreage programs, so this shouldn't have surprised anyone.)

Not only that, but in the south, farmers grow winter wheat and soybeans on some of the same acres. (As soon as the winter wheat is harvested in May–June, the farmer quick plants his beans.) If these double crop acres were counted as wheat acres and enrolled in PIK, the farmer wasn't allowed to plant anything on them at all. There went a couple million more soybean acres. The loss of soybean acreage was sped up by the fact that the USDA was so anxious to slash production (and support prices) that it was accepting just about all of the acreage that the farmers were interested in packing into their PIK bids.

To make a long story short, this was just not figured out by the market, not to mention individual grain analysts like myself. The USDA was scheduled to release the final results at 2:00 P.M. on June 29, 1983—namely, its official estimates of that year's planted acreage. As I said before, the mood on the trading floor was bearish. The markets had generally

wandered lower during the last half of May and all of
June.

Corn closed the session on the 29th in pretty good
shape. The nearby contract settled at $3.17¾, close to
a two-year high. Soybeans were another story. They'd
wandered lower for at least a month and a half at that
point, and on the 29th the market seemed to give up.
The most actively traded (November) contract, made a
new low for the break and settled at $5.98 when the
closing bell rang at 1:15.

Since the Acreage Report was one of the most important reports of the year, anticipation was high.
Traders and brokers quickly settled the day's business, grabbed a quick bite to eat, and hurried back to
the trading floor to assemble around the Reuters and
CNS wire machines to wait for two o'clock.

The numbers were a shock. Both the corn and bean
acreage numbers were below the average trade estimates, but soybeans were below even the lowest
trade estimate. This in turn threw everyone's estimate
of the next year's soybean crop right out the window.
This one report made it clear that instead of producing
more than soybeans that summer than the market
needed, the United States would produce far less.
Phones immediately started ringing off the hooks as
brokers and customers from around the world called in
to get the news. "What's the opening call?"!

The answer was limit up. Speculators had gotten
comfortably bearish on false expectations. They were
caught leaning the wrong way, and scrambled to cover
short positions on the opening bell. Users who had
been expecting ample supplies and lower prices
jumped in to secure some of their upcoming needs just
in case prices trended higher still.

And, oh yes . . . did I forget to mention the drought?
It just so happened that there was also already a
full-fledged drought underway in the Midwestern
breadbasket. It had already been underway for weeks

by the time the acreage report came out on the 29th, yet it had been strangely ignored by a market obsessed with PIK and its bearish expectations for the bean crop. Soybeans had actually dropped in price during one of the hottest, driest months of June on record. That all changed after the big Acreage Report, and prices soared with this one-two punch.

The drought of 1983, the second big U.S. drought of the decade turned out to be worse than the first. It continued all through the month of July and in fits and spurts on through the months of August and September as well. Its effects were also felt closer to the heart of the corn and bean belts, than was the case in the drought of 1980. Chicago set a new record for most ninety-degree days in one summer.

The average corn yield dropped from over 113 bushels an acre the year before, to only 81 per acre. In 1980 yields had only dropped from 109, to 91. As a result corn rallied to over $3.75, again just a stone's throw from the all-time highs at $4.00. Beans had to race to catch up. They not only had to adjust for the acreage shock, but for the steadily dropping yield prospects as well. As usual, the peripatetic bean market overcompensated and the November contract raced from its close under $6 on June 29, to $9.67 a bushel in six very dramatic weeks.

By this time I was both an analyst and CBOT member. The trading floor was where I spent the biggest part of my day. My job had moved me off the floor prior to the 1980 drought, and I didn't make it back until fall of that year, so this was my first drought spent on the floor of the Board of Trade. I don't recommend it.

Things went from sleepy to frenzied, literally overnight. Before the report, all was low volume, coffee breaks, and long pleasant chats on the phone with favorite customers and brokers. After the report, even the most minor tasks had an edge of hysteria to them.

In fact there's no such thing as a minor task during

a drought rally. Customers who seemed genuinely fond of you a few days before are now waiting on the line to scream that they want a price on their market order, they want it now, and they're prepared to take their business elsewhere, thank you very much!

Their hysteria is understandable because prices are racing up and down, and they have no idea where they stand. The only problem is that brokers trying to fill their orders in the pit are so swamped that they may not send an order back for hours. You could take a gun into the pit and point it at the December corn broker's head, and you still might not get his attention.

The average size of orders doubled and tripled, and these bigger orders flew back and forth across the order desk in a blur. The slightest mistake in writing one could generate an enormous error for the customer or the house.

Phone clerks writing hundreds of orders a day may be forced into the ludicrous position of sending their last runner, a 110-pound girl, to fight her way into a writhing mass of 200-pound traders in the middle of the soybean pit.

Good friends that worked only twenty feet away were only seen once or twice a day, often racing across the floor with a stricken look on their faces. I'm sure that I gave others the same impression.

The traders in the pit probably had it the worst though. They were at the epicenter of that blur, trading millions of bushels. Often they went home with the sick feeling in the pit of their stomachs that comes from not knowing your exact position. Were they long, short, or flat? Would they come in the next morning to discover they had lost $50,000? This too is part of the game during drought markets.

The funny part was that there was plenty of everything around, just as there had been during the drought of 1980. Soybean and corn carryouts were both expected to be record large in September, drought or no drought, and usage was dropping as it always does when prices rise sharply. So why did the world's users need to keep scrambling and keep paying up for supplies in July and early August?

Ah! Therein lies the point of our story. Supplies of corn and wheat that the market needed over the short term were still firmly locked away in loan and reserve programs. And what about all the corn and wheat that was going to be released from those government programs in payment for setting aside planted acres? It too was still safely locked away so as not to depress prices. The first PIK payments weren't scheduled to start dribbling onto the market until late summer, and the bulk was scheduled for release much later.

Why not release some of it ahead of schedule in July to cool off the markets, and sustain the domestic and foreign customer base until harvest? That makes sense, but it would have been anathema to the central purpose of the USDA support programs. The goal was higher prices, and basically the higher the better. That goal was being met. The customer was in a tight spot, and paying up. Another big success was underway.

As of August 1 the customers were being forced to pay corn prices that were up 75 percent from the previous fall's lows. By mid August, bean prices were up 60 percent since the acreage report alone.

During the second and third week of the month, however, one of the first props fell out from under the six-week-old soybean rally. A 100-mile-wide band of the Soybean Belt running east–west through the mid-section of Illinois got two to four inches of rain. That didn't seem like much to soybean speculators who were drought-crazed by that time, but it meant a great deal to the soybeans. They are hardy little plants, and this particular band of rain happened to fall on some of the most important soybean farms in the world at just the right time to save the crop.

As a result, the average national yield bounced up to

about where it had been in the less severe drought year
of 1980, and the price of soybeans started to roll over
and head south as it always does after one of its
breathtaking rallies.

Prices fell a little slower this time, however. They
worked their way down from the high of $9.67 in
mid-August, to about $6.90 by mid-winter. The market
fell more slowly this time because it was only taking a
breather. There was going to be a second act this time
around. Another, stranger crop story had developed
meanwhile in Malaysia.

Malaysia was and is the largest producer and exporter of palm oil. They were one of the countries that
took advantage of the high-priced era after 1972 to
vastly expand production and processing of their one
big crop. By the mid-1980s they were starting to erode
the decades long dominance that soyoil had enjoyed
over the world's vegetable oil trade.

Malaysia suffered two related mishaps in 1983–84,
however, that sidetracked their ascendancy. The first
was a drought of their very own. It affected much of
Southeast Asia, and reduced the expected yields for
the very thirsty tropical palm trees. The second
mishap came with the introduction into Malaysia of an
insect called the Cameroon Weevil which is native to
West Africa. The Cameroon Weevil was imported because of its unique ability to interact with the palm
tree and *stress* it to higher yields.

It was unfortunately introduced when many of the
vast, newly planted plantations were too immature,
and already under plenty of stress from drought.
Yields of the palm fruit fell sharply, and Malaysia
found itself unable to deliver on its palm oil export
commitments. In the process, much of the demand
that palm had taken away from soyoil in the 1970s and
early 1980s came flooding back into the soyoil column.

India was a case in point. It has traditionally been
the world's largest importer of vegetable oils, and it

was forced to replace the imported palm oil that many Indians prefer, with soyoil from the United States and Brazil. Other importers who perhaps had switched to palm simply because it was so cheap, were also forced to switch to soyoil in 1984.

However, the drought and PIK had so greatly reduced the American soybean crop the summer before, there wasn't enough soyoil to satisfy the market. Prices therefore had to rally again to "ration out" some of the resurgent demand for soyoil, and that's what they commenced to do after mid-winter. Soyoil futures actually rallied right past the drought highs to within hailing distance of the all-time "price shock highs" of 1973. In so doing they dragged soybean futures back up to $9.

The highs came in May, and this second rally was hard to figure. The fact that there had been two separate soybean rallies within one year led a lot of traders to believe that the market for soybeans and its products had turned higher for good. In fact it meant the opposite. The second rally only occurred because of the growing importance of the palm oil crop after its decade of furious growth. If it hadn't grown to the point where it was on the verge of taking over the number-one spot in world vegetable oil trade, its temporary loss wouldn't have sent the American market soaring.

By the end of 1984 the truth became apparent. The damaging effect of drought and cameroon weevil passed completely. Whole new palm plantations came on-stream, and production rose steeply.

The cheap Malaysian palm oil poured onto the world market, deeply undercutting U.S. soyoil, and it easily recaptured demand it had temporarily lost in India and elsewhere. By 1984–85 it vaulted ahead of soyoil in terms of its percentage share of the world market in vegetable oils, a position soyoil had occupied for decades. The fact that the Malaysians could ac-complish this feat was all the more remarkable be-

cause the crop that they had to offer was substandard
in many ways. Palm oil is loaded with saturated fat
(more than twice the saturated fat of lard) while soyoil
is a relatively healthy product. It ranks behind only a
few very healthy oils such as safflower, sunflower, and
corn oil. This unlikely victory is very much to the credit
of the Malaysian government, but some credit has to
go to the USDA.

Once again the USDA's timing had proved to be
almost eerily bad. Not only had they again initiated a
giant acreage reduction program in a year of terrible
drought, just like the Dust Bowl, but in so doing, they
had missed their golden opportunity in 1983–84 to
retrieve market share that had been lost to palm oil.

On top of the bad timing were those same old flaws
that had helped create opportunities for Malaysia and
others in the first place. Soyoil and the soybeans it
comes from had a difficult time competing against the
much cheaper palm oil based on price, as I've already
mentioned. On top of that basic price disadvantage,
USDA support programs now guaranteed that
American soybeans that the oil came from were consistently more expensive than soybeans produced in
Brazil and Argentina.

The break that followed the highs of May 1984 was
more like the breaks after past soybean rallies; it was
hard and fast. Beans dropped to under $6.10 a bushel
by late July, a loss of nearly one-third of their value in
less than three months. By year's end they had
wandered on down to $5.60, and the handwriting was
on the wall for all to see.

While the palm oil goings-on were occupying
soybeans, the corn market stumbled through one more
spring and summer of artificially tight supplies. The
United States stuck with its stretched-out schedule of
releasing PIK grain, and that limited the free supply
until late summer 1984. The nearby futures contract
bounced along between about $3.40 and $3.65 until

July, not too far from the drought highs of 1983. It
seemed as though the supply was genuinely tight because of the previous summer's drought, but at the end
of the summer there were still over 1.0 billion bushels
left, and a huge crop ready to be harvested.

This was the last summer the USDA was able to
create an illusion of scarcity. The United States sailed
into another string of surplus years in corn, wheat, and
soybeans. It was worst for corn. There were over 1.0
billion bushels of corn left over from the 1983 drought
crop, over 1.6 billion after the 1984 crop, over 4.0
billion at the end of the 1985 crop year, and nearly 5.0
billion bushels at the end of the 1986 crop. Five billion
bushels is more than the entire coarse grain production of either the USSR or populous China!

A surplus has its good points of course, but we already know that these advantages were diminished by
the policies of the USDA. It still tried to support the
world price by depriving it of grain that it could easily
get elsewhere for less. Most of those billions of leftover
bushels therefore poured into the loan program (in the
case of beans), and into the farmer-owned reserve in
the case of corn and wheat. What can I say?

The corn that was tucked away in the farmer-owned
reserve was of course safe from customers for years
and years, courtesy of the Farmer Owned Reserve of
1972. Each summer, the price dropped off a little
waterfall. The supports temporarily and artificially
tightened up the supply just a bit during spring and
summer, until the flood of newly harvested corn pulled
the rug out from under the market in August and
September. Then the programs would begin to sop up
the new surplus and the cycle began anew at an even
lower level.

Despite the expense and effort that the country was
going through with its now massive farm programs,
farm numbers were dropping off a little waterfall each
year too. Foreclosures soared during this period to the

highest levels since the Great Depression (a time by
the way when there had been a whole lot more farms
around to foreclose). By the mid-1980s, the grain
farmers with the heaviest interest payments often
needed prices that were 50–75 percent above the
prevailing free market price in order to turn a profit.

If they stored their grain in hopes of higher prices to
come, that just added to the cost. They were just going
to end up dumping it at an even lower price the next
year, and a bigger loss. If farmers took out government
loans instead, that just added another loan to the
already ludicrous pile that average farm families had
somehow racked up in the prior ten years.

One more difference was that by 1984–85 the friendly local banker was no longer so friendly. Bankers who
had helped fuel the debt bomb ran for cover, and it was
they who therefore tended to officially pull the plug.

Things got considerably less go-go in the Chicago
futures markets too. Wave after wave of layoffs came
among those brokerage firms that were dependent on
the grain futures trade. Visitors standing in the observation gallery still seemed to marvel at the hustle and
bustle of it all, but to those of us in the trading community, each day's activities just looked like two or
three thousand unnecessary people standing around
waiting for someone to phone in an order.

In Chicago, jobs and even whole companies disappeared for good, just like they were elsewhere in the
country, and just as they had ceased to exist in the
auto, steel, and electronics industries. I like to call it
the rolling recession, and it would soon roll on into the
oil patch.

We grain analyst types focused more of our energies
into teaching the act of futures "hedging" to farmers,
as one last attempt at financial salvation. Bankers and
brokerage firms urged farmers to master the art of
hedging in the futures to, "lock in a price." Unfortunately, the futures market didn't oblige by trading

at a higher price. Futures simply represented another place for the weaker farmer to "lock in" his loss.

The ubiquitous farmer marketing seminars conducted during those depressed years tended to start with the tricky bit about the farmer figuring his cost of production per bushel. If the balance sheet was free of debt, then this part was a minor discipline that needed to be dispensed with before the seminar moved on to more sophisticated concepts. It might cost the most efficient farmers only $1.40 to produce a bushel of corn in a good year on good land in central Illinois.

If the balance sheet was debt-heavy, however, the bottom line could be double that basic cost or more. These farmers might as well have put down their pencils and notebooks and gone home. We saw a lot of pained expressions on the faces of attendees that I assumed at the time was just confusion or boredom. In retrospect, however, some of those looks must have been despair—realization that there was no trick to this hedging business that changed the arithmetic they could do at home.

For a great many, the suspense was lifted quickly. The downtrend in the total number of U.S. farms that began again with bin-busting crops of 1982 kept right on going. By 1985 nearly another quarter million farms were lost—10 percent of the 1981 total in just four years.

15

1985

The winter of 1984–85 was the next milestone. It was time for another debate over another new farm bill, another golden opportunity to take the old stuff down off the shelf and have a good look at it.

This time around, the debate began as front-page news. The extent of the farm crisis and the fact that it was not going away had become obvious by late 1984. It could no longer be finessed by higher loans and targets or exotic acreage programs. This sense of immediacy caught the attention of the national media.

By that fall and winter it had already waded deeply into the mess, klieg lights blazing and notepads waving. Serious-looking reporters and even network anchors could be seen trailing camera crews through barren fields, picking up hands full of soil, staring silently into the distance, and interviewing sad farm couples around the kitchen table. It was hard to watch.

Even Hollywood had gotten into the act with three save-the-farm movies starring some of the biggest names in the film industry. Already out by January were Jessica Lange and Sam Shepard in *Country* and Sally Field in *Places in the Heart*. Coming soon to theaters everywhere were Sissy Spacek and Mel Gibson in *The River*. So the debate was geared for high theater.

Act One featured confrontation. On one side was the Reagan administration, and on the other was the Capitol's vast agricultural policy apparatus and the farm lobby. The lead was played by the young and yuppyish David Stockman, former congressman from the state of Michigan, and then budget director for the Reagan White House. He came to the stage with a reputation as a cost-cutting zealot who appeared to be completely immune to delicate political and social sensibilities on Capitol Hill. He was perfectly cast.

The Reagan administration wanted to slash farm subsidies to help reduce the deficit. It wanted to put its free-market principles to action in the farming industry and put an end to a system that it considered anachronistic and counterproductive. The strategists at the White House anointed David Stockman to be their ball carrier, and so designated, he girded his loins and went off that January to do battle against the wheezing giant.

At first no one could be certain what direction the wind would blow, so a lot of people were lying low. The farm crisis was the worst since the Great Depression, and it was widely acknowledged that national farm policies were at the very least ineffectual. Most of the old policy voices who had framed the old system seemed to sense their vulnerability. They wisely waited for Stockman to make his move.

In the minds of the Reagan administration, that left the field wide open. Stockman's job was to move quickly into the void and pull the parameters of the upcom-

ing debate to within the Reagan framework. He chose
to do so with an all-out assault that came during a
Congressional testimony that stretched through
January and February of 1985.

The assault had two prongs. One dealt with the farm
policies themselves. Stockman drove through to the
conclusion that the country and its farmers were better off without them. He went so far as to forcefully
propose that most if not all farm subsidies should be
eliminated, or at the very least, slashed to the bone. As
tough as all of this sounded, it might have struck some
real pay dirt, if it hadn't been for prong two, which
consisted of an equally spirited assault on the farm
community itself.

Stockman also pointed out, correctly in many
respects, what an unbelievable deal many of the
nation's more successful farmers had enjoyed over the
past couple of decades. He pointed out (correctly again)
that the mountainous debt some farmers had amassed
was entered into by consenting adults, that 40–50
percent of the nation's autoworkers had lost *their* jobs
from 1978–85 and nobody had bailed them out, and he
concluded that farmers ought to take their hits just
like any other small business that couldn't sell its
merchandise at a profit. This all made sense.

He also came to the more dubious conclusion that
there were too many American farmers in 1985, just as
there had been too many autoworkers in 1978. I call
this one dubious because the number of autoworkers
had only peaked seven years earlier, while the farm
population had peaked way back in 1916, at nearly six
times its total size in 1985.

And he offered no alternatives. Old policies had been
useless, indebted farmers had been fools, and by im-
plication they were supposed to dry up and blow away.

That was the gist of his comments at any rate, and
they initially left many members of the Congress in
stunned silence. The farm community and its congres-

sional representatives had never been spoken to in quite this way before.

It was too much for them. It was also too much for public opinion, and there was a backlash. In attacking farmers, Stockman had attacked one of the most sacred of all American cultural icons, and icons have a way of striking back. Even Stockman's mom took to the airwaves from Michigan to distance herself and her own political career from her outspoken son.

David Stockman's frontal assault therefore had a different effect than the one intended. Instead of staking out the parameters for debate, he provided fuel for the revival of the farm lobby. And he became a perfect foil for the subsequent public-relations counteroffensive. His role was recast by the opposition as the embodiment of the heartless Reagan Revolution: a cold fish who would not only let the poor hardworking farmer go down the drain, but who would gladly give him a great big push (sort of like the villainous Mr. Potter from that American film classic, *It's a Wonderful Life*).

Mr. Stockman abetted the efforts of his opposition by playing his part to the hilt, whether from sincere conviction or because he just relished his role as chief Washington iconoclast. But by early February he had shot off the last of his ammunition. After that the farm lobby and its congressional supporters regrouped, energized from having withstood the initial assault.

Act Two: Congress felt cocky enough to press for a debt-relief package which the House passed and sent to the president on March 6. Its use of the term "relief" was a bit questionable, since its thrust was to make government loans available that spring which were not scheduled to be available till fall. This was to give farmers the money they needed to plant.

In a previous generation, this might have made perfect sense, but not in 1985. Some farmers were already drowning in debt; Congress wanted to add to it and enable them to carry the new debt a few months longer than originally scheduled government loans.

Senators from the farm states even went so far as to filibuster to block the senate vote on President Reagan's nomination of Ed Meese to be attorney general. They wanted the president to agree to support their debt relief bill. He vetoed it instead, but eventually accepted a compromise package.

On March 7 a New York Times/CBS Poll showed broad support for aid to farmers. As the month went by, more poll results indicated the public overwhelmingly supported farm aid. In some cases Americans even voiced willingness to pay added taxes or higher food prices if necessary to help the family farmer.

Actually the most meaningful counterattack came from within the Reagan administration itself, from the secretary of agriculture no less.

A prominent member of what was known as the progressive wing of American agriculture, John Block was a very big, very modern, and a very rich leveraged farmer. In the 1970s his type of operation was held up by the USDA as the model of all that American farming ought to be. His nomination was an affirmation, the Reagan administration's further endorsement of big farming.

The Block "home farm" in west central Illinois alone contained three thousand acres, along with a hog feeding operation and much more. Mr. Block had built all this since 1960 on the base provided by his father's three hundred acres. When nominated in 1980, he was a rich man and a big customer of the farm subsidy system. That seemed to make sense in 1980. No sooner was he in office and ready to enjoy the fruits of his success, however, than things started going sour.

On top of the home farm, he and various partners had speculated in the purchase of thousands of additional acres in Illinois and Minnesota. Farmland prices peaked in 1980, dropped slightly in 1981 (for the first time in ten years), and then fell like a rock in 1982. That obviously left land speculators in a whole heap of trouble, and Mr. Block was one speculator who was in debt to the tune of several million dollars. Estimates at the time *started* at $5.1 million, and Block himself confirmed annual interest due of $694,000.

By early 1985, one of his major partners had already been forced to declare bankruptcy. Another had received a federally backed (FmHA) loan of $400,000, a loan made to help these rich men hold onto their speculative investments. Bad debt transformed John Block from another multimillionaire in politics, into another worried farmer populist.

But this worried farmer was in a key position to influence policy. He weighed in during late January in favor of the status quo with a proposal to gradually reduce the loan and target rates, as opposed to "slashing" or eliminating them. He brought out the old Nixon slogan of a more "market-oriented" farm policy, and he prevailed. "Gradualism" was quickly adopted by the administration as a workable modification of the old subsidies.

For my money, the emotional climax of Act Two came on May 7 with the remarkable press conference/testimony of two of the female leads of that year's save-the-farm movies, Sissy Spacek and Jessica Lange. They were accompanied by the ubiquitous Jane Fonda. (Where Sally Field was that day, I don't know.)

House Democrats staged this event to revive the public's interest in the farmers' economic plight, which had started to flag. One of the organizers, Congressman Thomas A. Daschle of South Dakota, said the event would help educate America. Imagine.

Ms. Lange seemed to be chief spokesperson. She and Mr. Daschle both admitted up front that the actresses knew little or nothing about farm policy, but she added that since her experience in filming *Country* she had come to relate to farmers in a special way and could "feel their pain."

Ms. Spacek said, "It is heartbreaking to witness their anguish as they watch their lives being stripped away." She didn't say whether this observation had occurred on network television, or simply on the set of her film. (I wonder if she included the stripping away of the vast holdings of Secretary John Block's partnerships.)

Ms. Fonda mostly sat and listened, occasionally dabbing away a stray tear. The group concluded by saying that they didn't know what should be done, but pleaded with the legislators to do "something" to help save the "family farmer."

Well it was all over but the shouting. The fact that this kind of circus could occur after months of debate and years of farm crisis said a lot. The debate was going nowhere. In the face of tremendous odds, family farmer mythology and inertia had again carried the day.

As usual, other potential players like the big grain exporters, processors, successful farmers, and the trading community in Chicago kept silent. Perhaps they all took a reading of the completeness of the Stockman defeat and the continued power of the farm lobby and were awed into silence.

Act Three: all anticlimax. It consisted of hammering out the details, making those gradual modifications prescribed by Secretary Block. It's always a little dangerous to summarize an American farm bill, but I think it's fair to say that it had three general goals with regard to price supports.

1. Support (loan) prices would reverse the uptrend that began in earnest in the early 1970s; annual *decreases* were scheduled over its expected four-year duration.

2. Production would be slashed as it had been in the

1960s, with aggressive long-term paid acreage reductions.

3. As production declined, the government would gradually push its stocks onto the free market in the hopes of eventually getting out of the business of storing grain.

One had to read between the lines, however, to get the real point. The United States was planning to shrink its farm economy to fit its shrinking share of the world market. The policy establishment had vaguely acknowledged the folly of raising loan and target rates in a competitive world. It even acknowledged the need to push grain stocks onto the market, but it held onto its fantastic belief that the federal bureaucracy had the skill required to rebalance the U.S. supply and demand with new acreage reductions. The USDA had never shown the slightest hint of possessing this skill. On top of all that was the inane belief that a few nips and tucks would halt the powerful trends working against the American farm economy and its export market share.

As for the acreage set-aside itself, it too was fairly standard operating procedure. Farmers were to be paid in cash to take acres out of production, and not in kind. How much did the USDA plan to shrink things? The goal was to attract a whopping 40–45 million acres to a Conservation Reserve Program (CRP), and they were to be taken out of production for ten years. Too much acreage had been the problem that produced the glut, and not our unwillingness to sell our crops at the world price.

As for the big goal of reducing agricultural subsidies, there was a lot to be said for the idea. It was in fact a good idea that was long overdue. Unfortunately, it was so long overdue that it had ceased to be a good idea.

While lower subsidies would theoretically make American crops more competitive in the world

marketplace, the process was scheduled to occur on a
very gradual basis. If, for instance, world prices happened to go down at the same gradual rate, the United
States would simply remain as uncompetitive as it had
been in the first half of the decade. If world prices went
down faster than the supports, it would end up losing
ground even faster. Might we not have to shrink our
farm economy again someday to fit an even smaller
role if this happened?

The other half of the problem was that many farmers
had already layered on huge debts based on expectations of high supports ad infinitum. Now that all of
that debt was locked in, the scheduled lower rates
were guaranteed to pull the rug out from under a few
thousand more of them each time the supports were
lowered. You could have charted it.

Furthermore, the worst single element of farm policy
was preserved and extended—the farmer-owned
reserve. If the competition could continue to produce
and sell grain below the new support prices, the
United States would continue to abandon more market
share to it. When that happened, the American farmer
would do what he had done for most of the previous
eight years: enroll his surplus grain in the farmer-
owned reserve where it would pile up for years and
take out a government loan.

In all fairness, it must be pointed out that there was
one ray of hope in the 1985 farm bill: its renewed
interest in the environment. The CRP acreage program was designed to mostly attract acreage classified
as highly erodible. It mandated that farmers who were
signed up for price supports have in place a conservation plan for all of their erodible acres by 1990. It also
had provisions aimed at preventing participants from
starting to farm any more highly erodible acres (sod-
busting), and from draining and planting more wetlands (swampbusting).

All in all though, this was another missed oppor-

tunity, and a failure on the part of the policy establishment to raise its eyes and see the world as it really
was.

I was inclined when I started to write this book to
paint David Stockman's role in agricultural policy in a
fairly good light. After all, he was out there on his own
telling a very destructive and inept group of law-
makers and lobbyists that they were destructive and
inept. There's a lot to be said for that.

Upon reflection I would vote for a different verdict.
Mr. Stockman and the Reagan administration were
there to lead, and 1985 was by far the best opportunity
since the 1930s to bust things open and start over.
Instead they chose to tell people how dumb they had
all been (true enough), and then told them they ought
to just take their lumps.

I'm not sympathetic to the farmers' position in the
policy debate, but who can blame their reaction in
1985? Since the late nineteenth century, they had
devoted their collective energies to the search for the
political formula that would guarantee every farmer a
fair profit. Since 1933 they had ordered from a menu
of federal farm programs that promised to try and
deliver those fair prices. Farmers were committed to
defending them.

Along comes the farm depression of the mid-1980s.
This was a time of fear for farmers, and they came by
their fear quite honestly. Many were in danger of
losing it all. At such times human beings are not
inclined to let go of cherished, but flawed ideals. Often
they will cling even tighter to the source of their
problems, unless someone leads them toward en-
lightened thinking.

The times therefore called for firm and gentle leadership, for "tough love." David Stockman and others in
the administration could have chosen to point out to
farmers that the basic *design* of their price supports
was undermining the weaker farmers among them.

Fruitful dialogue could have ensued.

Instead they got a bull in a china shop. Mr. Stockman proposed something that was unthinkable in farmers' minds, to sweep farm subsidies off the table. Furthermore, he didn't even pretend to believe this was for the good of the troubled farm population itself, that it was part of some plan to save farms and farm population.

On the contrary. His stated goal was to make farmers run the race even faster, to be cut off and left alone in the desperately competitive world sprint, up to their eyeballs in debt. He and the administration were telling us who they wanted to emerge from this depression. Big and well capitalized should survive (the John Blocks). The others no longer had a place.

Mr. Stockman and the other hard-liners were just plain wrong about this basic premise. There were not too many farmers in 1985. On the contrary. A problem that apparently didn't seem obvious from their vantage point on the banks of the Potomac was that there were already too few farmers, far too few. By then only 2.5 percent of the U.S. population was still farming, and the vast majority of farm assets were concentrated into the hands of half that many.

Stockman had a rigid dogma to which he adhered, just like the farmer. He preached free markets and competition, no matter the result. This was every bit as flawed as the farmers' search for "parity" and "fairness" through the manipulation of the free market.

16

THE GENERIC CERTIFICATE

Planning aside, the process of whittling down the surpluses would not begin for another year. As the finishing touches were going into the 1985 farm bill, summer crop weather in the United States was nearly perfect. Corn and soybean yields soared to new records of 118.0 and 34.1 bushels per acre respectively.

This would have been exceedingly good news in most of the rest of the world where abundant food supplies are an asset, and crops are meant to be used and sold. From the perspective of the USDA, however, this was more bad news.

The USDA's acreage reduction efforts had yet to begin in earnest, so those record yields were being multiplied by very high acreage numbers. By harvest the bins were full again. Surplus corn was poured onto the ground and covered with a tarp because there was no place else to put it.

At the end of the 1985–86 crop year (September 1986), carryover stocks for all major crops therefore stood at brand new records: 536 million bushels of soybeans, 4.040 billion bushels of corn, and 1.905 billion bushels of wheat. Another record yield in corn the following year served to raise the carryover to yet another record: 4.882 billion bushels. For surplus grain, all roads now led to the reserve and loan programs, and so that's where the bulk of the record carryovers ended up.

The process started feeding on itself. Even the formerly proud American soybean producers wanted more government help. In the past, they had tended to be in the upper crust of "grain" farmers, priding themselves among other things on being relatively free of the need for long-term price support programs. Soybean loans were issued for only nine months duration, so the beans under loan got redeemed and sold fairly quickly. It had been almost like a free market, so it had been healthier.

By 1984–85, those days were a memory. The soybean farmer asked for and got extensions on those nine-month loans. They were "rolled over" into new nine-month loans, or extended to twelve-month terms. As a result, soybeans and their products became progressively even less competitive against South American soybeans, soymeal, and soyoil. Starting in 1985 and extending into 1986, it was actually possible on a couple of occasions to import Brazilian soybeans and their products into coastal areas of the United States for less than it cost to obtain them locally. This was even the case in the rich lower Mississippi Delta where soybeans are produced in abundance in fields a short truck haul from port. Poor soybean oil seemed to be barely in the running against cheap and growing supplies of Malaysian palm oil by this point. Despite the quality problems some 900 million pounds of the stuff made its way into the United States in 1986.

Other examples of America's loss of farm competitiveness in the mid-1980s became almost absurd. China, with its more than one billion people had begun to modernize and decentralize its farm economy in 1978, and by 1985–86 this was bearing fruit. Formerly a needy importer, China had become a minor export competitor for the United States, taking away little chunks of feedgrain and soymeal business. Some of this was Japanese and South Korean business, which was understandable enough, but some examples hit closer to home.

China intruded into our Mexican feedgrain business, a market that the United States thought it owned. It turned out that China could bring small quantities of sorghum to its small and inefficient ports, sometimes literally in peasant carts, load it onto small and inefficient ships, and transport it all the way across the Pacific to Mexico for less than the cost of shipping U.S. sorghum that was sitting piled on the ground a short 500- to 600-mile train ride from the Mexican border. A couple of cargoes of Chinese feedgrains even landed on the West Coast of the United States itself.

One of the big grain companies imported a cargo of Argentine wheat and landed it in the Mississippi Delta area for less than the cost of competing wheat supplies that were being produced in the surrounding fields. India delivered 500,000 tons of soymeal to eastern Europe, undercutting American soymeal in the process. Saudi Arabia, which is composed of mostly desert sand and rock, produced its first exportable wheat surplus. It started getting a little weird.

Abundant world supplies naturally put heavy pressure on free-market prices, and most broke below lows that had seemed like ancient history to traders and analysts in Chicago. Many of us had come to think of a two- to three-year price history (chart) as being pretty darned long-term, but after 1985–86 we were all scrambling to find charts that went back much further. What we needed to know was where the next layer of support would be if soybean futures broke below $4.50 a bushel, or if corn dropped below $1.50.

Prices in every market traded below the depressed levels that had farmers so up in arms back in the mini recessions of 1976, 1977, and 1979. Farmers who hadn't even considered themselves a part of the problem in those earlier price troughs were now not only part of it, they were being foreclosed. Prices were so low that it's possible a majority of grain and soybean farmers were operating at a loss for the first time since 1932.

The enormous amount of energy and national will needed to make a dent in the farm problem at this late date could no longer be raised. That energy had been assembled in early 1985, but squandered.

Land prices continued their slide, and that alone dragged many farmers into the loss column. They had started to roll over in 1981 with an average drop nationally of just over 2 percent that year. This was followed by a drop of 8 percent in 1982, 9 percent in 1983, then 6 percent in 1984, 15 percent in 1985, and yet another 14 percent in 1986.

Rising land values had been the ultimate backing for much of the farm debt built up in the 1970s, and falling land values proved to be the ultimate cause of foreclosure. (In Iowa the average price of farmland fell 59 percent between 1980 and 1986.) Each decline pushed another layer into insolvency, and so the rate at which farmers were getting peeled off accelerated as the decade wore on. The farm population dropped from 5.850 million in 1981, to 5.754 million in 1984, 5.355 in 1985, and 5.226 in 1986.

Some farmers had refused to participate in price support programs in the past, either out of a sense of pride, or because they didn't like the restrictions involved. By 1985, however, even these farmers were signing up in droves. After a decade of pricing farmers out of world markets and adding to the farmers' already voracious borrowing habit, the USDA had managed to greatly expand its constituency.

Not too surprisingly, the private banking industry continued to desert the overextended. Their attack of cold feet was evident most everywhere by 1983, and the condition only got worse by mid-decade. Banks got entirely out of the business of extending farmers who were clearly insolvent.

Those farmers who could stay afloat a bit longer via increased participation in the loan and reserve programs, did so. Of course the more government loans that got written, the more grain that went into government programs and off the market. This in turn kept the U.S. prices above those offered by the competition, and so they continued to undercut U.S. exports. Ergo, sightings of Chinese sorghum on the West Coast.

Farm policy became unworkable, so in late 1986 the USDA responded with yet another new wrinkle in farm policy. Not an overhaul of the flawed building blocks mind you, but a new angle on an old idea that it hoped would be able to flog the underlying variables into delivering the desired performance. (I can't help but cringe as I launch into a description of yet another new and convoluted program. Hang in there. This will be the last.)

The 1985 farm bill gave USDA the discretion to pay farmers for acreage set-asides either in cash, which they chose initially, or "in kind." Since the USDA budget was at an all-time high by late 1986, and funding for whole new programs was not likely to be forthcoming, the USDA returned to the concept of a payment in kind (which in fact had been extravagantly expensive in 1983.)

In order to facilitate its latest payment in kind, the USDA began to issue something called a generic certificate. For my money these generic certificates were the ultimate in American-style farm programs. Each certificate, or "cert" as they were soon called, was printed by the government of the United States with a specific dollar denomination. They could then be used to redeem any of the available commodities owned by the CCC. They were essentially a new form of very liquid currency available to the farm economy.

Once again farmers were to be paid for not planting. As in 1983 they were to receive government-owned commodities. In this case, however, they were not necessarily being given the same commodity as the one that they were agreeing not to plant. They were paid with a set dollar amount of certs which could be used to redeem any or all of the grab bag of commodities that the CCC had in storage around the country.

In addition to wheat, corn, sorghum, and soybeans, certs could be used to purchase oats, barley, rough rice, upland cotton, nonfat dry milk, butter, and cheese. The amount of dollar-denominated certs one needed to purchase these commodities was determined by the government (CCC). The USDA regularly published a catalog that listed how much of each commodity was available, where it was stored, and how much it would cost in certs. Holders of the certs simply listed the commodities and quantities they wanted, and made the necessary arrangements to take delivery.

On its surface this complicated program might have overwhelmed and dismayed participating farmers. A corn grower in Hector, Minnesota was hardly interested in assuming title to a truckload of cheese in Newark, New Jersey. However, the certs were freely negotiable, just like money, so the market quickly found a way around this snag. Traders simply bought the certificates from the farmer at a markup, and in turn sold them to those who might just want that cheese.

Certs became another financial instrument, and a large secondary market emerged to trade them. If there's one thing this country does well, it is to trade and speculate in financial instruments.

Traders and brokers loved certs because it gave them something else to trade. The major grain companies loved them because it freed up new commodities for which they could then find markets. The farmer loved certs most of all. He was not only being subsidized with a widely accepted form of currency, but he found to his delight that the secondary market for certs paid him more than the dollar amount printed on the face of the certificate.

Certs were traded at a percentage of par (face value). The new secondary market soon discovered all sorts of reasons for added value, and they traded as high as 35 percent over par. For instance, the holder of a generic certificate could find areas where there was a certain commodity in CCC storage. He knew that he could purchase it for a set amount published by the USDA. He often discovered that the free market in that area would pay him far more than he had to pay the government because the government had undervalued that commodity in its latest catalog.

Farmers were also allowed to use certs to redeem their own commodity loans at what amounted to a discount. Let's say the farmer had put 10,000 bushels of his own corn under loan, and stored it in his own silos. That tied up valuable storage space and he was restricted from selling until the loan matured. To get around this he could: 1) agree to set aside a portion of his normal planted acres, 2) get paid for doing so with generic certificates, 3) use those certificates to pay off the government loan ahead of time at a discount, and 4) empty out the silos and sell the 10,000 bushels of corn.

The USDA dished out the certificates at a measured pace, and the sooner the farmer got his, the more chance he had of stumbling into windfall profits. Farmers could often redeem the loans and sell off the loan corn at a big fat profit if the supply of corn happened to still be artificially tight in their area. Why would it be tight in the midst of a glut, you ask? Most of the surplus was under loan. Most of your neighbors probably didn't have certificates yet to pay off their loans, and release their own grain under loan. Therefore the supply was artificially tight, and you could grease in and sell your loan corn ahead of the pack. It was called the "pik 'n' roll" after the basketball play of the same name.

If that 10,000 bushels of corn was in a commercial elevator, so much the better. You could fill out the papers in town, cash in your chips, redeem your government loan, and not have to bother loading up a truck. It all took about a half an hour. The darned certs were so versatile, and the secondary market for them was so liquid, that you probably could have used them to buy a new car!

Since the certificates were issued in no particular order, they and the windfall profits they sometimes brought went to rich and poor alike. The farmer who scored was as likely to be a wealthy corporate farmer with little debt and deep pockets, as it was a new young farmer barely hanging on, up to his eyeballs in red ink.

Another reason perhaps that certs traded above par had to do with the basic world price equation itself. For whatever reason, the world agriculture markets were in the process of putting in a major low (or a "big bottom" in the parlance of futures traders) during these depressed years. This major low started coming in during late 1986, just as the generic certificate program got underway.

There were a variety of reasons for the turn in trend. Demand had grown as it normally does during a prolonged stretch of low prices and rising population. World production of grains and soybeans had also started heading lower, so the total supply was shrinking as well. The big 1985–86 crops had been the peak. Total world production of coarse grains (corn, sorghum, barley, oats, millet) hit a record 841.8 million metric tons that year. Two years later the total had dropped by 55 million tons to 786.9.

Was there a drought in China or another crop failure in the USSR that explained this drop in world production? No, it was all a part of the plan, the USDA's plan to slash American crop production.

In the summer of 1986, the USDA lowered plantings with a modest paid set-aside, and production dropped a bit. Then they got much more aggressive with the next plantings by using the generic certificates to generously pay the farmer to slash acreage even more. It had worked. That 55 million-ton drop in world coarse grain production was all accounted for by lower production in the United States. In fact U.S. production dropped by nearly 60 million tons over that stretch.

That's right. The rest of the world's production had increased by 5.0 million tons. Other exporters were still gradually increasing production of grains, just as they had consistently done for more than two decades. American farm policy had spent much of the 1970s and the early 1980s making the United States into the world's most expensive source of grain, basing farm policies on debt and taking supplies off the market. Now that the damage was done, and the higher costs locked in for the guy with all that debt, it was purposely shrinking itself while others continued to expand. It followed something dumb with something even dumber.

The implications of all this are painfully obvious, but to the eyes of the framers of American agricultural policies they were still being masked. Export demand picked up temporarily because the government was unloading grain and soybeans that had previously been locked away, and so the export numbers started to improve. Government stocks started dropping, and prices were trending higher. What could be better?

Once the surpluses were worked off, and U.S. planted acreage was shrunk down to a proper size, the export subsidies and the total supply were scheduled to wind down. The surplus would be gone, and lower production would stay at the new low levels, magically in balance with future demands.

It's not as if I harbor any illusions about the general level of political debate in this country or the attention span of the American public, but after all the theatrics of 1984 and 1985, certainly someone should have been flicking on lights in various dusty corners of the nation's farm policy and asking some of the more obvious questions.

For instance, if we think it's possible for the United States to find the new export customers needed to use up the surplus of grain sitting in government hands, why not just go ahead and try to keep those customers after the surplus is gone?

Since the farm bill's plan is to reduce plantings by 40–45 million acres, sell off much of the surplus stocks, and then keep acreage down for ten years so as not to build another glut, isn't there a built-in dilemma? When the old surplus is gone, won't the new demand still be there in some form? How will the market satisfy that new demand with no surplus and 40–45 million fewer acres under cultivation? Won't there be some sort of shortage until the other exporters of the world produce enough to replace what we've decided to stop producing?

Wouldn't crop prices need to rise by quite a lot in order to squeeze out the new short-term demand that used it up? If that were the case, wouldn't the American consumer be among those forced to pay up to squeeze out that new demand? Doesn't this mean that American consumer ends up paying for agricultural policies twice, first with the $25 billion or so in tax dollars that go into the USDA budget, and then at the grocery store?

Why exactly are taxpayers paying these billions of dollars every year to a tiny and often wealthy slice of the population in the first place? Is it to bring ourselves higher food prices and eliminate our historic supply of cheap food?

Let's jump ahead to spring 1987. Let's say that farmers have completely cooperated with the USDA by reducing planted acreage, but the competition overseas increases its acreage and yields as they have done so often. Won't we be left with the same world surplus that we have today? Under the circumstances, won't the competition just continue to undercut us in price? Won't our surplus again find it's way into government loan and reserve programs?

If that happens, will the USDA stick with its policy of slashing American acreage again and again to bring the world supply and demand back into balance? Just how much are we willing to shrink the American farm economy? Should we go so far as to become a net grain importer because somebody, somewhere, is willing to plant more acres, and produce food more cheaply than our disastrous farm policy allows an American farmer to do?

Let's say things go just as planned. The "problem" of a food surplus is eliminated, planted acreage is sharply reduced for all U.S. crops, the consumer's food bill rises just a bit as a result, and the USDA finally juggles the world supply and demand back into balance. All the balls are in the air at the same time.

What if in that year of policy success there just happened to be another big American drought? Or a big drought in the USSR or China for that matter? How high would the market need to rally to adjust for both the absence of the government-held surplus and a major world crop failure in the same year? Might this not cause a price shock?

Maybe you think my drought question depends too unfairly on 20/20 hindsight. Perhaps. But when the bill was being written in the summer of 1985 it had only been two years since the Grain Belt had experienced one of the worst droughts of the century, and that had come only three years after the one in 1980. Drought ought to have been somewhat salient in the minds of policymakers. It certainly was among traders in Chicago and farmers in the countryside.

Anyone at the USDA or in Congress who was thinking about the potential for drought in that year of acreage reduction, should have been struck by an historic irony. The great drought of 1983 had been accompanied by a supremely ill-timed acreage reduction effort. The Dust Bowl droughts of the 1930s had followed hard on the heels of the first acreage reduction program of 1933. Here we were planning another such program for 1987–88 in the middle of a very dry decade. A betting man might have noted the remarkably bad timing of the USDA, and put his money on another drought.

At any rate, the USDA did in fact prove successful in reducing acreage as planned. Acreage reduction is something they do very well. On this go-around, corn acreage dropped from a near record of more than 83 million acres planted in 1985, to fewer than 77 million in 1986, 66 million in 1987, and then about 67 million in 1988.

Soybean acreage was on an even longer downtrend. It had peaked at more than 71 million acres way back in 1979, and had slowly worked its way lower from there. By 1987, total plantings had dropped to only 57 million acres, and the 1988 total was about the same.

As I mentioned earlier, the futures market had changed direction by then. Instead of trending consistently lower, it started trending higher. In the case of soybeans, the lows of about $4.70 were in place by early fall of 1986. As usual, the corn market took a little longer to exhaust its downtrend. Corn's big low came in late February 1987 at about $1.42 a bushel. Whether the change was due to the lost acreage or the long-term price cycle is hard to say, but both markets trended nicely higher from there.

By spring planting time in 1988 futures prices had been moving higher in all major markets for well over a year. Corn rallied up to around $2.35 by mid-May when the bulk of the corn crop was in the ground. Soybeans stood at what seemed like a dazzling price of about $7.40 by May 16 when soybean planting is normally about 30–50 percent complete. In the case of beans, this price represented an increase of nearly 60 percent from the big lows of late 1986.

Remarkably, this uptrend had occurred right in the teeth of the USDA's program of gradually dumping surplus stocks of soybeans onto the market. Annual usage had risen dramatically from the depressed year of 1984–85 when the latest farm bill was in the works. The USDA had in fact found all of that new customer business that it needed to sop up the surplus, and it had found it at steadily higher prices.

Imagine. As soon as the USDA determined that it needed to unload its dreaded surplus, it was being transformed by the market into an asset that was greatly appreciating in value each year. I've said it before, the USDA has lousy timing.

By the end of that crop year, it expected to have surplus stocks of soybeans down to a very manageable 275 million bushels or so. That total was even getting to be on the smallish side given the expected usage of about 2.050 billion bushels. One surplus was already gone.

That was the supply situation at planting time in 1988, a time when the market is always in the process of turning at least one eyeball on the prospects for the new crop. What about the new crop? Soybean acreage was going to be 20 percent off its all-time highs that year—again according to plan. If crop weather was favorable, and yields were near their all-time highs, the USDA projected a total soybean crop of 1.905 billion bushels.

If you are counting as we go along, you may have noticed that this was about 150 million bushels shy of what I just said was the usage being projected (by the USDA) for the 1987–88 crop year. That projection stood at 2.050 billion bushels. If usage happened to increase as it had been doing over the previous three years, we would be short by even more than 150 million bushels. If weather was just a little less than ideal and yields were only average, we could be over 250 million bushels short.

Which takes us back to the surplus stocks. They were down to only 275 million bushels or so, and that meant things were likely to get good and tight. Some people, perhaps a lot of people at the USDA and on the farm, no doubt thought this was just great. Farm policy had bought a bull market, and the bull market had started to make that tiny slice of the population prosper. Acreage had been slashed as planned, and now the world would have to compete, to pay up, for a limited supply of American soybeans.

Unfortunately, this is where the "blessings" of higher prices go sour. Agricultural markets do not allow their surplus stocks to just get wiped out in a nice and efficient process. The players start to get very nervous when they realize competition is heating up. Those who can, pay up to lock in their needs. That raises food bills. Some start to trim their usage plans a bit because their profit margin suddenly looks a little too tight. Others drop out altogether. Still others decide to buy cheaper soybeans from Brazil and Argentina instead.

If prices start to rise during summer and autumn in anticipation of tight supplies, those South Americans still have plenty of time to get more acres planted so they can handle some of the added business. And users of soyoil can turn to Malaysia for cheaper palm oil.

People don't just line up to pay whatever you want for that last bushel on the shelf. They go elsewhere, spend the money on something else, or do nothing. Business dries up. The short-term joys of higher prices are quickly replaced by the long-term struggle to woo back lost customers. This was an old lesson by the late 1980s.

Surplus wheat stocks had been slashed too, from 97 percent of annual usage in 1986, to only 45 percent in 1988. Corn stocks, the last to go, were next. They had reached a staggering 4.882 billion bushels in 1987. The USDA projected that it would shave over three quarters of a billion bushels off that total before the new 1988 crop corn started coming in about three months later.

Since the USDA had also paid farmers to set aside about 17 million acres that year (20 percent of the corn base), the corn crop was going to be a lot smaller again in 1988. With luck it would be as much as 1.5 to 2.0 billion bushels below expected usage, so that much more would get shaved off the corn stocks by 1989. Soon the whole problem—that darned food surplus—would be gone.

But none of these scenarios would be realized that year. There were not going to be any record yields, or even any normal yields. By planting time in May, it was already very dry and it was getting very hot. By early June, the soil was bone-dry for hundreds of miles in virtually every direction one might choose to travel out of Chicago.

The first drought of the decade, in 1980, had been focused in the southwestern and western Grain Belts. The second in 1983 had been worse. It covered a larger area and shifted the problem over to the right on the U.S. map, to the center of the Grain Belt. The third drought, in 1988, followed this trend. It expanded and intensified. It not only hit the center, the western, and the southwestern Corn and Soybean Belts, it hit hard across the North and East as well.

Some fields were planted twice and still failed to come up. Most fields were able to germinate, however, and crops managed to grow after the newly emerged plants sent root systems plunging deep into the soil to tap the layer of moisture stored farther below ground from the wetter winter.

Modern corn and soybean seeds are a marvel of hybridization and genetic engineering. They produce plants that have a remarkable ability to hunker down and conserve moisture once the early root system develops, and this ability was tested to its limit in June 1988. Temperature records fell on a weekly and even daily basis across 1,000–1,500 miles, represented by the red blob that shifted a bit from side to side each day on the *USA Today* weather map.

Futures prices in Chicago vaulted higher faster than they had at any time since 1972–73, after the USSR pulled off its "Great Grain Robbery." Soybeans traded limit up for days at a time. They rallied from the mid-$7 range where they had spent most of May, to $8, then $9, $10, and finally hitting their ultimate high of about $11 on June 23.

The corn story was about the same. Yield projections dropped on an almost daily basis from mid-June through early July. The rally in corn lasted about two weeks longer than it did in soybeans, and it eventually peaked at about $3.40. Users of all crops were facing a supply situation much more acute than the tightness planned by the USDA. The world had been lulled by surplus into the habit of keeping inventories nice and low. Now they had to scramble to rebuild stocks, or just get what they needed in the next couple of weeks.

The simplest way to cover needed supplies of U.S. corn, wheat, oats, soybeans, soymeal, and soyoil was by purchasing a futures contract before prices raced higher still. In the midst of a big rally, two major demand variables fight against one another: the scramble by those who want supplies at any price and those deciding to throw in the towel or make their purchases elsewhere. The higher prices go, the more people there are who leave the first group to join the second. Business planned in April for $7 soybeans, could no longer be conducted profitably at $10. If the price of your raw material goes up more than 50 percent in a few weeks and well over 100 percent in a year and a half, at some point you have to say, "I'm out."

Some foreign buyers also had reason to fear that grain purchased from the United States could not get shipped in time to meet short-term needs whether they technically owned it or not. The mighty Mississippi River was down over twenty feet below normal. Herds of barges loaded with corn and soybeans from Illinois and Iowa were going aground in the shifting river channels.

Barges that didn't get stuck waited longer to get through, and this waiting raised the cost of leasing or operating that barge. That increased the cost of each bushel on board. Newly loaded barges had to be filled well below capacity so they could float down the shallower river. That inefficiency added to the cost of each bushel for the foreign buyer.

As the drought gained momentum, the Great Lakes too began to drop. Lake Michigan, which had hit its highest levels in a hundred years during the winter of 1987, started falling farther and faster than it had since Europeans first arrived in the area to keep records. That in turn formed the background for a rather strange plan by Governor Jim Thompson of Illinois. It was his idea to try and refloat those stranded barges. He called a press conference in which he offered to divert more water out of Lake Michigan, and into the Chicago River. Billions of gallons of additional fresh water would flow from the Chicago River,

through the Sanitary and Ship Canal, into the Illinois
River, and thence on down the Mississippi.

Other, cooler heads calculated that this grand gesture to the barge owners might raise levels on the
lower Mississippi by all of six inches. I suppose Mr.
Thompson knew perfectly well that there wasn't the
slightest chance of his gesture being fulfilled, since it
takes an edict by the U.S. Supreme Court and agreement among all states bordering the Great Lakes to
alter the water flow at Chicago.

Among those cooler heads were all of the other gover-
nors of all the Great Lakes states. They all went on
record with an emphatic no, and the country was
spared the spectre of hundreds of billions of precious
gallons flowing down Illinois rivers and canals,
evaporating into the parched air, and passing within
miles of communities whose shallow wells were drying
up only to see if we couldn't raise a few barges owned
by corporate giants and push our dwindling food supplies out of the country a little bit faster. (There's an
awful lot to be said for all those little checks and
balances.)

Demand for grain was being eliminated in ways
other than stalled river traffic and price rationing at
the Chicago Board of Trade. Cattle producers in the
western Corn Belt had animals that were ready to
move off parched pasture lands, and into feedlots to
eat corn and soybean meal. That's when they make
their final and most rapid weight gains, the last
several weeks before slaughter. As cattlemen
reworked their feeding cost numbers, many realized
that the skyrocketing price of corn would wipe out
their profit margins and put them well into the red if
the animals were put through the much more expensive feedlot process that June and July.

Cattle were therefore slaughtered ahead of schedule
to cut losses. Plans for herd expansion later in the year
were shelved too because the profits weren't likely to

be there on down the road. That left the cattle producer in the ironic position of watching his prices drop hard and fast due to distress slaughtering of cattle as the price of other crops, such as corn, skyrocketed. As more and more cattle poured into the nation's slaughter-houses, prices fell even faster. It meant fewer animals would be around eating up corn and soymeal come fall and winter.

This loss of demand gripped the soybean market first. It was badly overextended by the time it reached $11 on June 23, and it started to slide from there despite the fact that the drought continued in full force into that first week of July. The corn market had more staying power in part because it was not as overex-tended, and in part because the drought was by then doing some irreversible damage to corn yields. (Bean yields can still bounce back in late July–early August.)

Along about the second week of July, the dry pattern started to break up just a bit. Although the July rains still fell far short of normal, and temperatures remained very high into early August, the increased precipitation rescued many a soybean field and prevented the corn crop from being a total loss. The combination of lost demand, slightly improving yields, and the fact that the markets were by then loaded with long speculators brought on a total collapse in price, a crash that compared with the biggest price breaks in U.S. crop history.

Soybean prices fell from their peak of $11.00, to about $7.40 by the first of August. They staged a rally of nearly $2.00 from there, but by mid-October they were right back down near $7.40. On the way down, corn was the more restrained one as usual. It eventual-ly fell to about $2.50, but it took until the end of November to do so.

Market analysts, brokers, and farmers started to sift through the fundamentals trying to explain the crash and project the odds of a bounce. It was clear by fall that the "rationing" effects of the rally on demand had been stunning, and nowhere was this more clear than from a look at soybean numbers.

The total U.S. soybean supply for the coming year fell to about 1.775 billion bushels—stocks plus production. That total falls far short of the more than 2.0 billion bushels that were used in each of the previous two crop years. If we add the fact that the system needs to end the year with at least 150 million bushels in the "pipeline" just to keep the system functional, it means the world should have been over 400 million bushels short of its needs in 1988–89—about 20 percent short.

Yet after a rally of only about five weeks, demand had been slashed to such an extent that prices fell all the way back near their pre-drought levels, and they stayed there for months on end. That usage was gone, gone, gone. It had taken a shocking increase in price, but supply and demand had been rebalanced. The drought of 1988 demonstrated for good what a two-edged sword any great price rally can be.

The loss of demand reflected more than just an exercise in the elasticity of demand in a rising market. It also showed how tough the competition had become. There was a great big farm exporting world out there to which the food importer could turn. Part of its size and flexibility was a legacy of all those years when the United States had pulled its supplies off the world market, and handed market share and billions of dollars in profits to their competitors.

This time around, the USDA tried to preserve demand. During the height of the drought, it released its huge stocks of corn and even its relatively scarce stocks of soybeans at an accelerated rate. It made it clear that this was to preserve domestic herds and export business. It also made it clear that government corn from past crops was still in ample supply (still true enough), and that it would be made readily available to the market throughout the upcoming crop year.

The USDA had learned its lesson from the drought/PIK rally of 1983 when it hanged onto its record supplies while the market raced higher, and demand evaporated. Still, I must admit to feeling queasy as I listened to announcements of aggressive steps to preserve markets. There we were in the midst of what was probably the worst one-year drought in American history. The USDA had eliminated just about all of the surplus in soybeans and a big chunk of the surplus in wheat. It chose 1988, the worst one-year drought in history, as the time to finally wise up and start dumping grain on the market to preserve demand.

It was perhaps the riskiest food decision since 1946–47 when the United States decided to keep pumping out the postwar food aid, despite the fact that it drew U.S. stocks down to dangerously low levels. This time the effort was to preserve market share and domestic livestock, something it should have considered over the previous ten years. My nervousness came from thinking about the almost eerily bad timing that has always plagued farm policy.

If the dryness of June had lasted into mid-August, it would have been a much different story. We would have been dumping grain and soybeans in June and July that the country would need badly before another crop could be harvested in the fall of 1989. But some rain did fall. Yields did struggle a bit higher from the expectations of June. Combined with the loss of demand, supplies turned out to be adequate. Apparently the gamble paid off, and here we are.

Now that the dust has settled on another great drought, and the volatility has been squeezed out of prices for a bit, where do we stand? What's the bottom line of our story?

The American agricultural and economic giant of the 1940s, 1950s, and 1960s created and controlled

markets and seriously thought it could control prices
as well. By the late 1980s, however, it has been pretty
much reduced to just "one among many." Expansion
and modernization of farms, processing plants, and
port facilities in Brazil, Malaysia, Western Europe,
Australia, and Argentina is a finished work that will
not go away. The world's customers were thoroughly
trained over the years to find other sources when the
United States withdrew or voluntarily priced itself out
of the market.

Yet that doesn't bring us to the heart of the matter
nor does it identify what it is that keeps the United
States out of step. Not even a grasp of the century-old
farm populist rhetoric will satisfy this dilemma. Why
is the United States so absurdly mistake-prone in its
farm policies while others are not?

I think it boils down to this: we don't seem able to see
ourselves for what we are. Many other countries know
themselves and act accordingly. They look sensibly at
their strengths and weaknesses and then proceed from
there.

Brazil and Argentina see themselves as the debtors
and low-cost producers that they are. They therefore
aim to produce, process, and export as much as possible to earn capital needed for investment and the
occasional interest payment. This makes sense.
Western Europe (the EC-12) correctly sees itself as a
high-cost producer that has experienced widespread
starvation twice in the twentieth century. They desire
a high degree of self-sufficiency, and they know this
will cost money in a low-priced agricultural world
dominated by the United States and other low-cost
producers. They've spent a lot, but they have largely
erased their competitive disadvantages.

Australia and Canada are longtime players, old
hands who can produce a limited number of products
(mainly wheat) in a more hostile climate than that of
the United States. They both aim to produce and

market as much of these basic crops as they can without injecting volatility. The modest and consistent subsidies these countries employ have helped them to boost production and exports by directing the money to the farmer. Income, not debt.

What is it that we see in ourselves? We see ourselves as a farm exporter, but also as the lynchpin of NATO. We can compete, but only with kid gloves lest we offend the tender sensibilities of our allies. They suffer no such qualms. We understand the need for farm subsidies, but America is the land of rugged individualism and free markets. Subsidies therefore have to be masked as financial arrangements. The free market has to be "helped along" with elaborate interventionist schemes. It's embarassing, and it's these sorts of conflicts that have put the United States into its decline across the spectrum.

Maybe this makes the drought and the vulnerability that it has exposed a potential "blessing in disguise." In 1988–89, the United States lost only about 10 percent of its business in corn, the biggest and most valuable of its crops. In large part this is because the USDA simply didn't have time to eliminate the corn surplus, as it had the one in beans where we lost 20–25 percent.

These days you clearly need to light a bomb to get the attention of the American public and Congress. Maybe the drought was the bomb needed by farm policy. If the drought can kindle interest among those outside the same tired circles, that can only be to the good. If a drought can make the reality of this tougher world manifest itself sooner, we will be better off in the end, having suffered through it and survived to learn from our mistakes. But if we still don't learn, if we remain unable to get a grip on our food policy, then we deserve the results.

17

SO WHERE ARE WE HEADED FROM HERE?

What's next? What is to become of American agriculture? It's always risky to try and look into the future, but this is an important question and one that we can in large part answer.

If the story of farm policy teaches us anything, it teaches us that powerful, frightening trends are underway. Most have been around a long time. They are straightforward, relentless, and fairly easy to observe and measure. It is the outcome of these great trends that we need to project.

I think it's safe to assume that these profound forces are in no danger of a sudden death. Powerful trends that have been underway for decades aren't likely to stop dead in their tracks just because we're approaching the end of this book.

By following the bigger trends, we can see fairly large patches of the road ahead. Not much of what we can see is reassuring.

The Family Farmer

Arguably the most important of the big trends involve the decline in farm population and the number of American farms. These numbers refer to people, and they involve a important element of our society.

History is clear enough on this score. Farm population has been declining with only the briefest of interruptions since 1916, and the same has been true of the number of farms since 1920.

The years since 1981 have demonstrated that both of these ancient trends are very much alive, and still briskly headed lower. In 1987 the number of people living on farms in the United States dipped below 5 million to 4.986 million—probably the first time that it's been that low since the first decade of the 1800s!

Even at these very low levels, the trend is by no means simply inching downward. In the six years after 1981 alone, the farm population registered a whopping decline of about 15 percent. By 1987 it amounted to only 2.0 percent of the total U.S. population.

As low as that figure is, we can legitimately predict that it will fall even lower still. Less than one week after the 1988 national election, the Farmers Home Administration (FmHA) sent notices to 83,000 farmers telling them they faced foreclosure of their farms if they failed to take steps "soon" to pay off or refinance their low-interest subsidized loans. Since four out of five of them hadn't made a payment on those loans in at least three years at the time of the notice, the outcome for a majority seems pretty clear.

If in fact each of those farms is to be foreclosed, and if each one of them shelters the 3.28 persons that the Census Bureau tells us are in the average farm family today, these notices represent over 272,000 people.

Their loss alone would lop another 5 1/2 percent off the already tiny farm population that remained in 1987. This alone would take the farm population down to less than 1.9% of the total U.S. population.

Consider too that the average American farmer is far older than the average American—nearly thirty-eight years old versus only thirty-two for non-farmers. That's a huge demographic spread. Farmers also retire at an earlier age than those in the general population because of the physical nature of the work, so attrition is about to accelerate dramatically regardless of economic conditions or drought.

Who do you suppose will take over the land? Large young families who are interested in getting into farming, and who just happen to have the nearly $1 million in start-up capital needed for a new farm that will be big enough to be "competitive"? I think not.

As farmers retire, their farms will be absorbed by larger and wealthier farmers and family farm corporations with the money to finance multimillion-dollar expansion. Or perhaps they will be added to existing farms owned by financial institutions, a process that accelerated in the 1970s and 1980s. Maybe they will simply be left to non-farm children or relatives living in places like Chicago and Manhattan.

That last one sounds a little better, but it isn't. Farm programs make cash and commodity payments to the owner. Why should the taxpayer pay to support the holdings of persons of inherited wealth who do not work the land? By improving the ability of an absentee owner to acquire and carry investment property and inherited wealth, it moves land ownership more and more out of the reach of the poorer tenant who does the work. It also locks land ownership and the whole business of farming forever out of the reach of any non-farm families that might want to get into this fine bedrock business, and raise one of those decent farm families that everybody seems to like so much.

There are plenty of other small and midsize variables that have contributed to the downtrend, and the evidence tells us that most of them are also still alive and well, and likely to contribute to still more downward momentum.

Then there is the composition of the farm population numbers. Small as they are, they are all statistically inflated. Official Census Bureau farm numbers include as a farm anything that produces and sells over $1,000 worth of farm goods each year. Throw out the very small and very part-time farm operations, and you'll find that the full-time farm population has already dropped far below the official 2.0 percent of the U.S. population, whether or not there are any more foreclosures, and whether or not any older farmers die.

So just how small is the number of "real" farmers? Is it 1.8 percent of the total population? 1.6 percent? 1.4 percent? The only problem is where to draw the line. I think we can safely say that the majority of the food produced and consumed in America comes from farms owned by less than 1 percent of the population.

And so what's wrong with that, some of you may be asking? (Few, I hope.) Since ancient times and throughout the world, history has repeatedly told us that the extreme concentration of land and food production is a key element in the loss of freedom and prosperity among the majority of the people.

Rome began its great history not as the despotic imperial system with which we often associate it, but as a functional republic. One of the underpinnings of the Roman government was its large class of landowning farmer/soldiers. They gave early Rome its muscle and its deeply practical culture.

As the Republic expanded around 200 B.C., advanced farming methods were imported from Greece and Carthage, followed by vast numbers of slaves imported from newly conquered territories. This enabled wealthier landowners to rapidly expand their farms into

great estates which it was now possible to man with
the huge new slave population. The dispossessed small
farmer class trekked to the city where it became the
backbone of the mob of malcontents that plagued
Rome's government for centuries. This added dramatically to the gradual disintegration of the Republic and
its replacement with Imperial Rome. Substitute slaves
for technology, and our farm story is effectively the
same.

The USSR is another good case in point. Farm assets
were heavily concentrated even in the days of the
Tsars. Then it was in the hands of the aristocracy, but
there was also a large landowning peasant class. The
agricultural system did nothing to foster individual
freedoms, but it was dispersed enough to be productive, and Russia was the world's largest exporter of
food from the late eighteenth through the early twentieth centuries.

After the revolution, the state started to covet ownership of the land. Stalin finally accomplished almost
total state ownership with his collectivization moves
in the 1930s. It was this process that removed the
USSR from the ranks of exporting countries. It has
ironically turned the great wheat exporter of history
into the world's largest wheat importer. As was the
case with Rome, this hasn't weakened the military
power of the USSR, but it has depleted its treasury
and impoverished the culture. As Gorbachev tries to
restructure the Soviet Union, he must constantly
return to the moribund state of affairs in agriculture.
It is the engine of the Soviet economy, employing up to
a third of its population, and the car won't start
without it.

Britain is still another example. The concentration of
farm assets locked it into a rigid class system that has
proved to be a drain on the British people now that
their empire is gone. The process began in earnest
with enclosure—the purchase and exclusive use of

former common lands by rich farmers and the aristocracy. Enclosure began in the 1500s, but gathered steam in the 1600s and 1700s.

Much of the formerly stable population was forced to migrate into the growing industrial towns and cities of England, which were headed for an Industrial Revolution, and they experienced a life of grinding poverty. A sad end for the descendants of the proud English yeomen.

The specifics are very different, but in every case the separation of the common man from the land ownership and food production was a critical element in the loss of shared prosperity and individual freedoms. All three of our examples continued to have fine *systems* of equal justice for all after the common man lost the land, but in practice justice often eluded him. Freedom is a very fragile thing; it needs to be planted in something that will sustain it. Land ownership among the many is a major prop that helps a free nation to maintain its foundation and integrity.

In the case of the United States, the 98–99 percent of the population who do not produce food, are far too dependent on the tiny minority who do. This is in direct conflict with the original farm policies that attempted to spread and maintain land ownership as widely as possible, policies in which the people of the United States have already invested enormous sums of public money.

Right now the dependency of the majority seems fairly benign, but any significant dependency will darken with time.

The Farm Itself

As the number of American farms declines, the average size of an American farm is growing. Since 1920, the total number of farms has fallen from over 6.5 million, to under 2.2 million. Over that same stretch of time, the average size of a farm has risen from less than 150 acres, to nearly 450 acres.

To some, this may sound like wonderful progress, and it did seem that way for a long time. One doesn't need to look too deep, however, before some gaping flaws appear.

For starters we need to remember how misleading that number is. It includes anything that produces and sells over $1,000 worth of farm produce each year. If we again throw out the very small and very part-time "farms" that inflate all of the basic numbers, we see that the size of an average farm in the United States is also understated.

The average size of the commercial farms run by full-time farmers that produce the vast majority of the country's food are more like one thousand acres in size. Since the 1960s at least, the average size in the category of "real" farms grew much faster than the official average that included farmettes. So what's wrong with bigger and bigger farms? Usually quite a lot.

Did the farm get big by gradually combining a series of smaller farms, and then obliterating every pond, marsh, and tree row that stood in between? Most did.

Did it buy the most powerful equipment as it grew—huge new tractors that were only efficient if the farmer plowed and planted in straight lines, right up the side of the hill, instead of contouring around it to hold the soil in place? Saving fuel and planting more acres in a day is a pillar of the religion of farm productivity. Taken to its logical extreme, saving fuel justifies an almost unlimited abuse of the land and its vegetation over the short term. For that reason alone, the creation of larger farms will always tend to increase the rate of soil erosion.

Yet it appears that the amount of land one man can plant and harvest has finally peaked. Farmers have started backing off from the very biggest tractors and planters. At some point, the weight of the machinery packs down the soil so much that it prohibits the emergence of seedlings. So the trend has exhausted itself, right?

No. Variables other than bigger machinery have made farms too big. Each farmer has been and is in an all-out competitive sprint. In the past, fellow family farmers raced each other, but now the largest corporate farms compete with each other, with the Western Europeans, and with the vast palm oil plantations of Malaysia. Unless we interrupt this process with new policy, bigger farms will remain the best way for Americans to stay in the sprint. Already the trend has simply reorganized itself. Farms are now getting bigger under the banner of large corporate entities with hired managers and lots of hired hands. There's no upside limit to this potential.

There are plenty of illustrations. A good one lies in Newton County, Indiana, about seventy-five miles southeast of downtown Chicago. In that particular county in the heart of the Corn Belt, Prudential Insurance is the biggest "farmer." It owns more than 26,000 acres (40.6 square miles) on which it grows corn, soybeans, and winter wheat, all very fine things, and I suspect that they're being grown as "efficiently" as a huge financial corporation can manage.

In order to efficiently increase this particular farm's yields (and therefore profit per acre), Prudential has at least 207 deep wells capable of feeding huge commercial pumps that can irrigate most of those 26,000 acres at the same time. They can irrigate them around the clock as well if they so choose, and in the past that is just what they have done.

Many of the thousands of people who live on the periphery of this huge corporate estate have claimed for years that irrigation has frequently resulted in sharp drops in the surrounding water table. During summer growing months, water tables have dropped as much as seven to twelve feet over a single weekend.

Water tables don't stop at the property line, and this pumping has quite literally deprived neighboring people of accessible and drinkable water. It has deprived them by draining and harming the water supply that is under their own land. A lower water table can leave the water that remains in a shallow well too full of sulfur and iron for human consumption. In some cases wells have simply dried up. (Big farmers who have been accused of draining local water tables traditionally fall back on the position that non-farmers ought to simply dig deeper wells. Ordinary citizens apparently are expected to participate in the competitive world farm sprint too.)

Newton county agrees that there's a connection to the activities of the Prudential farm, and it has ordered those 207 wells capped, but there may be more wells than the 207 that are registered. There is also no strict ongoing procedure to ensure compliance, even for those wells that have been identified by the county. This large farm, like most large farms that irrigate, is a bad neighbor indeed.

The bigger and better capitalized a farm, the greater its ability to introduce and concentrate a monstrous level of technology into a local area, if it so desires. If it isn't even owned by local citizens, the urge to use its muscle to run amok in search of higher yields can be irresistible.

It takes an even larger and more determined power like the federal government to restrain wrongdoing on such a scale. Historically, the federal government and farm policy has instead played the role of collaborator.

The Topsoil

This leads us to another great trend. The country's storehouse of fertile topsoil is eroding at a rate far exceeding nature's ability to replace it. This process has been a component of American agriculture since

Europeans first started settling and planting in New England and the mid-Atlantic states.

For instance there were subtle, but critical details to which the first farmers failed to adjust. Rainfall in England had come in smaller, steadier amounts than it did in *New* England. In the British Isles, the raindrops themselves were actually smaller in size on the average, the volume of rainfall tended to be spread out, and so it packed less force when it struck unprotected soil. Multiply that micro force times the millions of drops that fall on each acre with each storm, and you get a glimpse of the effects of water erosion.

Soon the imported farming practices that had easily protected soil during the gentle rains of the British Isles were overwhelmed by nature in the New World. Erosion wasted the farm landscape in New England, but at that time land was cheap and plentiful. A farmer that got eroded out, just pushed west or south.

Farming in the South soon fell into a more sophisticated version of "slash and burn." Continuous cotton production not only depletes the soil, it generates rapid erosion, especially when it isn't rotated with crops like hay or oats that are better able to hold down the soil.

By 1800, however, cotton was the biggest cash crop in America by far. Many cotton farmers therefore made the economic decision to push the land to its limit, in search of the cash flow that "King Cotton" produced. In the process, millions of acres in the South were stripped of their topsoil, gullied by deep erosion, and rendered useless. Like the early Yankee farmer, cotton producers simply moved on.

Topsoil erosion seemed less of a problem out on the prairies of the Midwest and Great Plains as they were being gradually settled in the mid-1800s. The land tended to be flatter, the topsoil was deeper, and farming practices on smaller family farms were gentler than those practiced on the larger plantations made possible by slavery in the South.

Whatever the rate of erosion in the nineteenth century, it certainly accelerated after the World War I price shock stimulated plantings. Farming expanded onto steeper hills, thinner topsoils, and the semiarid western fringes of the Grain Belt. Farms got slightly bigger as farm animals were replaced by more productive tractors. Fields got bigger too, and bigger fields are more vulnerable to wind erosion.

The devastating culmination of the World War I expansion came during the Dust Bowl droughts of the 1930s when all of the newly exposed land was subjected to the worst series of droughts in generations. The wind erosion that followed could lift millions of tons of exposed topsoil into the air in single great storm clouds, and the country lost millions more arable acres.

Federal conservation measures that were formalized in the 1940s and 1950s probably slowed the rate of erosion on a national basis, but most agree that it still exceeded the replacement rate on average. By the late 1960s the rate of erosion had taken off again nationally as larger equipment invaded land that had been idled by USDA set-aside programs, and ran more roughly over much of the rest.

In 1982 the USDA made its most recent inventory of the nation's land resources. Cultivated cropland totaled 376.5 million acres, and the average loss of topsoil per acre was put at 8.1 tons per year! That's 8.1 *tons* per acre. Topsoil can replenish itself, but only at a rate of 1–5 tons per acre per year.

In the Midwestern breadbasket alone more than 109 million acres, some 47 percent of all cropland, was considered inadequately protected. This is the same cropland that was called on to "feed the world" in 1917, 1945–47, and again in 1973. There's not much doubt in my mind that these acres will be needed to do the same thing again someday. But will the soil that covers those acres still be there?

The Water

The availability and quality of groundwater (meaning underground) probably needs to rank as our top water priority, but this an area that is tough to measure. There are plenty of other water-related numbers that are nearly as important and troubling, however.

For one, the mighty Mississippi dropped by more than 22 feet below normal in spots at the peak of the 1988 drought. This is not a book about the drought of 1988, but it's worth pointing out that this was not an entirely isolated event. Studies show that the average levels of the river had been gradually dropping over the previous ten years as well!

The Mississippi is not just another river. In concert with its tributaries, it is a watershed for some 1,231,000 square miles in the center of the North American continent, including the cropland that produces some 90 percent of the nation's corn and soybeans. If the dropping levels of this river reflect a long-term trend toward drier weather over that entire watershed, it's a huge problem for the country.

The other really big water system in the center of North America is of course the Great Lakes, the largest reservoir of fresh water on the earth's surface. In the winter of 1986–87, Lake Michigan reached its highest recorded level in over a hundred years. During the winter storms of that year, waves were actually pounding at the base of some high-rise apartment buildings along the northern shoreline of the city.

However, as soon as the city noticed the high water, the trend turned. I remember a friend saying at the time that it seemed like nature was just topping off the water supply before a long dry spell began. Sure enough. A task force formed to study the problem, and

the lake's level began to drop. It proceeded to drop at
the fastest rate ever recorded over the following
eighteen-month period, a total of some three feet. It's
still at those lows, and to me this also has the earmarks of a trend.

I'm not sure that we need to force these events into a
specific conclusion, except for one. We know that we're
damaging and depleting our groundwater. This is obviously a grave mistake, even if Chicago were up to its
ankles in lake water. If lower lake and river levels tell
us climate is getting drier in the central United States,
we hardly need to be busily polluting what's left with
farm chemicals.

And what about that pollution? Half the shallow
wells in the state of Iowa are now tainted by residue
from pesticides. Traces of certain banned pesticides
have remained in wells tested six years after their use
was halted. The Environmental Protection Agency
claims pesticides have fouled groundwater on which
half the population of the United States depends for its
primary source of drinking water.

Other areas of the farm economy besides grain and
soybean farmers are to blame. Vegetables and fruit
come to us bathed in chemicals known to cause things
like birth defects and cancer. Each year the states
report that more groundwater has become tainted
with residue from agricultural chemicals, and that
where levels have been reported in the past, they are
increasing.

Time studies of chemicals in groundwater in major
agricultural areas also tend to show that chemicals
percolate down from one layer of the groundwater
supply to the next, just as plain logic would make we
non-experts assume. Each year more agricultural
chemicals appear in groundwater, they appear in
greater concentrations, and they appear over an ever
wider area.

I don't think there's much more that needs to be said

about the water pollution, except this: farm chemicals also seem to be building up in another natural resource. Studies show that most Americans have built up residue from a number of farm pesticides within their own bodies. These levels too seem to be growing in concentration, in the number of chemicals involved, and in the number of individuals affected.

Most of us have heard plenty about chemicals and pesticides in our food, so ignorance is probably not the deciding factor. I'm not sure why we have allowed this disgraceful activity to start and continue. Maybe we should mull over the fact that for most of the past 120 years, the American farm economy has produced more food than it could use or sell. Why we thought it necessary to poison the water (and the soil) for the past forty years to boost yields while we struggled to curb overproduction, is beyond me.

Maybe some small part of the public's acceptance of farm chemicals is based on sympathy with the mythological family farmer as he struggles to get by. If it is, let's knock out that misconception. The bulk of the chemical bath we all experience comes courtesy of farms owned by well-capitalized corporations and a tiny class of landowning and relatively wealthy farm families.

Land Values

The value of good farmland tripled and quadrupled during the 1970s. After its peak in 1980, however, prices plummeted. This proved to be the final straw for many a farm debt portfolio that was secured only by the rising value by the land.

Between 1981 and 1986 the value of all farmland in the entire Corn Belt (the USDA officially includes Ohio, Indiana, Illinois, Iowa, and Missouri in this category), dropped by an astonishing 52 percent! Try to imagine the value of your house dropping by 52 percent. That drop incidentally was about equal to the drop that took place from 1916 until 1933.

Prices for good farmland began to firm in 1987, and in 1988 the best soil in the Midwest vaulted higher with one-year gains of over 20 percent being reported in some farm counties. That's good, right? Perhaps, but I'd like to point out that there are considerable clouds inside this silver lining.

1. On the way down, land values knocked the props out from under the younger farmer, along with giant speculators like John Block. As it did, land very much tended to move out of the hands of remaining small and midsize farmers, and into the hands of bigger and wealthier farmers and corporations.

This is all water under the bridge, but what happens if land surges in value from now on? It locks land ownership even more securely into the hands of the relatively rich and few who bought out those that went under.

Every time these increasingly concentrated farm assets appreciate in value, it takes them further and further out of the reach of would-be farm families of average means. If this were to continue it would firmly lock ownership into the hands of that 1–2 percent.

2. On the other hand, the rising prices may be a fluke. The first jump in price, like all quick bounces in a big downtrend, is sometimes a red herring. Much of the bounce was backed by pure land speculation such as the mini-syndicates that bring together a bankrupt farmer with a small group of lawyer and doctor type investors who buy the land for a speculative investment and then "hire" the farmer as a tenant to work the land.

Land speculations historically have a checkered record. Having sucked in more "weak longs," prices might well end up taking out the lows of 1986–87. This is a problem.

Weather

Long-range weather is a topic that needs to be handled with care. Theories tend to get wildly unscientific at the drop of a hat, but it's also a subject that can't be ignored.

The hottest theories today seem to revolve around the concepts of a global warming trend, a greenhouse effect, and sunspot activity cycles. They all basically imply that the earth's atmospheric temperatures are rising, and that this will result in hotter and drier weather in North America, perhaps into the middle of the next century. This is still very much subject to debate, but there's a large body of evidence to suggest that 1988 was the warmest year of the century, on average, worldwide.

Even if we err on the side of conservatism, however, and leave the long-range projections aside, some plainly observable weather developments are cause for concern. There is, for example, the severe drought pattern of the 1980s. The years 1980, 1983, and 1988 each saw a major drought that hit the nation's food-producing solar plexus. Each one came with increasing severity, and each affected a wider area than the one before it.

There is no precedent for a triple and worsening drought pattern with three- to five-year spacings in this century, and so we really ought to think of this too as a potential trend.

If it is, and if the breadbasket, the granary of the world, is hit with still another drought that's comparable in severity to either of the last two (or worse, as the pattern suggests), then the country has made its long series of blunders at the worst possible time. It has begun to deplete water tables and aquifers, and it has encouraged large-scale farming methods that are perfectly designed to speed the process of wind erosion under very dry conditions. (The 1982 erosion survey didn't even include the last two droughts.)

If, on top of these plain facts, those who are predicting the greenhouse effect are correct in saying that the earth's atmosphere is warming, or if sunspot theorists are correct in saying that activity will peak in the years 1990–92, and if all of this does in fact point to warmer and drier weather in central North America, then all of the already alarming trends—the soil erosion, water depletion, farm foreclosure, and loss of rural population—could accelerate from dangerous, to truly spectacular proportions.

I'd like to say that there are some other trends that we can throw into the mix that compare in scale with these and which point out some bright spots ahead. In all honesty, though, I can't think of one.

18

REGAINING GROUND

In 1990 the time will come again for Congress to revise farm policy and reset the course of American agriculture for the next four to five years.

As you know, we've been here before. We've come to farm bill time in a state of wartime emergency, in a state of (price) shock, in times of glut, and even with a broad national consensus that the farm economy was broken and in need of being fixed. Each time, however, there was a common danger, those structural flaws, running through the farm policy process and in the end outweighing all other influences.

Time and again, and against some pretty steep odds I might add, the old ways have hung on. Farm policy has spent sixty years on a quixotic quest for the magic formula that would expunge the evils of low prices and torture the market into delivering that fair and just price.

The worst of the New Deal and populist dogma has been enshrined, and to it is now being added the worst aspect of the dogma of the Reagan Era, the notion that those few family farmers who remain in this mean race should now be left alone to run even faster against the competition of giant corporate farms and the more intelligently subsidized competition abroad.

On the face of it, it's hard to imagine that 1989 will be any different. There is nothing on the table to stop the chemical downpour from entering our drinking water. Nothing on the table will come even close to getting the national erosion rate back under the rate of replacement. Nothing will reverse or slow the evaporating farm population, stop the depletion of groundwater, or recapture lost export market share.

At best, the signals indicate glacial movement in the direction of restricted chemical use and a vague desire to wean the farm economy off all subsidies.

Great. Now that the farm population has been hacked down to only 1–2 percent of the U.S. population, and nobody but the very wealthy have any hope of gaining access to a life that's supposed to form part of the bedrock of American society, we just give up and abandon the few bits that are left to concentrate themselves further into the hands of giant corporations and a hereditary, landed aristocracy. Good plan.

I'll tell you what *I* think. It is time to make the big move and clean house. I know I said that there didn't seem to be any reason for hope in the early stages of this latest farm policy debate, but the farm policy establishment is not where we should look for hope. If we've learned anything from our story, it's that changes will probably never come from within.

In a perverse sort of way, the source of hope may be found in the sheer magnitude of the mess. Surely, all one needs to do is flick on the lights. How could the mess ever defend itself? For me, that's reason enough to feel hope.

During the Third Battle of the Marne in 1918, Ferdinand Foch sent an inspiring message back to the Allied High Command: "My center is giving way. My right is pushed back. Situation excellent. I am attacking!" Foch knew that no matter how bleak circumstances appeared on the surface, the enemy had done its worst damage. Victory was at his fingertips. The exhausted German armies would collapse around him if only he attacked. For my money, the farm policies of the United States are in the same boat as the German armies were that day in 1918. Farm policy might just be a wide open door, ripe for the old Ferdinand Foch reversal.

I said at the start that no area of national policy has the same kind of power for good or ill as does farm policy. So far this book has concentrated almost entirely on the ill because that's what needs to be exposed. But I'd like to clarify my intentions. In no way do I limit farm policy's potential for good to just the stopping of its bad practices. I think that this powerful tool's potential for good is very nearly equal to the potential for bad that I've spent the bulk of my time describing. I think we can do better than to simply stop losing ground. We can reverse many of these trends.

Farm policy touches hundreds of millions of acres and more than a thousand small towns. It can actually help in the restoration of both. It can make those towns start to grow and prosper; it can attract families who will not have to peddle themselves to some foreign manufacturer in the hope of getting it to build a factory there.

Farm policy can give an enormous shot in the arm to things like reforestation, which we not only need to stabilize soil, but which can preserve moisture needed by the rest of society and provide wood that may be needed for the homes of our grandchildren. Farm policy has the potential to start reassembling that critical, but lost part of the American bedrock, the family farmers. It can even be a way to house and sustain many of the homeless.

Situation excellent!

Step One has to be to make sure we're thinking straight. Many have charged into this swamp in the past, and got lost. We need a compass, some rules of the road, and a clear head. We need to have a firm grip on some basic assumptions. Such as:

1. Most programs on the agricultural policy menu are and have been ruinous, particularly the loan and acreage set-asides. Most programs should be thrown out with no debate.

2. The authors of those policies—the farm lobby, Agriculture Committees of the House and Senate, and the USDA—have lost their franchise. This policy huddle has produced fruit poisonous to the farmer, the environment, the nation, and its resources. This power structure is every bit as misguided and inbred as the ones that have ruled China and the USSR for the past generation. It's just been lucky enough to exist within the context of a richer, freer society. Given the past results and the propensity for bizarre timing, even the most serious-sounding policy reforms must be viewed with the utmost suspicion, if they come from the inside.

3. Farmers are not even remotely alike anymore. Even Midwestern grain farmers vary enormously. They range from corporations like Prudential Insurance, to the poor farmers near Waterloo, Iowa, who needed the proceeds of a food drive to get through the winter of 1988–89. In between are a block of medium-size farms operated by men and women who may still fit the mold visually, but who are in fact very wealthy individuals who may do only three months of concentrated farm work each year. We need to keep this reality firmly in mind whenever

farm rhetoric starts whizzing through the air. Which group are we trying to protect, subsidize, expand in number, etc.?

4. Modern American agriculture as it stands today is a positive force only because it produces food. Its side effects all tend to be devastating. For decades agriculture has assaulted the American environment on a scale that is unmatched by any other industry, and we can only assume that it will do more of the same if it is left to its own devices.

5. Non-farm taxpayers have both the responsibility and right to be directly involved in the formation of agricultural policy. It was the lack of informed input from outside that made possible many of the disasters of the past.

This "right" does not depend merely on either morality or the public good. Scores of billions of dollars have already been paid to the holders of farm assets. There is a debt owed. Taxpayers already own the right to make certain very specific demands. Farm policy is a social contract of great importance, and it ought to be treated like one.

6. Higher prices do more harm than good. They encourage heavy borrowing and are a burden on the lower third of society as well as the welfare system. Lower prices in a free market bring enormous dividends on every front.

Assumptions are all very well and good, but they're just the first step. Where do we head with them? What's the goal? What exactly do we want farm policy, this powerful force for good, to accomplish in America?

Good questions, and they can only be answered with a set of goals that are as clear and tough as our assumptions. These goals need to be very specific, and plainly in the best interest of the nation as a whole. They need to be very ambitious, and above all *measurable*. If they aren't all these things, we'll just end up lost in the same old swamp.

Here are my basic goals for the nation's farm policy:

1. To produce a surplus of grain and oilseeds
(soybeans). This surplus should be continually available to the free market at free-market prices. Sounds
obvious enough, but over the past sixty years these
two elements have rarely, if ever, been put fully into
play at the same time by farm policy.

2. To reduce the average rate of topsoil erosion in
every farming county to below the rate of natural soil
replacement. It has to happen eventually, or we'll
run out of soil.

3. To eliminate all further pollution of U.S.
groundwater with nonbiodegradable agricultural
chemicals. Even if this happens, the chemical
residue that is already in play will work its way into
untainted groundwater. The situation will certainly
get worse before it gets better. How much worse is
the only question.

4. To reverse the sixty-eight year downtrend in the
number of American farms. More to the point, to
create one million new small farms which are in-
dividually owner-operated. Small farms, in and of
themselves, have a far more desirable impact en-
vironmentally and socially than do large farms
worked by hired hands and tenants. This is
Americana 101.

5. To reverse the seventy-three year downtrend in
the nation's full-time farm population—specifically,
to more than double the present population of less
than five million, to at least ten million. This would
still be only 4 percent of the total U.S. population.

This does not mean including more tenant farmers
or adding migrant workers to the census numbers.
Nor does it mean adding farms that produce less
than the minuscule $1,000 of produce per year that
the Census Bureau currently uses as its cutoff. It

means adding to the farm population more than five million individuals who are part of families sustaining themselves by tilling land that they own.

6. To discourage the creation of more large farms and the expansion of existing ones. Extreme concentration of farming assets has occurred in virtually every large society throughout history. It has always been a destructive process in the end.

In no way should we interfere with the property rights of large landowners. Instead, the goal should be to design policy so that it increases the competitive position of the businesses that are most desirable, the smaller farms, over those that are least desirable, the very large farms.

7. To generate a vast increase in the sheer mass of vegetation in the center of the North American continent. Today it probably stands at its lowest ebb since recovery from the last Ice Age. Vegetative mass reduces erosion rates and helps wetlands to do their job. Its residue helps create new soil.

If billions more trees are planted as a result of farm policy, it could be the lumber that various locations need for housing in fifty years. It can shelter more wildlife, help to cool surface temperatures, and perhaps even influence local precipitation.

There you are: specific, ambitious, and measurable goals. Furthermore, they are plainly in the best interest of us all. They are even in the best interest of the present farm population.

Of course even the strongest set of goals still isn't enough. With any set of objectives comes the need for means to implement them. Step Three therefore should be the policy initiatives needed to make up a new agricultural policy for the United States.

The following plan is hard to judge on individual points. It should be judged in its entirety, and I firmly believe that it will take the entirety to give us a chance

of achieving the basic goals. (Keep in mind that the
harm generated by past farm policies came from the
sum total of existing farm policies.)

With that in mind, let us begin with a crucial question. Should the United States continue to subsidize
farmers at all—specifically, grain farmers?

You may be surprised, but my answer is yes. An
emphatic yes. There are great trends underway, and a
vast array of variables continues to reinforce them.
History tells us that things like erosion and concentration of ownership seem to occur almost naturally. Yet
they cannot be allowed. That's a dilemma, and the idea
of laying down ambitious goals that run counter to
powerful historic trends, without the benefit of some
well-aimed dollars, makes no sense.

Besides, the American farm must compete against
the likes of the Federal Marketing Boards in Canada
and Australia, and aggressively subsidized exports
that are pouring out of the EC-12. It must compete
against cheap Brazilian soybeans flowing from incredibly cheap new frontier lands that get put to the
plow there each year, and against the huge commercial palm plantations and processors in Malaysia.

If American farmers, even large and well-capitalized
farmers, are cut loose to compete on their own against
a heavily subsidized and very tough world, they will be
swimming upstream. Even those seemingly secure
farmers who might clamor for the removal of all
federal subsidies today, could find to their surprise
that they will be the next layer that gets peeled away.
Other farmers of the past also thought themselves big
enough and well capitalized enough to stay the course,
and in the end wound up being just that much more
grist for the competitive mill.

Not only that, but U.S. support programs have already put in a good fifteen years of hard work that has
put the remaining farmers at a disadvantage by shifting market share and development capital to competi-

tion overseas. To spend years creating disadvantages, and then cut loose weak and strong farmers alike on the basis of some sort of dogmatic principle, is piling a big mistake on top of the old whoppers—another example of exquisitely bad timing by farm policy.

So just what form should this subsidy take? Perhaps our cue ought to come from a place where farm subsidies have earned some substantial dividends for the society involved. I'm thinking of the EC-12 in particular. Those twelve nations of Western Europe have used their farm policy and the money spent on it to carve out a remarkable international success for themselves, and they've done this against some pretty long odds.

In recent years the EC-12 has often spent about the same amount on its farm programs as has the United States, roughly $25 billion per year. With that level of expenditure they've managed to: A) maintain a relatively prosperous farm population that is *four times* the farm population of the United States, and B) make dramatic advances in market share, transforming themselves into a major exporter in wheat, protein meal, and feedgrains.

This is all the more to their credit since they've done so with generally poorer soil, less of it, and a shorter growing season than that of the United States. (It's also worth noting by the way that the soil of Western Europe seems to be more firmly in place than that of the United States after as much as two thousand years of fairly intensive cultivation.)

This remarkable achievement comes because their farm subsidies are designed to be just that—subsidies. They consist of high price guarantees paid directly to farmers as income, and not as part of a convoluted system based on debt. Furthermore, the commonsense goal of EC farm policy has been to create a large surplus, and then use it or subsidize its export. In this way they support their large farm population, preserve and create jobs, reduce the need for imports, and so forth.

The United States has subsidized exports over the years too, but often as a sideline to the primary goal of reducing production and trying to force the free market to move higher by taking supplies off it or slashing acreage.

I don't want to spend too much time lionizing the Europeans. The Common Agricultural Policy (CAP) of the EC-12 has a few kinks in it too. CAP may have been guilty of shagging far too much money into the hands of some already prosperous people, but my point is that they gained enormously, while we lost enormously. Should we look to the losers for solutions, or the winners?

We've actually had a similar plan of our own waiting in the wings for decades, that in its purest form would have the same general effect. Typically, we've felt compelled to think of it in terms of creating debt, so it has been called a "marketing loan."

In its unvarnished form, the marketing loan is simply a guaranteed price. If the farmer sells his crop below the guaranteed price, he gets paid the difference in cash. If he sells it above the guarantee, he keeps the entire sale price, and the government is not required to pay anything. There are no restrictions on when or where the farmer can sell. No government storage payments, generic certificates, set-asides, or five-year price support loans. Debt is not created to facilitate the process. It's a plain old subsidy.

There are a number of questions you could ask at this point. For instance, how high should these loan guarantees be? Should they remain at the relatively low levels of 1989? Should they go even lower still, as many suggest, go back up to the 1985 highs, or what? I believe that the only way to put farm policy to work is to substantially raise them. I think increases of up to 50 percent are in order.

Raise them, you ask? Here we are with the farm assets of the United States squeezed into the hands of a relatively wealthy 1–2 percent of the population, and now I suggest that we ought to throw substantially *more* tax dollars their way? Well, that's not exactly what I meant.

The question is, should these higher subsidies be made available to all farmers and landowners? My answer is no! Since the creation of new small farms is our goal, subsidies should not go to *any* large farms or absentee or foreign owners—the entities whose rapidly growing role needs to be reversed.

Should all smaller farmers be subsidized simply because they are small? The answer is another emphatic no! Farm policy must be designed so that it extracts some tough provisions from participating farmers, provisions that will become the active agents for reversing many of the damaging trends underway.

In order to be eligible for the high guaranteed price, small farmers should therefore meet the following requirements:

1. They should cease planting without compensation on all acreage classified as highly erodible by the USDA. Farms with such acreage should only become eligible after the loss of topsoil on it is brought below the rate of replacement for at least two consecutive years. The USDA already inventories this land and the erosion rate. This can be measured.

Current farm programs pay the farmer (or wealthy urban and foreign investor in farmland) to stop planting such acreage, in effect paying people to stop a destructive activity that generates off- site cleanup costs for the taxpayer. This is a bit like extortion, and it's not the business that the government should be in.

2. All subsidized farmers should be required to use low-input and conservation tillage techniques ap-

propriate to their region, the soil type, and the crops in question. This includes such steps as using cover crops to hold soil and replenish nitrogen naturally, crop rotation, leaving crop residue after harvest to hold the soil through the winter, and curtailing fall plowing. The measurable goal is the same as for Point One. Erosion must be held below the rate of soil replacement.

Low-input farming fits with a rapidly growing trend among farmers in any case, so this is not some pie-in-the-sky idealism. Farmers by the thousands are proving that intensive management (and sharply reduced use of chemicals) can increase profitability, maintain high yields, and sharply reduce soil erosion. Farm policy has to take this emerging trend and run with it.

3. Reduced use of chemicals cannot be just a vague goal. I'll go one step further. Chemical use per acre should be strictly limited to perhaps half the levels common ten years ago, or lower. It is overuse of fertilizers and chemicals that promotes runoff into the local water supply and increases the cost of farming.

Compliance should be enforced by a variety of means such as spot checks and requiring farmers to submit receipts for chemicals and fertilizers purchased. Cheating to remain eligible for subsidy monies should be treated as a criminal act, like other forms of fraud.

Grain and soybean farmers are already learning to use methods that reduce chemical application by as much as 50–75 percent from the levels commonly applied in the early 1980s. This is done by monitoring the need for pesticides and herbicides as the growing season progresses, and then applying them in small doses as needed.

This is akin to the fairly new practice among diabetics of closely monitoring their blood sugar levels (as well as diet) during the course of the day, and then administering insulin in small and appropriate doses. Not only does this greatly reduce the insulin needed, but it is far more effective in controlling the disease.

All evidence suggests that nature itself can be enlisted in the battle to control insects and plant diseases, just as the body is now used to help control diabetes.

4. Subsidized farmers should be required to halt all irrigation via the pumping of ground water. Limits should also be set for participating farmers on elements such as the volume and placement of drainage tile. Many farmers have greatly increased water runoff on their land in order to make sure the land drains and dries more quickly after a rain.

This allows them to plant and harvest more quickly under wet conditions (another efficiency), but it also means that our thirsty water tables and wetlands are deprived of needed water. This is a ludicrous situation in the decade of great droughts and falling water tables. It's also unnecessary; today's equipment can get a crop planted and harvested in a few days, even under fairly wet conditions.

5. Participating farmers should be required to plant either a hedgerow or tree row along at least two-thirds of the perimeter of every field above a prescribed number of acres. That size can vary depending on crop and region; 160-acre enclosures for corn and soybeans, and 320 acres for wheat should be the absolute maximum. This will greatly reduce wind erosion, help hold existing soil moisture, and greatly increase the overall mass of vegetation across the center of the continent.

The USDA, along with other federal agencies, should begin an aggressive program to produce the vast quantity of young trees and bushes needed, and it should provide them to the farmer free of charge.

If they die of drought one year, we should plant more
the next. Even nonsubsidized farmers should receive
them free of charge, provided they're used for
windbreaks. It's in the public interest.

6. Subsidies should be restricted to farms that are
at least 90 percent owned by one individual, by
partnerships of no more than three individuals, or by
corporations that are limited to members of an immediate family. Foreign ownership should be completely restricted from participation in any subsidy
program.

Furthermore, individuals should be limited to
ownership interest in just one subsidized farm, no
matter how small that interest is. Otherwise, larger
farms could be divided up and family members par-
celed out with fractional ownership rights ad
nauseum. A small group of individuals could receive
inordinate amounts of tax dollars—a little here, and
a little there. That's how it's done today. This restric-
tion will also reduce the danger of paying subsidies
to non-local investors (the farm partnerships
dominated by urban professionals, for example), who
could otherwise make small investments in several
farms and receive lots of small checks.

Farmers who are eligible in all other respects, but
who rent a small portion of their land, should be
allowed to rent very limited amounts of land (25
percent or less) from a larger entity that doesn't fit
the ownership requirements. In such cases, payments should be made only to the renter (the farm
worker). All fields should fit all the other requirements, whether rented or owned, and the subsidy on
rented land should be limited to three years. Otherwise the subsidy money would simply flow to the
large landowners as rent.

7. Subsidy payments should also be restricted to
those whose primary residence (voting registration)
is in the county where the subsidized farm is located,

or in an adjacent county in case of overlap. This will further skew subsidies to the ones doing the field work.

8. New entries into the already existing Conservation Reserve Program (CRP) should be halted. Under the present system, we are paying farmers to not engage in an undesirable activity—namely, farming of highly erodible acres.

It is in society's interest to restrict or ban harmful behavior, not to reward people handsomely for stopping it. The fact that the current acreage program often makes these payments to wealthy individuals who have recently purchased land, who are holding it as part of an investment portfolio, and may be residing elsewhere, makes it all the more onerous.

In fact there needs to be a moratorium on all paid set-asides for at least the life of the new bill. We need to enforce proper use of farmland and rebuild the surplus.

9. Institute a moratorium on the foreign purchase of U.S. farmland. With the farm economy on the defensive, and the remaining farm population aging, land will flow to the great pools of capital that have been accumulated by wiser countries. This will also hold down land inflation, and allow this plan to work.

I think the sum total of these points will yield very desirable results. It will improve the environment on several levels—water quality, groundwater retention, and soil erosion to name just the obvious ones. It will also restrict participation (and the profits the subsidies will bring) to only those farms that are already smaller. These farms can afford the man-hours per acre needed to accomplish intensive crop management because the farm family doesn't need to pay itself an hourly wage.

Participants will tend to be those who have less invested in things like irrigation pumps, elaborate

drainage systems, and the biggest equipment needed
to handle the biggest fields—namely, the smaller
farms. Smaller farms will also find it less of a burden
to surround smaller fields with hedgerows simply because . . . well, because they're smaller. All of this puts
at a disadvantage the larger farm that might need to
hire additional skilled workers who could handle the
low-input management and smaller fields. That's
good. That's what farm policy ought to do.

However, we need one more catch so that the individual subsidy checks don't start getting too big.
There should be a limit to the number of acres in a
subsidized farm. It could vary with the crop and perhaps with the fertility of the soil, but the limit should
be relatively low: no more than 320 acres in the case of
prime land in the Corn Belt, but perhaps as high as
640 acres in the western Wheat Belt. Farmers could
plant more acres besides those being subsidized, but
the additional acres should all conform to all of the
conditions above, even though they are not earning a
subsidy.

This is more than just an attempt to steer public
dollars away from the rich. It is also a conscious effort
to skew the competitive advantage *toward* the small
family farmer. It quite frankly needs to be the goal of
federal farm policies to create an environment wherein
the very largest landowners are prodded to reduce
holdings of farmland and look for better investment
opportunities elsewhere. How else could the country
create a million new small farms?

Would this policy generate a reduction in large corporate holdings of farmland? I believe it would

If the higher subsidies can attract sufficient acreage,
and if those farms are paid to keep supplying the free
market with an ample and cheap supply of grain, it
could cut deeply into the profit margin of farms like
Prudential's forty square miles in northwestern Indiana once the drought ends. Under this system, they

would eventually be put at a competitive disadvantage and they'd look for more attractive investments elsewhere.

Will high subsidies for smaller farms quickly generate another glut that would explode the USDA budget? Would they start forcing the larger farms with less capital than a Prudential into foreclosure? I think not. First, it will take time to generate the extremely large numbers of participants it would take to severely pressure the market with oversupply.

Even the most attractive subsidy rates and the most aggressive policy of farm creation would probably attract only 30–35 percent of the nation's cropland over the life of the upcoming farm bill. When you consider the restrictions on chemical and fertilizer use, the land that would be taken up in tree rows and hedgerows instead of crops, and the fact that participants cannot plant on eroding acres, it's clear that a high rate of participation by farmers would keep planted acreage below the high levels of the early 1980s. No matter how high this program's subsidy rates, and no matter how high a percentage of the farmland that gets enrolled, it's awfully difficult to imagine it resulting in a protracted glut in and of itself.

If we are to experience another glut because of higher yields, however, and if prices again plunge as a result, then the United States had better have a system in place that can deliver the goods to world customers as cheaply as anyone, and still ensure that the farmers who sold them are able to earn enough of a profit to be there to plant again the following spring. This system could do that.

And what if a big surplus returns, and as a result the price of farmland resumes its 1980s downtrend? Let's say it falls right back down to the big lows of 1986, or lower.

There is always that danger, but if this happens, it has its advantages. It creates an opportunity to generate a far larger number of new farms over the short term. And depressed land values would be incentive for eligible farms to enroll in the program. This in turn would continue to spread benefits that society and the environment could reap under this system. Lower land prices should also encourage those farms that are too large to be fully subsidized to shrink themselves to get on board. A large farmer might enroll the maximum amount of land allowed in order to boost their bottom line with the subsidies it provides. In that case, the rest of their land would be required to conform with the low-input measures, so society and the environment would gain that much more.

Let's say prices are so depressed that the large farm is still unable to support its nonsubsidized acres, even though the maximum allowed are earning the subsidy. Well, that large farmer might be compelled to sell those nonsubsidized acres. That land might just be accessible to a family from outside the farming business *if* the USDA has a program in place that facilitates the process of creating small farms.

Believe me, I suffer no illusions that a majority of middle class American families are out there eager to become small farmers. The vast majority no doubt would cringe at the prospect. But I do believe that 1–2 percent might be really interested if they ever dreamed that it were possible. Wouldn't 1–2 percent of the families living in an urban or suburban setting be interested in the business of farming if they thought for one minute that they could afford the land and make a decent life at it?

I'm sure that a tiny percentage of Americans want an alternative lifestyle for their young families. If this group amounted to just 1 percent of the total population, a tiny percentage, it would include nearly 2.5 million people. Those 2.5 million people could generate

500,000 of the desired goal of one million new farms. A somewhat depressed land market would therefore be a golden opportunity. It can help to relieve the cost-of-housing spiral in our urban job-creating centers.

There's another, even greater potential here. I believe that farm policy, specifically this farm policy, is even a feasible outlet for the growing population of homeless. As this group has grown in size, it has come to include more young, healthy, and otherwise "normal" nuclear families. What do we plan to do with them? I see only a few options in the existing system. We could just let them rot. We could put them into heavily financed homes in one of the big urban job markets. (Wasn't that a race they couldn't stay in to begin with?) We could dump them into our unsuccessful welfare system and public housing, where solid families would be exposed to the influence of gangs, drugs, and the fractured families already living there.

Or we could do something of lasting benefit to all of us. We could take these languishing American assets—the intact nuclear families with no shelter—and generate for them a workable option outside the sometimes unwinnable financial race occurring in the great urban centers. The federal government can itself create new farms and make it a priority to put homeless families on them.

Furthermore, it should turn them over to homeless families at no cost for the land, or with a mortgage listed at a small fraction of the value of the land.

It should prohibit these families from selling the land for an extended period (ten years or more), so they don't just sign up to cash in. If they abandon it, they lost it. The government should also prohibit lenders from foreclosing on the land itself for farm-related debts. This was wisely the case for original homesteads, and it should be for today's as well. This little provision should force the local banker to rein in his

natural itch to start shoveling debt when he finds a
willing victim. (The banker can foreclose on the crop
only.)

The federal government can acquire the needed
lands in a variety of ways. It could buy down bad farm
debt from any of the local and national farm lenders
and troubled thrifts who hold it—buy it at a discount
to the face value, and then turn it over at an even
bigger discount, in order to get the new homestead
farm on its feet.

In addition, the government could commit to spend-
ing four to five billion dollars per year on direct purchases on the open market.

Large corporations, even Prudential Insurance, who
would be purposely locked out of this subsidy system,
might be induced to write down the value of part or all
their holdings of farmland for the good public relations
it brings, or for tax considerations by local and state
bodies that would benefit from having more local small
businesses trading and investing in the local community.

Some sort of upturn in the farm population is im-
perative. It is both shrinking and rapidly aging. This
problem won't solve itself.

We could head off in a host of different directions
from here. I could explain how this system would help
overcome shortages in times of drought and grain
robberies alike because land is not going to be locked
away in a huge acreage program when the shock
comes. I could explain how this would enable the
country to be better able to hang onto its water and
land resources if the long-range weather theorists are
right, or if the drought cycle simply continues into the
1990s. We could crunch all of the numbers and show
how the higher price guarantees, heavy farmer participation, and the biggest world glut might still leave
us with a smaller USDA budget than a couple of recent

years have seen if all the other policy junk gets scrapped.

I could write at length about how many jobs and new products are created with a cheap and accessible supply of grain that is free to move around and get used at any price. I could point out the painfully obvious social benefits of abundant and cheap food to a stable, law-abiding society. How cheap grain makes for cheaper end products like red meat and corn sweeteners and ethanol. How saner farm policies might have prevented the shortage of dairy products that may curtail school lunch programs this fall. How corn processing plants actually create more energy than they use (through cogeneration). How small profitable farms are in a better position to start cutting through the consolidation that now plagues the entire food market. How a bigger farm population can cut through the layers of processors, and give the average citizen more direct access to the sources of their meat, poultry, and dairy products because a small farmer might then live nearby.

I could point out that in this day of chemical food, when 20 percent of the shelf space in your super-market may soon be controlled by just one consumer products company, this system can provide safer basic foods to more people. We could look at how small towns and school districts can revive with more younger families, and how a few more kids might be able to grow up in a more traditional family setting with one or both parents around each day.

Every way you look turns up some new benefit to be reaped from well-designed farm policy and more carefully aimed dollars.

I could go on and on, but I think I've said enough. The present flawed farm policies and all of the damaging current trends they have spawned could go on and on too. I can assure you that they will, unless we decide

to stop them. It will take a conscious decision. Like so
many of the decisions facing our country, this one is a
test.

Most would no doubt conclude that we are certain to
fail this and other such tests. This may well be true,
but let's be clear about one thing. It doesn't have to be.
There are clear ways out. Why not follow Marshall
Foch's example, and just attack?

INDEX